Just Mary

Mary Grannan's first CBC publicity photograph, 1939.

Just Mary

The Life of
Mary Evelyn Grannan

Margaret Anne Hume

Foreword by
Gwendolyn Davies

THE DUNDURN GROUP
TORONTO

Copy-editor: Jennifer Gallant
Design: Jennifer Scott
Printer: Friesens

Library and Archives Canada Cataloguing in Publication

Hume, Margaret Anne

    Just Mary : the life of Mary Evelyn Grannan / Margaret Anne Hume.

Includes index.

ISBN-13: 978-1-55002-597-2
ISBN-10: 1-55002-597-X

    1. Grannan, Mary, 1900-1975. 2. Authors, Canadian (English)--20th century--Biography. 3. Muggins, Maggie (Fictitious character). 4. Radio writers--Canada--Biography. 5. Television writers--Canada--Biography. I. Title.

PN1990.72.G73H84 2006   C813'.54   C2005-906955-4

1   2   3   4   5   10   09   08   07   06

Conseil des Arts du Canada   Canada Council for the Arts   Canada   ONTARIO ARTS COUNCIL CONSEIL DES ARTS DE L'ONTARIO

We acknowledge the support of the **Canada Council for the Arts** and the **Ontario Arts Council** for our publishing program. We also acknowledge the financial support of the **Government of Canada** through the **Book Publishing Industry Development Program** and **The Association for the Export of Canadian Books**, and the **Government of Ontario** through the **Ontario Book Publishers Tax Credit program**, and the **Ontario Media Development Corporation**.

Care has been taken to trace the ownership of copyright material used in this book. The author and the publisher welcome any information enabling them to rectify any references or credits in subsequent editions.

J. Kirk Howard, President

Printed and bound in Canada.
www.dundurn.com

Dundurn Press	Gazelle Book Services Limited	Dundurn Press
3 Church Street, Suite 500	White Cross Mills	2250 Military Road
Toronto, Ontario, Canada	Hightown, Lancaster, England	Tonawanda, NY
M5E 1M2	LA1 4X5	U.S.A. 14150

For my father,
Albert Mair MacLean,
with love and thanks,
and in fond memory of my mother,
Mary Barbara Fraser MacLean.

Author's Note

When quoting from Mary Grannan's letters and scripts, I have corrected typographical and spelling errors without using *sic* because of their high frequency. Punctuation marks, however, have been transcribed exactly as written, with the exception of two-period ellipses, which have been changed to three-period ellipses. Since she used ellipses frequently, I have put my own ellipses (to indicate omissions) in square brackets.

Table of Contents

Foreword
by Gwendolyn Davies

At the beginning of this biography of Canadian children's writer Mary Grannan, Margaret Anne Hume vividly describes rushing back to her Grade 2 classroom in Prince Edward School in Moncton, New Brunswick, to hear her teacher read the next exciting episode of Grannan's classic creation, *Maggie Muggins*. Her anecdote struck a personal note with me, for I too was once a little girl in the Moncton area and I too eagerly looked forward to episodes of *Maggie Muggins*. But unlike Hume, I was part of the radio generation in Canada, the group that, between 1946 and 1954, listened with raptness to the language pyrotechnics, lively dialogue, and multiplicity of Grannan voices that characterized both the *Just Mary* and the *Maggie Muggins* episodes.

My visual Maggie Muggins, with her carrot red pigtails and freckles, was a product of my radio imagination. Hume's Maggie Muggins was given physical dimensions by television, a medium that changed the way in which Grannan conceived of her voices and her scripts. Speaking to Canadian literary critic John Moss in Fredericton in 1972, Grannan noted that, in the days of radio, she had complemented James Annand and Beryl Braithwaite as Mr. McGarrity and Maggie Muggins respectively by doing all the other voices: "I had Fitzgerald Fieldmouse and

Grandmother Frog and Reuben Rabbit, and Benny Bear and so on and I had to do all those voices myself — and the way I did it, I would take, I remember, the mouse as red. I'd mark red along the edge and the frog was green and somebody else was blue — so I knew the colours, so reading I could change from one voice to the other voice." But television was quite different, she noted. "I could take Fitzgerald Fieldmouse to the moon on radio," she explained to Moss, but "in television you had to have that puppet there and you had to have the moon fixed ... there were just 3 puppeteers and I had to work it out ... it was a matter of working out the timing to move the people who had the puppets."[1]

In spite of the challenges of change, Grannan revelled in the fame that the *Just Mary* and *Maggie Muggins* stories brought her. As Hume explains in this biography, Grannan cherished winning the Beaver Award for distinguished service to Canadian radio, an Honorable Mention from the Institute for Education by Radio at Ohio State University, and the International Mark Twain Society of Saint Louis Honorary Membership (in company with Rudyard Kipling, Thomas Hardy, Sir Arthur Conan Doyle, and Franklin D. Roosevelt). She was a consummate professional, impressing CBC officials with her ability to write for either radio or television, meet unexpected deadlines, and introduce inventive new ideas. Her ability to turn CBC broadcasts into books or books into CBC broadcasts marked a development in the history of publishing in Canada.

Fourteen hundred avid admirers would turn out in a Canadian city in the fifties to hear Grannan and her current Maggie Muggins read, and her books eventually sold over four hundred thousand copies. Astutely aware of the popularity of her Maggie Muggins creation, Grannan approached the Reliable Toy Company in 1947–48 with the concept of a doll. By the end of 1948, the first year of its release, eleven thousand dolls had been sold. I well remember the Christmas of 1948 when I agonized over whether to ask Santa Claus for a Barbara Ann Scott doll or a Maggie Muggins doll. In the end, Santa brought me a Barbara Ann Scott doll, complete with blue lace skating costume and white figure skates, and my friend Elaine, next door, a Maggie Muggins doll. In retrospect, the fact that two such important Canadian cultural icons were successfully commercialized as dolls speaks volumes about

Canada's sense of nationalism in the postwar period. It also reminds us of Grannan's astuteness in recognizing the degree to which her literary creation, Maggie Muggins, had captured the hearts of a generation. She had created, as she indicated to John Moss in 1972, "a little Canadian folklore child."[2]

Hume's biography of Grannan points out all the foibles, strengths, and brilliances of Mary Grannan's personality and career. She loved large hats, bangles, and extravagant clothes and was always stylishly attired, whether in a sound booth or on a publicity tour. She enjoyed people, and, in spite of working incessantly, created enduring friendships with CBC personnel such as J. Frank Willis, who produced some of her radio programs, and a series of *Maggie Muggins* associates who informed her professional life. She had an instinctive capacity for recognizing the versatility of language that made her a success in both radio and television. And, grounded in her school teaching and New Brunswick heritage as she was, she had a kind of practical sense of how to do things that made her absolutely adaptable to the CBC's needs as it moved from radio infancy to television experimentation.

Given Grannan's influence on Canadian children's culture in the post-Depression and postwar periods, it is remarkable, as Hume has noted, that no one has hitherto written her story. Therefore, admirers of the *Just Mary* and *Maggie Muggins* episodes will be deeply indebted to Hume as they read this biography, for she has meticulously sought out those who knew Grannan throughout her career and has included many personal letters that reveal the private side of Grannan's rise to success. She also explores Grannan's sheer mastery of the three storytelling media — print, radio, and television — that made her imaginative and verbal impact so broad and enduring. Not least of Grannan's successes, as Hume narrates her story, were the remarkably positive benchmarks that she created for children as part of the fabric of her narratives. Maggie Muggins's signatures, such as "Tra la la la la la la lee" and "I don't know what will happen tomorrow," will remain timeless credos of how Canadians of any age can cheerfully address life.

Gwendolyn Davies, Ph.D., FRSC
University of New Brunswick

Prologue

Maggie Muggins was an unforgettable part of my childhood. The image is still vivid. The year was 1956, and I was standing in the hallway of our house on Givan Drive in Moncton, New Brunswick, looking at the clock on the kitchen stove. As the clock hit 1:15, I felt a surge of excitement: it was time to return to school for the afternoon session. My scurrying feet carried me swiftly the one block to Prince Edward School and, at the sound of the bell, down the broad hallway to my Grade 2 classroom. I settled quickly into my seat, sitting at attention with my hands clasped together, for what was causing my exuberance was about to begin. Our teacher, Mrs. Steeves, began every afternoon by reading a *Maggie Muggins* story by Mary Grannan, and I could not wait to find out what mischief Fitzgerald Fieldmouse would get up to next.

We seven-year-olds knew the characters of the *Maggie* stories well — young Maggie with her red pigtails and freckles, her animal friends in the meadow, like Fitzgerald Fieldmouse, Grandmother Frog, Petunia 'Possom, and Big Bite Beaver, and Maggie's wise old friend, Mr. McGarrity, who helped her solve the problems and crises that arose each day. The reason for our great familiarity was that *Maggie Muggins* was more than just a series of books. It was a popular CBC television show, which had begun in 1955, and had been a CBC radio program from 1947 to 1953. Although *Maggie Muggins* first appeared as a small book in 1944, it was the radio and television broadcasts that turned the story into a success. The subsequent books were adapted from the broadcast stories. So, as we children listened to our teacher reading the *Maggie* stories, we could visualize them because we had watched them on television.

Television was a recent phenomenon in our lives, and CBC Television was only four years old. During those first years of broadcasting, when few people had television sets, all the neighbourhood children used to gather at the one house on the block that did.

"What's television?" the wide-eyed innocents would ask the more worldly children. "Why, it's a piece of furniture with moving pictures and it tells stories," came the reply. In the late afternoon, we would all gather at the house with the television set. We would sit cross-legged on the floor directly in front of it and stare in wonder at *Howdy Doody* and later *Maggie Muggins*.

After my family got our own set, I remember my father patiently explaining to me why the picture was sometimes fuzzy. It did not help my tears and frowns. He eventually built his own aerial, called a *yagi*, from wood covered with heavy aluminum foil. I watched in fascination as he and our neighbour assembled it and wondered how this contraption placed in the attic would work, but indeed it did.

Television quickly became a part of our daily lives. My brother and I read the schedule and speculated what the shows might be like. We imagined that the local Moncton show called *The Bunkhouse Boys* was likely children jumping on bunk beds and were quite disappointed when we discovered that the show only featured people singing and playing musical instruments. And we were absolutely convinced that the male ballet dancers we saw on television were naked from the waist down, not believing our mother when she said they were wearing tights. Subsequently, we put on our own ballet, jumping on the beds with my brother appropriately undressed.

Among those early television shows we watched, *Maggie Muggins* was a favourite of mine. I revelled in the humorous adventures of the spirited young heroine and enjoyed the lively puppets with their quirky personalities. As I watched the shows, my interest peaked when the scene shifted from Mr. McGarrity's garden to the mouse house in the meadow, for that was where the action began — and the trouble.

Beyond the show and the books, I had an extra reason for thinking that *Maggie Muggins* was special — Maggie's creator, Mary Grannan, also came from New Brunswick, albeit Fredericton. Even at that young age, I felt a sense of awe and pride in the accomplishments of someone from my own province.

The years passed, and childhood joys were not forgotten but tucked away, as I tried to break free from childhood and grow up. In the fall of 1967, I began studies at the University of New Brunswick in Fredericton. During my years there, my mind was occupied with things of the moment — what assignments were next, when the next break was, what was going on during the weekend, and what boys I liked. As I wanted to plan my future, I had bigger questions to think about, such as what career I wanted and whom I wanted to marry. Things from my childhood were far from my mind then. What I did not realize during my years in Fredericton was that in a little white house across town lived Mary Grannan, creator of *Maggie Muggins*. She was retired then and lived a quiet life. I wonder if I ever walked by her house — it was certainly possible. If I had, she might have looked out the window and noticed me. If I had known she was there and I had summoned up the courage, I might have knocked on her door and said hello. What a missed opportunity that was, for she died in 1975, four years after I left Fredericton.

In the fall of 1988, I was once again at university, this time McGill in Montreal. With my children in high school, I was returning to study to become a librarian — a mid-life career change. One day, as I learned how to search for information in computer databases, I entered the name "Mary Grannan." I had become curious about this writer of stories from my childhood and thought I would find out something about her. I was stunned when the database search produced no information. Later, I continued the search in older print indexes and found some dated magazine articles about her that outlined a basic sketch of her life.

The essence of the reporting laid out a simple story. Mary Grannan, originally a schoolteacher from Fredericton, was a much-loved children's broadcaster on CBC Radio and later CBC Television from 1939 until 1962, when her shows were cancelled. *Maggie Muggins* and *Just Mary* were her best-known broadcasts. Her books, based on the radio and television tales, were bestsellers through the forties and fifties. During those peak years, she was a popular and well-known personality throughout Canada.

Brief by necessity, the magazine articles skated over the surface of her life story, avoiding the bumps and rough patches of which I learned later. I longed to discover more details about her, what she was really like, flaws as well as perfections. How did she manage to leave a traditional teaching role in a small town and go to Toronto to become a national broadcaster at a time when such a move was highly unconventional for a woman? Why did she do it? How did she overcome whatever obstacles were in her way? What was her journey like as she moved from teaching to broadcasting in the pioneering days of radio? What excitement did she find in her daily life in Toronto? Was she truly unusual or were there many like her? How did she cope when it was all over and she returned to Fredericton? Why is it that today so few in Canada know who she was, given the extent of her popularity for two decades in the mid-twentieth century?

The faithfulness of a young fan and the loyalty to the memory of a daughter of my home province launched me on a road I had not expected — to research and write her biography. The journey took me further than I could have imagined and revealed to me a woman with more character and depth than I had first suspected.

Chapter One
The Departure, 1939

Nothing was going to stop Mary Evelyn Grannan from getting on the train to Toronto that Saturday evening, July 1, 1939. After twenty-one years of teaching Grade 1 in New Brunswick, she was leaving her hometown of Fredericton and going to Toronto to begin a new job in radio as a junior producer of children's programs for the three-year-old Canadian Broadcasting Corporation. Although she later described herself as feeling like a "frightened schoolmarm,"[1] she must have possessed a large measure of determination to bluster past the emotional roadblocks she faced at home as she prepared to leave.

Clouds of dust billowed up around Mary's mother, Catherine Grannan, as she swept the sidewalk in front of her home, a diminutive white house at 325 Brunswick Street.[2] The grey-haired woman in a cotton housedress and bibbed apron worked the straw broom with an intensity born of grief. Frowning and pressing her lips together, Kate braced herself for an impending loss as her middle daughter, Mary, stepped out the front door with suitcases in hand and headed to the waiting taxi. Pausing to embrace her seventy-seven-year-old widowed mother, Mary said goodbye and promised to write home every day. As the taxi drove away, Kate again tackled the dusty sidewalk, while Mary's younger sister, Helen, cried in the doorway.

"I was heartbroken," Helen said later. "I thought I wasn't going to live at all with Mary gone. It was very sad."[3]

Not wishing to handle tearful goodbyes at the train station, Mary had asked her family to stay at home, and she got into the taxi by herself. She must have held back her own tears as the taxi travelled one block east along Brunswick Street, turned south on York, and proceeded four and a half blocks to the Canadian Pacific Railway station. Pulling into the yard, the driver stopped in front of the station's west-end portico, with its stucco gable, red tile cross, and suspended sign that read "Fredericton." He opened the door for Mary and helped her out of the car. Carrying her luggage, he accompanied her as they walked along the wooden platform, a hollow muffled sound marking their steps. They passed under the great overhanging eaves of the impressive building, whose red tapestry bricks were arranged into decorative lines and patterns, and entered the oak-panelled ladies' waiting room.

For just under thirty dollars, Mary purchased her ticket for the overnight journey to Toronto, which would involve a change of trains at Fredericton Junction and Montreal.[4] After checking all her luggage except the overnight bag, Mary returned to the platform to wait for the 5:35 train.[5] She stood tall, her five-foot, seven-and-a-half-inch willowy frame straight, with shoulders back, reflecting years of teaching correct posture to her pupils. In the classroom, Mary would place a yardstick at the back of her waist and hold it there for a few moments by encircling it with her bent arms.[6] The long, flared skirt of her dress extended to mid-calf, giving an added sense of height. A jaunty hat covered most of her short dark brown curls, with only wisps sticking out around her ears.

The late afternoon sun was warm as she waited; the temperature had peaked at sixty-seven degrees Fahrenheit that day.[7] Extra holiday travellers milled around on the platform, for it was Dominion Day and the first day of school summer holidays. In the small capital city of ten thousand, people were friendly and knew most of their neighbours. As Mary greeted those she knew, she beamed a broad, infectious smile, her blue eyes sparkling, her prominent cheeks rosy apples.

This Dominion Day, however, the usual gaiety of summer holidays was dimmed by forebodings of war in Europe. The day before, Fredericton's local newspaper, the *Daily Gleaner*, had borne ominous front-page headlines: "The Breach Between Britain and Axis Powers; British Pledge to Resist Aggression; Europe Drifting to Serious Crisis" and further down the page, "Germans Have Been Definitely Warned."[8]

Two and a half weeks earlier, King George VI and Queen Elizabeth had graced Fredericton with a whirlwind two-hour visit as part of their month-long cross-Canada royal tour.[9] Their goal was to firm up Canada's support in the event of war. With public buildings decorated with flags and bunting, citizens and dignitaries welcomed their Majesties with all the pomp and ceremony they could muster. Interestingly, the graceful and beautiful Queen Elizabeth, who charmed citizens all across the country, was the same age as Mary. Both were thirty-nine years old.

So, as the country paused in between the glory of the royal visit and the coming horror of war, Mary began her journey from the safe and secure employment of teaching to an uncertain new career in radio broadcasting. She could succeed ... or fail. There were no guarantees, and she would have the added stress of being on probation for three months. For two years, she had eagerly sought a position with the fledgling CBC, but when the written offer finally came, she found herself thinking very carefully about leaving her secure teaching position.

"There is as yet no pension scheme or collective insurance," General Manager Gladstone Murray wrote to her, "but we are hopeful of arranging this before long. Nevertheless, it should be borne in mind that this is a new business without the elements of security with which you are familiar in the teaching profession."[10]

Since the country was just emerging from years of depression, a person did not quickly give up a good, steady-paying job, and furthermore, Mary contributed to the financial support of her mother and Helen. Wisely, in case the whole thing did not work out, Mary opted for some safety by taking a year's leave of absence from the Devon School Board. It would be embarrassing to have to return to her small city and teaching, but at least she would have employment to fall back on. So, it was with a mixture of excitement and anxiety that Mary waited for the train.

"I will leave here on Saturday, July 1," she had written two weeks earlier to Mr. Murray, "hoping with every mile that I will be able to please you with my efforts."[11]

The train arrived, its bell clanging and steam engine chugging slowly and hissing steam as it backed its four wooden coaches into position. Since this was a branch line, the train had turned around earlier at the wye. With a piercing squeal and a *whoosh* of air escaping from the brakes, the train came to a stop and the conductor alighted on the platform.[12] Mary boarded the train along with the other passengers and settled into a seat for the forty-minute ride to Fredericton Junction. A nearby gentleman offered to put her small bag onto the overhead rack. The conductor called out "All aboarrrd!" and the journey began. The CBC and Toronto lay ahead, and in all likelihood, Mary never envisioned how successful she would become.

Chapter Two
Birth of a Storyteller, 1900-1914

With a slow *clang-clang-clang* of its bell, the train pulled out of the station, taking Mary on the first leg of her trip. The coaches were warm, but the breeze from the open windows was cooling as the train picked up speed leaving the city. Since it was still daylight, the coaches' Pintsch gaslights were not yet turned on. The conductor passed down the aisle collecting tickets, and soon the *clickety-click* of the wheels along the track assumed a regular rhythm. Although Mary was leaving behind the city of her birth, parts of Fredericton and its people would travel with her and take up residence in her stories, for many of the tales to come would be coloured by people she knew and experiences she had at home during the first thirty-nine years of her life.

Born on the doorstep of the twentieth century, Mary Evelyn Grannan was ushered into the world on February 11, 1900, on a cold, wintry Sunday in the small, picturesque provincial capital situated on the banks of the frozen St. John River.[1] This woman who was later to become prominent in Canadian radio and television broadcasting was born a year before Marconi received the first wireless transatlantic signal and six years before Canadian Reginald Fessenden produced the first wireless voice broadcast.[2] With Queen Victoria still on the throne of Great Britain for one more year, Mary was born at the end of the Victorian era and would see through her lifetime some great changes and events in the world around her.

The Canada into which Mary was born had a population of approximately 5.3 million people, and New Brunswick, around 330,000.[3] The newspaper headlines at the time of her birth were dominated by the Boer War in South Africa, and early that year Canada sent over a second contingent of volunteer soldiers.[4] Beyond its interest in and contribution to this war in a distant land, Canada, under the leadership of Prime Minister Sir Wilfrid Laurier, was experiencing growth in the Canadian West, partly through its expanding railway connections across this vast country. With the continued development of resources and an increase in manufacturing, Canada was on the verge of a time of prosperity.[5]

Mary's birthplace of Fredericton was established as the capital of New Brunswick in 1785, the year after the British colony was created by the partition of Nova Scotia. From its origin, the city was influenced and shaped by the presence of government, military, university, and church, as well as the influx of Loyalists leaving the American colonies at the end of the American War of Independence. In the mid-nineteenth century, Irish immigrants arrived, fleeing the famine at home. The city became a central market and mill town, using the St. John River as its main means of transportation until the building of railways, which began in 1869. At the beginning of the twentieth century, large steamboats, schooners, sloops, and wood boats still plied the waters. As well as transportation, the river offered the city beauty, character, and the threat of flooding in spring.[6]

In 1900, when Mary was born, horses and carriages travelled Fredericton's dirt and gravel streets, which the city gradually started to pave with concrete a few years later. While people walked the sidewalks of the business district on paved asphalt, many in the residential areas still escaped the mud on wooden planks. The city had replaced the gas streetlights with electric lighting seven years earlier, although it took many years before electricity reached all the houses, and many continued to use kerosene lamps. The telegraph and telephone had been brought to the province in the mid-nineteenth century, and Bell Telephone had begun installing telephones and setting up an exchange fifteen years earlier. Most of the houses of the time were wooden, while many of the public and commercial buildings were made of brick or stone. Perhaps reflecting their rural roots, most residents of the city maintained vegetable and flower gardens and many also kept animals, such as chickens, goats, horses, and even cows and pigs.[7] The gentle nature of Mary's stories and the presence of many animals reflected the Fredericton of her youth.

When Mary arrived in the family, her father, William Peter Grannan, was thirty-three years old, and her mother, Catherine Teresa Haney, thirty-nine.[8] They were older and mature parents who had married four years earlier in 1896 after a long courtship. Helen said:

> My father and mother went together for ten years. My father and his sister shared a house or a flat or something. When my parents decided to get married, he went to his sister and said he was going to get married. And she said, "Where are you going to take your bride?" And he said, "Well, I'm bringing her home here." She said, "When she moves in, I move out." So, that settled that. So, he got a little flat somewhere and moved out. He was earning $7.00 a week at the time. I guess it must have been quite hard to pay the rent, but they got along. So, the children, the three of us, were born downtown and I don't know where, but in a flat.[9]

The family was living on Regent Street when Mary's older sister, Ann Margaret, was born in 1897,[10] and by 1903, the year Mary's younger sister, Helen Julia, was born, they had moved to 213 King Street.[11] It is unclear exactly where they lived the year Mary was born. The family had a modest income and lifestyle, but the young sisters appeared well dressed in family photographs. "Like many families in those days," Helen wrote, "the Grannans were not overburdened with worldly goods. Modest as were our means, we three girls enjoyed a comfortable and secure life."[12]

Mary's parents shared an Irish heritage and Roman Catholic faith, although Billy's family had arrived in New Brunswick at least a generation earlier than Kate's. His parents, John Grannan and Julia Shortill, were both born in Royal Road, York County, New Brunswick, and John maintained a farm at Douglas near Fredericton when Billy was born in 1867.[13] Kate's parents, Patrick Haney and Ann McChey, were both born in Ireland and likely immigrated to New Brunswick during the Great Famine migration. Patrick worked as a labourer, and he and Ann had six children, the youngest of whom was Mary's mother, born in 1861.[14] The Irish heritage was a strong influence and fascination for Mary and became a common theme in her stories.

Mary's father was a small, quiet man, "but he had a great sense of humour," said Helen.[15] He was fond of reading, wood carving, drawing, and bicycle riding.[16] Among his many influences on Mary, his humour, book reading, and drawing were significant. Billy instilled in Mary at an early age the importance of books and the love of reading, and these were vital factors in her development as a writer. With her father's example and guidance, Mary also learned drawing and artwork skills, which she developed and used throughout her life in both her play and work.

A carriage builder by trade, Billy Grannan was employed as a wheelwright at Patrick McGinn's Wheelwright Factory at 93-95 King Street and was paid an annual salary of three hundred dollars, according to the 1901 census.[17] In the 1870s and 1880s, Fredericton was the centre of wagon and carriage building in New Brunswick, and Patrick McGinn's Wheelwright Factory, in business since the 1860s, specialized in heavy wagons.[18]

In addition to woodworking, Billy had a second vocation for which he was well respected in the community. He was a fireman and became captain of the No. 2 Hose Company of the Fredericton Fire Department.[19] With many wooden buildings built closely together and an unfortunate number of arsonists in its midst, Fredericton suffered so many fires in the nineteenth century that Austin Squires in his *History of Fredericton* said that the city was known as the "City of Fires with a fire every Saturday night."[20] By the time Billy joined the fire department sometime in the late nineteenth century, it had been reorganized, with the fire protection laws having seen numerous revisions. There were five hose companies, which continued to pull the hose reels by hand until 1902, when horse-drawn hose carts began to be used. Although the department brought in the first truck in 1916, fire horses were in use throughout Billy's time with the department.[21] During their courtship, Billy and Kate's evening walks together were frequently interrupted by the fire bell, sending Billy running off to fight the fire while Kate found her own way home.[22]

"[The firemen] got paid once a year," Helen said. "I don't know how much it was now, but I know this. It was the one time of year that my father could afford to buy a bottle of liquor. And I think he gave us each a dollar out of the fireman's pay — Ann, Mary, and me."[23]

In contrast to Mary's small and quiet father, her tall, red-haired mother had a strong-willed and forceful personality. Although Kate's sisters had trades — Mary Haney was a dressmaker, and Margaret Flanagan was a milliner — she may have remained at home, helping to look after her parents until her marriage at the age of thirty-five. Kate ruled the Grannan home with a firm hand, but she also had a playful side and regaled her children with bedtime stories, many of them the Irish tales she had learned from her own mother. Books were important to Kate as well, and it was she who bought most of the books at auctions and brought them home. She "played the bones," using dried meat bones to make rhythmical music, and was noted among family and friends for her dramatic exits from the room after pronouncing her opinion on a matter. With a quick tongue and a sense of humour, she had a quip for her neighbour who frequently complained when they met over the clothesline.

"Ah, Mrs. Grannan," the neighbour said, "I'm not feeling well. I think this is the day the Lord is calling me home."

"Many are called," Kate replied, "but few are chosen."[24]

Kate's influence upon Mary was complex. On the one hand, Mary was governed by her mother's overbearing nature, especially when she was younger, but on the other hand, Mary herself became a similarly strong-willed and forceful presence. The alternate side of Kate — the playful, humorous, and storytelling side — was an enormous influence on Mary, encouraging the growth of her imagination and sense of humour that was so essential to her later writing and such an integral part of her

character. The traditional Irish tales Mary heard from her mother frequently found their way into Mary's stories, as did Kate herself.

How did Mary see herself as a child? When Mary dramatized her
childhood in a biographical radio play she wrote to celebrate her tenth
anniversary in national broadcasting, she portrayed herself as an energetic and excitable child with a curious mind and an impetuous nature
who grew up in a household with a profusion of storybooks, a father
who loved to read to his children, and a mother who charmed her girls
with dramatic oral stories. In the fertile ground of a free and unstruc-
tured playtime, Mary's imagination and creativity grew as she amused
herself and her sisters with make-believe and wove stories into their
play. Fictional though it was, Mary's radio play nevertheless provides
genuine insight into her character as well as her family interactions:

59 ANN:	But I thought we were going down to the green. … Mum, do you know some-thing … Mary makes up the silliest things down at the green.
60 MARY:	I do not.
61 ANN:	You do too. Mum, you know that big willow tree on the green, the one you and papa used to sit under before you got married?
62 MOTHER:	Yes…
63 ANN:	Well there's a great big hole in it, and yesterday when I was picking cat tails down by the river Mary told me she went inside the tree and she found a pair of stairs in there … and she went down there and there was a toy room down there full of all sorts of toys and things.
64 MARY:	I did too … and the stairs were glass just like Cinderella's slippers…
65 ANN:	And she said she talked to a rabbit, Mum.

66 MARY: And I did too, didn't I, Mum?
67 MOTHER: I wouldn't be a bit surprised.
68 ANN: Do you believe it, Mum.
69 MARY: Sure she does. She makes up all kinds
                of things too ... and she makes up all
                those stories she tells us at night, don't
                you, Mum?[25]

The sisters spent many childhood hours playing together and entertaining themselves. They made dolls from clothespins or pieces of cloth they got from the dressmaker who lived upstairs, turned ordinary things such as scatter rugs into pretend canoes, drew and designed on paper alongside Father, and romped outdoors with their dog, Sport. Church was mandatory on Sundays, and afterward, in good weather, they went on family bicycle outings. All the girls took music lessons — Mary's instrument was the violin — although none of them pursued music into their adult lives. Art was the preferred activity, and they were all good at drawing.[26] The storytelling and book reading activities in the home were a large influence, and Helen experienced the effect it had on Mary.

"[Mary] told stories all her life," Helen said. "Ever since I was three years old and Mary was three years older than I, she told me stories. On the table in the kitchen, she'd make little scenes with paper. Well, if I didn't like [one] and started to cry, she'd stop that and start another one."[27]

In 1906, Mary's formal schooling began at age six at St. Dunstan's School on Regent Street, the Roman Catholic elementary school taught chiefly by nuns. In 1910, a class photograph taken in front of St. Dunstan's showed a demure young Mary in Grade 4. Her hair fell to her shoulders and was drawn back on the top into a large white bow. A hint of a smile played on her lips. The classes most years at St. Dunstan's were two grades to a room with the classes as large as fifty-two or fifty-three students.[28] According to Mary's biographical radio play, she tried her best to be first in spelling and she did win a prize some years. In 1911, St. Dunstan's opened a new school building located on the site of the former Roman Catholic cemetery.

It was in Grade 1 that Mary had her first opportunity to perform in public. At the Christmas school closing, she recited "I Lost My Dear Dolly":

> I lost my dear dolly
> And what do you think?
> They gave her no victuals
> They gave her no drink
> They left her uncovered
> All night in the cold
> My poor little dolly
> Not quite a year old.[29]

"[Mary] had a new doll for the occasion," Helen wrote, "but she was not happy because she desperately wanted one with a straw hat. Christmas morning and Santa Claus eventually arrived and, of course, like the scamp she was, she was downstairs first. There among Ann's things was a doll with a straw hat. Quick like a flash, she switched her toy piano for the coveted doll. She couldn't understand how Mum knew that the doll was Ann's."[30]

Dramatics were in Mary's soul from a young age. In the beginning, the backyard step at the end of the clothesline was her stage for singing and acting with her sisters.[31] School, of course, provided opportunities for her to take part in concerts. As she grew older, she eagerly attended local amateur theatre and performances by the travelling theatre groups and entertainers that visited Fredericton as part of their route, often playing at the Opera House. Helen perhaps relates Mary's enthusiasm best:

> My sister Mary's love for the world of make-believe
> came early. As a child she was stage-struck. Her blue
> eyes would go wide with wonder and longing as she
> lived every minute with the beautiful and distressed
> leading lady. In those days the stock companies played
> in the local theatre, and she coaxed, wheedled, or
> pouted until she got the price of admission.

I can see her yet — the round, proud little face so ready to burst into tears or light up with laughter. Her straight hair, always a cross for her to bear, pulled back tightly, revealing her small ears, and fastened securely with a ribbon. She sat there tensely, plump hands grasping the chair ahead, absorbing to the utmost this wonder world behind the lights.[32]

Mary was so fascinated by acting that she thought she wanted to become an actress, but she found no parental encouragement for this young dream. In her biographical radio play, she touched on the prevailing attitude she had encountered at home:

103 MARY: Mum, can I go on the stage when I get big?

104 MOTHER: Mary, the stage is no life for a respectable girl. We'll think of something nice for you to do when you get big. You study hard and we'll think of something.[33]

Early motion pictures had been shown in Fredericton at the Opera House beginning in 1899, and the first motion picture theatres opened in the city in 1907.[34] Thus, from the time Mary was a young girl, movies were positively a part of the life of the city. Mary was enthralled with them and re-enacted some of the plots on the kitchen table for Helen.

"[I remember] when movies were not too common," Helen wrote, "[and someone] — would I call him an entrepreneur, I wonder, or just someone out to try to make a buck — renting a vacant store in a small town like this, nailing kitchen chairs together with boards under them to make theatre seats, renting some celluloid film and having matinees for kids on Saturdays — admission 5 cents with a bag of hardtack as an added inducement. I've been to them — dragged by Mary, of course."[35]

Of all the various entertainments and delights of her childhood, the one that did more than any other to captivate and inspire Mary was the circus. Circuses began coming to Fredericton during the first half of the nineteenth century. During Mary's childhood, circuses came most summers, including Lemen Bros. Circus, Sells & Downs, Barnum & Bailey, Hargreaves, Norris & Row, Cole Bros., and Howes Great London Circus.[36]

The circus spectacle was the grandest entertainment of the year for children in small cities in the first part of the twentieth century. Only the circus exuded this scope of excitement, with its colourful, exotic nature, its daring and funny acts. And it was the most flamboyant and exciting part of Mary's childhood. She longed to be part of the circus, but when she expressed this desire the response, especially from Mother, was clear. Joining the circus was not something a respectable person did.

"We're not the kind of people who perform in a circus, Mary," said Mother in Mary's play.[37]

So, it was a summer treat, a fantasy. She watched the circus parade through Fredericton, and when it had passed her along one street, she ran to another to watch it all over again. It was a love and fascination she never outgrew.

In 1914, three circuses visited Fredericton: two arrived in town in June before school closed — the Mighty Haag Circus, on Thursday, June 18, and Wheeler Bros. Circus, on Saturday, June 27; John Robinson Circus visited on July 24. Years later, Mary related a tale to fellow circus enthusiast Jim O'Neill of Fredericton.[38] She did not tell him the exact date, but there was only one event that fit the description.

On Thursday, June 18, 1914, the slight figure of Billy Grannan appeared in the doorway of Mr. James A. Hughes's Grade 7 and 8 class at St. Dunstan's School. Mr. Grannan asked Mr. Hughes for permission to take Mary out of class to go see the Mighty Haag Circus. At a time of strict school discipline, this was undoubtedly a rare request, and Mr. Hughes, being principal of the school as well as the senior class teacher, probably gave an even rarer assent. The usual excitement and thrill of the circus gained an extra aura that day as father and daughter left the school hand in hand to attend the afternoon show of the Mighty Haag.

Under the Big Top at Queen's Park that beautiful spring day, a large crowd converged for the spectacle.[39] Their excitement had been building through the day. The Mighty Haag had arrived by train at the CPR station early that morning, and, with a good contingent of locals watching, its crew immediately began unloading the twenty-some double cars and proceeded to the performance site to erect the tents. Later that morning, at ten-thirty, Fredericton citizens beheld one of the finest circus parades to meander through their streets in many years.

Having made their way through the crowd to find their seats in the big tent, Billy and Mary, with her eyes twice as wide as normal, watched the spectacle unfold in two rings and on centre stage. The performance began with the grand parade into the tent accompanied by the stirring march music "Caesar's Triumphal March," played by the band. Ten dapple grey horses pulled an elaborate wagon that sported carvings of Columbus discovering America. Sitting beside the driver was the circus announcer, Doc Coates, wearing his Texas Western hat and frock coat.

"Hold your hosses," he called out, "the elephants are coming."[40]

Into the ring came gilded dens carrying wild animals, elaborately costumed riders standing on horses, bright and funny clowns of all sorts, the enormous and smelly elephants, the gently loping camels, and the jolly steam calliope. The Mighty Haag, noted for its superior menagerie, displayed fine quality horses and a large herd of ponies.

No sooner had the parade ended than the acts began. Bareback riders with the Green-Hollis equestrians performed on their elegant horses. High overhead, the aerialists, a family of six from Munich, swung and flipped in astounding acrobatics, making the crowd gasp. Back on the ground, a rope act was followed first by jugglers and then by trained ponies and dogs. The clowns arrived in all shapes and sizes and drew laughs with their antics, including a slack-wire act and crazy tunes played by the clown band. Then another high-wire act had spectators transfixed once again. The well-trained elephants performed next, and after one more juggling act came the finale — a camel race.

As the Big Top show drew to a close, Mary must have felt exhilarated. Not only was it a superb circus display, but it was also important enough that her father had taken her out of school to see it. Earlier that day, she may have pleaded and begged to attend. Mother, in her usual stern approach, probably rebuffed the request. But Father, with his soft heart, must have known how important the circus was to Mary. So, as Mary and her father wound their way through the throng and out of the tent, they must have felt a special happiness and closeness.

What may have aided the lasting impression of that day in June 1914 was the fact that this was the last summer of Mary's childhood in which circuses came to the city. Ten days later, on June 28, Archduke Franz Ferdinand of Austria was assassinated in Sarajevo. Within two months, Canada was at war, and no circuses travelled to Fredericton during wartime. The next year that they came was 1919, when Mary was a young working adult.

From the beginning, she was an artist seeking expression. Whether it was on the impromptu stage at the step in the backyard or on the stage at school, she loved to perform and to entertain others and was in turn captivated by the entertainment and spectacle of the circus, theatre, and movies. Her early life was a circle of stories told to her, told by her, read to her, and read by her. Stories infiltrated her play, the autonomous and self-entertaining play of children who were free to roam the neighbourhood of their small city, drop in to visit Aunt Mary or Aunt Maggie, or wander down to the green by the river. Mary was at liberty to amuse herself as a child, whether through imaginative play, games, or simply sitting on a fence, pulling a string attached to something meant to catch the attention of passersby. Amusing and amused by life, Mary found joy in all she saw, and she noticed extraordinary amounts of detail around her — little puppies with sad faces, kittens, ponies, and people. She had an affinity and sympathy for creatures and humans. The building blocks were there all around her — in her character, in her upbringing — laying the foundation for her later storytelling years.

Chapter Three

The Schoolmarm, 1914-1934

July 1, 1939

At quarter past six in the evening, Mary's train arrived at the station in Fredericton Junction, a small community to the south.[1] The short trip had been merely enough time to settle down from the rush of packing and leaving earlier that day. Along with the other passengers, Mary disembarked and filed into the wooden frame station house to wait for the connecting train to Montreal. Within twenty minutes, train number 41 arrived from Saint John.[2] Made of steel and air-conditioned, this train was longer, consisting of sleeper cars as well as coaches and a dining car.[3]

Mary boarded the train at the platform and walked through the interior until she located her assigned sleeping car and berth. Eight minutes after its arrival, the train had gathered up its passengers and departed promptly. It was barely up to speed when a waiter from the dining car passed by, sounded a *bing bong* on his small chime, and announced, "Second call to dinner." Jostled from side to side by the swaying of the train, Mary made her way along to the dining car.

With white, starched table linens and napkins, silverware, china, and flowers, the dinner service aboard the train was a welcome and pleasant diversion. Dinner prices began at one dollar, and Saint John harbour salmon was a standard feature on the menu for the train to Montreal.[4] Delicious smells emanated from the kitchen, while efficient and uniformed waiters seated passengers and took their dinner orders. Making small talk with her companions at the table, Mary enjoyed the meal and the scenery as the train moved through western New Brunswick toward Maine, the shadows gradually lengthening on the extended summer evening. Undoubtedly, her new job was foremost in her mind. During quiet moments when she was able to avoid conversation, she may have gazed out the window and conjured up possible new story scenarios for upcoming broadcasts. She had a long way to travel that night and the next day, but, upon reflection, she had already come a long way from her first employment.

Student Days at Fredericton High School and Provincial Normal School

In the fall of 1914, as Canada went to war against Germany, Mary began high school in the Grade 9 class taught by Ellen Thorne.[5] Fredericton High School at that time was located on York Street in a three-storey brick building that housed both elementary and high school classes. While Mary's elementary school had been a Roman Catholic institution, her high school was non-denominational and the only high school for the city of Fredericton. In this setting, Mary began to become friends with a wider circle of young people in the community.

From the fall of 1915 until the spring of 1917, Mary was in the Grade 10 class of the classics and history teacher John E. Page. Mary's studies in Page's class consisted of a traditional mix of English, Latin, French, arithmetic, geometry, algebra, history, geography, physiology, hygiene, chemistry, agriculture, and botany. Females greatly outnumbered males in her class by 1917, thirty-six to seventeen.[6] While some of the young men enlisted in the war effort, others left school to work on farms. As the war continued through Mary's high school years, Canadians' original patriotic enthusiasm for the conflict waned as they faced mounting losses of loved ones overseas and inflation and food restrictions at home. It was a sobering time to be growing into young adulthood.

While in high school, Mary faced the reality of choosing a career. She set aside her childhood dreams of circus, stage, and art and chose the noble and practical profession of teaching. She said that it was a choice based on her love of children and her own enjoyment of school as a child.[7]

"In those days during and following the First World War," Helen wrote, "it was only the very well-to-do who could send their children to university. In this town, there seemed to be three choices for young girls — Normal School (as [Teachers' College] was then called), nursing or business school. We all chose the first."[8] In fact, older sister Ann had first chosen nursing but left it for teaching.

Mary prepared for the Normal School entrance examinations and passed them in the spring of 1917. Since she did not write the junior matriculation or high school leaving examinations, she did not receive a high school diploma, although she may have received some type of high school certificate. This was a common practice at the time. She was present at the school closing exercises, participating in a reception for graduates by playing a couple of violin selections.

Two changes in Mary's home life occurred during her high school years. The first was a shift in her father's employment. As cars became more common in the city, the horse-drawn carriage trade in which Billy Grannan had been working began to dwindle. He turned his skills toward general carpentry, while he continued as a fireman.

The second change concerned their residence. It was likely while Mary was in high school that the Grannan family moved into the Haney home at 325 Brunswick Street. Mary's grandfather, Patrick Haney, purchased the house for the sum of two hundred dollars in 1879,[9] although the family may have been leasing the property prior to that date since Mary's mother, Kate, was supposedly born there in 1861. Built in 1850, following the great fire that had consumed the city, the house was originally a small two-storey wooden structure with an enclosed porch concealing the front door, a fireplace for cooking on the main floor, and a circular stairway going up to the second level.[10] At some point, an extension was built on the back of the house, and the door and small porch on the front side were removed and replaced by a new side entrance with a large veranda.[11] Since her Haney grandparents died before she was born, Mary knew this house through her childhood as the home of her mother's sister, Mary Haney.

On May 1, 1916, Mary Haney passed away and willed the house to her invalid sister, Margaret Flanagan, for her lifetime.[12] Upon Margaret Flanagan's death, the will stipulated that the house was to become the property of nieces Ann, Mary, and Helen. Given these circumstances as outlined in the will, the Grannan family probably moved into the house in 1916 to look after Aunt Maggie, and after her death the girls inherited the home. And so the house became Mary's home when she was sixteen years old, and it remained so for the rest of her life.

In September 1917, Mary began her ten-month course of studies in teacher training at the Provincial Normal School, located on Queen Street in Fredericton in a three-storey brick building built in 1876. In addition to teacher training classes, the school conducted a "model school" in the building for the benefit of the student teachers. Mary joined a largely female class of 272 students from across the province. She appears not to have been an exceptional student as far as her scholastic grades were considered. Her mark in "professional class" was 51, compared to the highest mark in the class of 64.9, and her scholarship average was 65.5, compared to 81.2. She graduated in June 1918 as a teacher second class.[13]

Teaching in the Country

Mary's first teaching assignment in the fall of 1918 was in Maplewood, a small community in the parish of Southampton, York County, about fifty kilometres northwest of Fredericton. She boarded there with Mrs. Murray Wallace and taught eleven pupils, aged seven to twelve, in a one-room school.[14] Many of the children had brothers and sisters in the class, so that altogether they represented the school-age children of about five families. It turned out to be a short first assignment, for the school was closed after seven weeks because of the Spanish influenza pandemic that swept the world following the end of hostilities in the First World War.

"[Mary] went [for] her first school to a God-forsaken place in the country," Helen wrote, "but wasn't there the full term because of flu epidemic. Much to her relief, I must add. She was definitely not a country girl. I wish you could have heard her describing some of the swains who tried to take her out."[15]

After spending the remainder of the fall term at home in Fredericton, Mary travelled in January 1919 to the coal mining town of Minto, about fifty kilometres to the northeast. Her sister, Ann, had been teaching in Minto at the South Minto School for a year and a half and had appealed for help with her extraordinarily large class. In her first year there, Ann had taught 104 students, but that year she faced a total of 122, ranging in age from six to fifteen.[16] The women divided the class, with Ann teaching the advanced group and Mary, the primary. The groups did not divide equally, however, and Mary was responsible for eighty-two children, quite a change from the eleven she'd had in Maplewood in the fall.

The South Minto School was a one-room wooden school located on the north side of the Fredericton-Richibucto road. Known locally as the C.P.R. School, it had nothing to do with the Canadian Pacific Railway; this was merely a local name given to the area of South Minto and its school at the time. Most of the children in the school were the sons and daughters of miners, some of whom were European immigrants. On Friday afternoons, Mary allowed the students to sing songs in their own languages. Their uproarious laughter while they sang left Mary with the impression that they were teasing her with some songs of dubious quality. She never learned the meaning of their lyrics.[17]

Ann and Mary must have enjoyed the experience of teaching together, especially since they were the only teachers in the school. Although the community was small, it featured a movie theatre, Cady's Theatre, as well as an ice cream parlour, which was a favourite gathering place after a movie.[18] While in Minto, the two sisters boarded at MacMann House, the town's main hotel, each paying board of one dollar a day. On April 24, 1919, a fire completely destroyed the hotel as well as all of their personal belongings.[19] When their mother received news of their loss, she bundled up replacement clothing and took it to them. While the experience of teaching in Minto was undoubtedly a rich one, their teacher's pay was not — Mary earned approximately thirty-seven dollars a month, and Ann, forty-two. Most of their earnings went to pay for board. When the school term ended, Mary and Ann had to request some money from home in order to purchase their train tickets back to Fredericton.[20]

"That summer when school closed in 1919," Helen wrote, "[Mary] went to work in a ladies' dress shop [in Fredericton, Murray's on Queen Street, and] was such a good saleslady that the owner tried to keep her on — she was artistic and could dress windows and paint show cards … but the Devon School job came up and she spent the next just about twenty years there."[21]

An Opening at Devon Superior School

Mary's interim employment at the dress shop ended when her search for a local teaching position turned up an offer. Fred LeR. Mawer, Secretary for the Devon School Board, wrote her a letter on October 23, 1919:

> No doubt you have received my letter of the 18th inst. stating that the vacancy in the Primary Department of the Devon Superior School has been supplied. However, the Teacher having accepted a School in St. John still leaves this department vacant, should you care to accept, the salary is $37 per month.
>
> Kindly advise me by return mail or Phone 629-22.[22]

Mary pounced on the opportunity. It was the beginning of a happy and fortunate employment, for Mary had found a platform from which she could nurture her artistic abilities.

The school, originally known as the Gibson School, was built in 1875 and became the Devon Superior School in 1917 when the town of Devon was formed from the villages of St. Mary's Ferry and Gibson.[23] The school was a two-storey wooden structure with four classrooms on each level. An annex was added to the building in 1917, two years before Mary arrived. Located on Union Street in Devon across the St. John

River from Fredericton, the school property was bordered by a railroad track across the back and a steep gully and stream along one side. Former students recalled that the school grounds were soft and springy when wet and speculated that sawdust might have been underneath. The classrooms were heated by wood stoves, and since the janitor lit these only once everyone had arrived, the rooms were chilly at the beginning of the winter days. The bathrooms in the basement were damp, smelly, and in poor condition, the basement itself being prone to flooding.[24]

Mary joined the teaching staff partway through the fall term as a Grade 1 classroom assistant, replacing the departing teacher, Florence Lint, in January. Mary set about at once to decorate the otherwise bleak classroom with her drawings and artwork. Classes continued to be large, and Mary's classes through the years at Devon averaged fifty-eight students, ranging from a minimum of forty-three to a maximum of seventy-six.[25] Discipline was strict, and teachers at the time strapped students on the hands as a means of punishment for misbehaviour, talking in class, chewing gum, or spelling mistakes. The basic lessons of Grade 1 were reading, spelling, writing, arithmetic, and drawing. For most of Mary's years at Devon, the children used slates for their work.

"When you started grade one," said Pat Barry (class of 1935–36), "you had to have a slate, slate pencil, a sponge (a real, natural sponge) for washing the slate, and a rag for a drying cloth. You had to get someone to rule one side of the slate with a nail — my father did mine. I had crayons also and drawing books."[26]

Recollections from former students contribute to a composite picture of typical activities in Miss Grannan's class.[27] The day began with roll call and a devotional reading, often Psalm 23, "The Lord is My Shepherd." Interspersed through the lessons were exercises — marches around the room, stretches and bends, and songs with actions, such as "Here We Come on Our Ponies." No matter what time of year, Mary threw open the windows occasionally to freshen the air. She kept a large abacus at the front of the room to help students learn to count, add, and subtract, and she led the children in drills of arithmetic and the phonetic sounds of the alphabet. Some recalled that she had a large wicker chair beside her desk, and on the desk she kept a stuffed cat and dog. Every once in a while, she would pick up the stuffed animals to engage the children with the nursery rhyme "The Gingham Dog and the Calico Cat." Students remember most fondly the Friday afternoon story times. Mary dramatized her readings, providing different voices for each character. This was undoubtedly a natural training ground for her to learn the art of storytelling to children.

In the following interview, as in most of her later interviews, Mary told of daily storytelling in the classroom:

> In school we always had devotional and then arithmetic, so when I began to teach I decided to have devotional, then a story, then arithmetic after; I thought it might make the day brighter. I read to the children from books that were available but there [weren't] enough of them, so I decided to write my own.
>
> I asked the pupils what they liked to hear about and so they wouldn't copy, I got them to come up and whisper in my ear.
>
> I also used experiences in my own childhood, my imagination and day by day incidents. Many of my pupils were the inspiration for my stories, and adults too.[28]

Mary may not have told daily stories from the beginning of her time at Devon but rather gradually incorporated them into the daily routine.

"After Psalm 23," said Mary Hayes (class of 1932–33), "Miss Grannan would tell some story about an incident or about something that happened."[29]

"Miss Grannan had the ability to relate to a six-year-old on his level," said Pat Barry. "She projected a sincere warmth."[30]

"She was really *good* with children," said Mae Savage Nicholson (class of 1934–35). "Her story times on Friday afternoons were great. … Mary Grannan made such an impression on me. … I have always loved reading my whole life because of her. Everything about her made that impression on me — she took reading seriously and took math seriously, too. … She was bigger than life. She had a presence that no other teacher had, even in high school. She was so *sure* of herself. She made us *want* to learn because she *wanted* us to learn."[31]

Stories in class were not the only product of Mary's imagination. She gained a tremendous reputation in the community for the school skits and dramas she wrote and directed for the Grade 1 and 2 classes as part of the year-end recital. These were performed behind the school on a wooden outdoor stage under a big tree. Parents and even neighbours who did not have children in the productions carried their chairs to the school ground to watch the proceedings. Mary worked in conjunction with the Grade 2 teacher, who was Nellie Blair for most of the years, and then her sister, Muriel Blair, for the last few. But it was Mary who was the driving force behind the productions.

"If you knew Miss Grannan," Mae wrote, "you'd know that she was 'in charge' of anything in which she was involved. She was a force unto herself and everybody recognized the fact. But that said, she was also very patient, kind, compassionate, generous, and considerate."[32]

Sometimes enlisting the help of her sister Helen, Mary made elaborate crepe paper costumes for the children and designed artwork to decorate the stage. "The Life of Laura Secord" was the play she wrote for June 1929.

"I was Laura Secord," said Mary Kessom Grandy (class of 1928–29). "I had a lot of memorization to do. On the day of the play, my cousin, Ray (Bunny) Burpee, was up in the tree making faces at me while I was trying to say my lines."[33]

Selecting a few students to play the larger roles, Mary tried to involve as many children as possible in the productions. The presentation by Grades 1 and 2 was only part of the recital, as all classes up to Grade 8 participated, and the year-end first-place certificates were presented on the same day. During the first few years, Mary likely would have drawn on the more usual recitations and songs, but the skits and dramas soon evolved.

For June 1933, Mary wrote a skit called "God Given":

"Up, up in the sky" solo.
Helen: Up, up, in the sky, the little birds fly.

Doris: And oh! How the little white cloudlets go by.

Vida: And the rest is so blue and so sweet and so clear,
         I wish a bit of the sky would drop right down
         here.

Hope: I could make me a blue dress and trim it with
         white.

Doris: And the red from the sunset would set me off
         just right.

Hope: Seems a waste for such colors to be so far away.

Vida: Let's borrow dad's ladder, and climb up some
         day.

Hope: Do you think we could reach it?

Helen: No, I don't think we could
         Let's write the colors a letter
         Think they'd answer?

All: I bet they would

Helen: Let's see now, I'll start it. (has pencil and paper)
         Dear shades of the sky,
         We love you. You're pretty.
         Drop in going by
         And tell us your story. Tell us what you see.
         Do you watch little girls, like Doris and me?
         Do you all get together, and play in the sun?
         Do the little stars wink at you?
         Oh you must be fun.
         Well we'll stop now, our letter
         Dear shades of the sky.
         Remember come see us.
         From the girls, and I.

The girls ask a robin to carry their letter to the sky. In response to their letter, the red, white, and blue colours come to visit the girls and relate the colours of the sky to the Union Jack. The skit ends with the patriotic declaration that the flag is "God given," and as the colours dance out singing, the girls conclude the skit.

Helen:	I'm glad that our flag holds the sunset
Vida:	I'm glad she's the white and the blue
Hope:	I'm glad that I live in Canada
H.V.H.:	We're glad we're Canadians too.
Helen:	But what are you glad for Miss Doris
	Do you know girls, she's not said a word
Doris:	I know, but I was just thinking
	That I had to get crumbs for the bird.
All:	We've forgotten the bird!
	" " " "
	" " " "
All Singing:	Little bird, we have heard
	A story that's a winner
	You sent it here, so my dear,
	We'll go and hunt your dinner.[34]

Exploring Her Creative Side

When she was in her early twenties, Mary started to take part in the annual St. Patrick's Day play put on in March by the St. Dunstan's Dramatic Society. Mary threw herself into these amateur productions with an infectious enthusiasm and earned favourable reviews of her acting. On March 17, 1924, she played the role of "Gilda Deveaux" in *Our Wives*. *Teen Talk* magazine later related Mary's story of being offered an acting job as a result of her performance: "[Mary's] love of dramatics led her to join the town's dramatic club where a character part was her first assignment. So well was Mary getting along in this field that an English Stock Company touring the country offered her a job. But Mother put her foot down. No daughter of hers was going to become an actress!"[35]

Discouraged by her mother from pursuing professional acting, Mary nevertheless continued her amateur performances and school dramas. With a few years of teaching behind her and perhaps a few dollars saved, she began to indulge herself by taking some long-desired artistic training. In the summer of 1927, Mary travelled to

Boston and took a commercial art course from the Vesper George School of Art. Subsequent to this course, she entered some exhibits in the local Fredericton Exhibition in 1929, including a paper doll display that was distinctive enough to earn a special mention in the local newspaper:

> This year the fine arts exhibit consists of oil paint-
> ings, portraits, landscapes, pastel work, water colors,
> charcoal heads, etchings, flags of the different coun-
> tries in wax, hand painted china, basketry, ham-
> mered brass, parchment lamp shades, carved wood, a
> landscape with a back ground in water colors and the
> building in birch bark, ottomans, fancy flowers, com-
> mercial work and fire screens. An interesting feature
> was an exhibit, The Life of Our Block in Dolls, orig-
> inated and painted by Miss Mary Grannen [sic], of
> this city.[36]

Other artistic dabbling followed. In June 1930, she supplied sever-al cartoons for political advertisements in the *Daily Gleaner* during a provincial election campaign. The cartoons were critical of the incum-bent government and the International Paper Company: one depicted New Brunswick forests stripped of all trees, "cleaned out" by the com-pany, and another portrayed the company as Goldilocks eating up all the local electric power.[37]

However, the main focus of Mary's artistic work remained in the classroom. Her artistic decorations there left a lasting impression on many of her students. "Entering Mary Grannan's classroom," said Mary Kessom Grandy, "was like walking into fairyland. The blackboards were filled with chalk pictures she had drawn. On one board, she might have something like Winnie-the-Pooh. She changed them periodical-ly and with the seasons. They were so beautiful."[38]

"The most wonderful thing," said Pat Barry, "was that Mary Grannan drew a birthday cake for you on your birthday — a great, big, juicy-look-ing cake on a pedestal. I just wanted to go up and lick it. 'Happy Birthday, Pat' would be written on the board when I came in that day."[39]

In 1928, she began to study privately with the elocution teacher from Normal School, Mrs. LeR. Mooers. The student book Mary kept for these studies showed that the lessons in elocution and expression provided some fundamental training in voice and acting:

<u>Expression</u>

<u>Oct. 22. 1928.</u>   <u>Devon</u>

<u>Lesson I.</u>

<u>Expression</u> is thought taking on <u>Embodiment.</u> Some persons choose the term Elocution. This means merely Oral Delivery, whereas Expression is mode of expressing Character + Thought.

An artist has as his instruments, palette, canvas, brush, etc. […]

We have as our instruments <u>Voice</u> and <u>Body.</u> These are the "tools" of Expression.

Voice and Body are representatives of the <u>Mind.</u> Mind then is the important factor in Expression. Voice and Body may be trained to obey the mind, and at the same time, call no attention to themselves as Voice and Body. Mind works in three ways, we might say, in, out, and around.

[…] Voice has range. Some thoughts are subordinate to others, and voice should be used accordingly.

<u>Posture.</u> Change in position, must not be noticeably dramatic, but must be natural, and done in such a way as to show audience, no planning of the change. The order of the change is 1) Eyes, 2) Head, 3) Chest, 4) Body, 5) Feet.

One must feel, admiration, contempt, sympathy, etc. for characters impersonated. If this feeling dominates, one is able to express the author's thoughts.

<u>PROBLEM. Lesson I</u>

Young Lochinvar by Sir Walter Scott

A Model Letter by Booth Tarkington[40]

Subsequent lessons addressed gestures, breathing exercises, transition from passive to active attention, and foot placement. Assignments for performance covered a range of poetry and prose, including Charles Dickens's "Fezziwig's Ball" from *A Christmas Carol*, Alfred Noyes's "The Highwayman," Pauline Johnson's "The Pilot of the Plains," sonnets by Shakespeare, and a scene from Shakespeare's *King Henry VIII*. Later lessons introduced readings with dialect, such as selections from Tom Daly's *Canzoni*.

In this small journal, Mary carefully printed her lesson notes and the selections she was learning to perform. However, partway through the book, she began to include some original compositions of her own:

Reluctance

I knew your worth,
And so — reluctantly, I gave you friendship —
Felt it grow.
And friendship ripened — fitted as a glove,
Reluctantly — I gave you love,
I felt your charm — your power to enthrall.
Reluctantly I gave you — all,
And once my heart within your wretched keeping
You crushed it — ah — then the reaping
Of a weak reluctance,
Lack of strength to quell,
A worthless love —
The outcome? Loneliness in hell.
MEG[41]

Mary's entries in the journal continued at least until 1933, although she may not have taken the lessons from Mrs. Mooers all of this time. A couple of her original pieces appear to have been written for her students to perform at the school closing concerts.

As well as the art and elocution lessons, Mary took typing lessons in evening classes at the high school from October 1929 until March 1930. While not an artistic endeavour, this was a skill she would need for writing stories.

Social Life Meshes with Creative Life

Whether it was a rule or merely a convention, female teachers of the time were typically unmarried. Once the women married, they usually resigned from teaching. Conversely, women who wished to work at their careers often delayed or even avoided marriage. Since career and work were important to Mary, she was in no hurry to find a mate. She had a close relationship for several years with Bill Shea, the son of Mr. and Mrs. Dennis Shea, who owned a plumbing business in the city.

"Mrs. Shea had a big home downtown and a maid," said Donald Roberts, a friend of Mary's. "[Mary] would go [to] Sunday dinners, and I think Mrs. Shea, from what I can understand, wanted the two of them to be married — they were both Catholic ... but Bill was the kind, I think, that was spoiled, and he didn't seem to Mary to be the type to hold down a job and be steady. He was a good-looking man. Anyway, Mary decided she wasn't going to marry him, although she liked him terribly."[42]

In September 1922, Ann Grannan began teaching Grade 6 at Devon Superior School. After a three-year interval since they had last taught together in Minto, the sisters must have been pleased to be together at the same school once again. During this time, they lived with their parents at the Brunswick Street family home, which they co-owned with Helen. In fact, Mary continued to live at home throughout her time teaching at Devon. One can imagine how the dinner conversation revolved around events at the school. Ann remained on staff there for four years, after which she eventually left Fredericton to accept a school position in Moncton.

Since most of the teachers at Devon Superior were single ladies, friendships among them were natural. At the same time as Ann arrived at Devon, Muriel Burtt joined the staff to teach Grade 4. She and Mary became especially close friends. Muriel was three years younger than Mary and was similarly anxious to develop her teaching career. Muriel had a boyfriend, Bill Walker, whom she later married, but she delayed marriage into her thirties so she could work. Muriel's daughter, Muriel-Ann, offers some insight:

I think it would have just been a choice to work, and these gals would have had their own money at a time when people didn't and they had a lot of fun. My mother ... was nearly forty when I was born. ... She would have been well into her thirties before she married. So, again by choice, [she spent] nine years with one man and [wanted] to [marry]. There was no other reason, other than she didn't want to stop working. ... My mom travelled across the continent while she was single and used her money for that. So, I'm sure it just gave them a life that they otherwise just wouldn't have had.[43]

Among their varied social activities, Mary joined Muriel at the Baptist Young People's Union, the BYPU, of the Brunswick Street United Baptist Church located near the Grannan home. It was there that Mary met and became friends with a primary teacher at the York Street School, Gertrude Davis, with whom Mary would soon become involved in local radio broadcasting. In recognition of Mary's active part in the BYPU, the group named her an honorary member, even though she was a Roman Catholic and not part of the Baptist congregation.

"And [Mary] said her mother would have a fit if she knew her Catholic daughter was in the Baptist Church,"[44] Gertrude said. Such religious barriers mattered little to Mary.

On school days, Mary and Muriel walked together to and from Devon twice daily because they went home for lunch. The bridge they took over the St. John River provided a pleasant walk in good weather but a cold and blustery one in winter. On the cold days, Mary wore heavy woollen overstockings to help keep her legs warm, which she removed when she reached her classroom.[45]

"[Mary] said her life consisted of [going] over the bridge and back, over the bridge and back, over the bridge and back,"[46] said Gertrude.

Muriel remained on staff at Devon Superior School until June 1927, when she left to take a position at the Charlotte Street School in Fredericton. By this time, however, the friendship between the two women was firmly rooted and continued their entire lifetime.

During the summer holidays, Mary spent many idyllic days with Muriel at the Burtt family property on Grand Lake, the largest lake in the province. When the city was sweltering from the heat, getting away to the lakeshore was a relief, but more than that, it was a lot of good-natured fun. The forty-five-minute car ride there was part of the anticipation. They drove along the north side of the St. John River until they reached McGowan's Corner and then travelled east along the dirt road. The driver would honk his horn to warn other drivers before entering the covered wooden bridge along the way, and as the car bumped along the planks of the bridge, passengers could catch flickering glimpses of sunlit water through the small spaces between the side boards — reminiscent of the jerky images of early cinema. The road was so dusty that everyone had to roll up the car windows when another car approached, its cloud of dust trailing behind it.[47]

The Burtt property was located at Palmer's Point, a short distance beyond Douglas Harbour and almost at midpoint along the western shore of the lake. Douglas Harbour was the locale for the Saturday night square dances. There was no dance hall — people came from all around to dance outdoors in the field in front of the little store. Old Mr. Ballantyne played the fiddle and sometimes Mrs. Ballantyne entertained everyone with her sword dance. Mary and Muriel often took part in the square dances there.

The Burtt family called their summer place the "camp" because in the beginning they camped in tents among the trees. Later, they built two log cabins with stone fireplaces, which they called the "big camp" and the "little camp." At the camp, the young people, the "gang" as they called themselves, swam and boated in the lake, played softball in the clearing between the cabins, and had corn boils for supper. In the evenings, they pushed aside the furniture in the big cabin, played phonograph records, and danced. In the clearing on the far side of the big cabin, Mary, Muriel, and Muriel's sisters slept in a tent with a good roaring fire built in front. They awoke in the mornings to the sound of older cousin Gladys Hall coming out of her tent.

"Is EV-erybody HA-ppy?"[48] Gladys would yell. It was a well-known phrase made famous by Ted Lewis, the New York orchestra leader, singer, and vaudeville performer.

On summer Sunday mornings at Grand Lake, the campers held informal church services on the beach. In their midst at the shore were a couple of Presbyterian and Baptist ministers who led the devotions. The campers made time for reflection as well as fun.

One summer, Mary the artist drew and painted portraits of everyone, including herself, on stiff paper and then cut out the figures. She painted one as a composite of the three Burtt sisters — Muriel, Jo, and Molly — and called it "Mujomol." Muriel's younger cousin Gwen Kitchen posed for her portrait in trendy beach pyjamas. The portrait figures remained tacked to the walls of the cabin for many years.

On Sunday, July 19, 1931, during one of those many weekends at the camp, everyone gathered near the little cabin for a photograph — the moment forever captured by the camera.[49] With Grand Lake and the trees in the background, they posed in a group, some seated, some standing behind: Muriel Burtt and Bill Walker, Mabel and William Burtt (Muriel's parents), Gwen and Nancy Kitchen (cousins of the Burtts), fellow Devon teacher Lois MacLaggan and her beau, Gladys Hall, Joe O'Connor, and Mary. Mary was seated on the ground beside Joe, leaning against him with her left arm draped over his right thigh. His right arm was around her, his hand grasping her right wrist, and his left hand held her upper left arm. She was laughing and appeared to be teasing him, while he was trying to restrain her. Her hat rested on his left knee.

Earlier that weekend, Bill Walker and Joe O'Connor had been delayed in their arrival at the camp, apparently because they were busy with a big sale at the Fredericton men's clothing store where they worked. In a mischievous mood, Mary had written a poem in her journal:

The Wind's Misfortune

A log house by the lakeside,
A log house there alone,
Desolate? Well hardly
Two maidens were at home
And the wind blew thru the bushland,
Vicious, venomous it blew,
And the females in the log house,

Were waiting there, for — who?
Blow wind, blow, blow
Bring Bill, bring Joe.

A log house by the lakeside.
How they cleaned the darn old shack
Washed up all the dirty windows
Dug out each crevice, every crack
And the wind blew thru the bushland
On that Thursday afternoon,
Maidens don their best clean blouses
For the boys were coming soon
Blow wind, blow, blow,
Bring Bill, bring Joe.

A log house by the lakeside,
The day is wearing fast away
No sign of Pontiac forthcoming
They'd welcome e'en a Chevrolet.
Watching, waiting by the window,
White caps rushing on the lake
Pondering if life is worth living
Decide the boys are just a fake,
Blow wind, blow, blow
Bring Bill, bring Joe.

A log house by the lakeside
Evening long and cold and drear
A murmur from one of the maidens
Gee, I wish my Bill were here.
Watched the lake, we, for a boat then
Feared he'd floundered in the gale,
For he'd told us — oh so plainly,
He was going to have a "sale".
Blow wind, blow blow
Bring Bill, bring Joe.

Night then settled by the lakeside,
And the maidens who'd been glum.
Came to, and at once decided,
They had just been very dumb.
Sat they up then, in their trundle,
Called out to that vicious blast
"If those guys are on their way now,
Blow the two damn rigs, right past"
Blow wind, blow, blow,
You can have Bill — AND Joe.

———

Written at "TAKUTEZE" July 16 … '31
Dedicated to William Walker and Joseph O'Connor,
Scovil Bros. in memory of their failure to appear, at
forementioned camp.
M.E.G.[50]

The teaching years were busy and happy times for Mary, filled with the serious purpose of instructing the young, joyful social activities with friends, and the advancement of her art through classes and amateur activities. Mary was viewed by her students as a teacher who could connect with a six-year-old on his own level, an enthusiastic and good teacher, and an artistic and inventive one. Mary's friends saw her as full of fun and wit.

"She was a clever, enchanting, amusing, entertaining, beautiful girl," said Helen, "and as Jack Ross (my Scottish friend) described her moods — either in the moon or the midden."[51]

"Either in the moon or the midden" — up or down, high or low, extremely happy or cast into the refuse heap. In a rare comment on Mary's disposition, Helen alluded to moodiness. In photographs, the twinkle and excitement can be seen in Mary's eyes, captured even from the back of the room. She could be alive with bursting energy and drive when in the midst of work or play, but apparently at other times she slumped. It was perhaps part of her artistic nature.

Chapter Four
The New Circus, 1935-1939

Sunday, July 2, 1939

When the sun rose on Sunday morning, Mary's train was travelling through the Eastern Townships of Quebec not far from Sherbrooke. She was likely awake and watching out the window by the time it crossed over the St. Lawrence River and passed through the communities of Montreal West and Westmount on the approach to downtown Montreal. It was around eight o'clock when she arrived at Montreal's Windsor Station, the imposing stone structure resembling a castle that was Canadian Pacific Railway's headquarters. She had almost two and a half hours before her pool train to Toronto left from Bonaventure Station a few blocks away — time enough for breakfast in the concourse and a walk around outside.

    Streetcars clattered by as Mary crossed the street, strolling by Dominion Square and the Queen's Hotel. Church bells could be heard now and then, and she may have been tempted to stop in for prayers at the nearby Saint James or Sainte-Jacques-le-Majeur Cathedral (later Mary Queen of the World). When the gates to pool train number five opened at 9:55, Mary found a seat in the coach. This was the final segment of her journey, her destination a mere eight hours away. The next morning, she would report for work at the CBC. For this long-desired opportunity, she owed a great deal of thanks to one man — J. Stewart Neill, whom she called her "great benefactor."

J. Stewart Neill and CFNB

In the city of Fredericton, J. Stewart Neill and his brother, John, co-owned their father's hardware business, James S. Neill & Sons, which sold, among other things, radio receiving sets. At first, Neill wanted to develop local radio for the purpose of selling his radio sets, but he became so enthusiastic that it took over his and his family's lives.

Radio experimentation flourished during the first two decades of the twentieth century, following the first wireless transatlantic signal by Guglielmo Marconi in 1901 and the first radio broadcast by Reginald Fessenden in 1906. The first radio station in Canada, XWA, began in Montreal in 1919, and throughout the twenties radio stations multiplied in rapid succession across the country.[1] Radio, the first broadcast medium, the first means of voice and sound mass communication, astounded people around the globe, as the invention enabled broadcasters to reach large numbers of people simultaneously over wide physical territory. In Canada, with its population strung across a vast land, radio began to draw people together as never before.

With a ten-watt transmitter, Stewart Neill started his radio station, called 10-AD,[2] from his home on Waterloo Row on January 12, 1923, playing records and providing commentary. At first, there were only about five households in Fredericton that received his broadcasts. Several upgrades of power boosted his output and gradually more households in his broadcasting range began to have radio receivers. His audience was occasionally increased when tiptoeing family members left the party line telephone off the hook for others to hear.[3] Jack Fenety, friend and later manager of the station, recounts a story from the early days:

> Stewart Neill did a program called "From the Classics," and he did this from his studio in his home on Waterloo Row. He played RCA Victor Red Seal

records — they were about twelve inches in size, whereas the standard records were eight-inch ... and they were John Charles Thomas and the New York Symphony, and so on and so forth. And one day, he fainted. Of course, the station was off the air. When the record finished playing, there was nothing but dead air. And all thirty-five local people with radios phoned the telephone company to find out what happened. So, they got in touch with Mrs. Neill. ... She went in and there was Stewart on the floor. She thought maybe he had died, but anyway, it turned out he had just had a fainting spell.[4]

Neill changed the name of his station to CFNB and eventually moved the studio out of his home in 1927 or 1928 to the corner of York and Queen above his hardware store.[5] While his brother ran the store, Neill focused on the radio, searching for local talent and becoming friends with others in radio broadcasting across the country.

Thus, it came to pass that Mary Grannan's world intersected with the world of Stewart Neill and radio when the Canadian Teachers' Federation planned to use national, regional, and local radio broadcasts as part of the first national Education Week in 1935. With the theme of "Education: Highways to Life," prominent leaders from government and the field of education had airtime to broadcast their speeches and comments. The Governor General Earl of Bessborough, Prime Minister R.B. Bennett, the Honorable Mackenzie King, and Mr. J.S. Woodsworth spoke during the week's first education broadcast on February 4, their addresses broadcast nationally by the Canadian Radio Broadcasting Commission (CRBC).[6] After the impressive beginning, provincial and local educators took their turns, while a local Fredericton group decided to do a program of their own. At the planning meeting, Mary and fellow teacher Gertrude Davis were selected to do the local broadcast.

"That's when we started," Gertrude said. "We did the broadcast together."[7]

Rather than an address to the radio audience, Mary wrote a dialogue in which she and Gertrude discussed primary work, apparently with the participation of some of Mary's students. Broadcast on CFNB on February 12, the skit received a positive response from the community, including a note of official thanks from the Devon School Board. When Stewart Neill heard the broadcast, what immediately caught his attention was the distinctive voice of Gertrude Davis. As a trained pianist and singer, she had a musical voice with unusual characteristics that performed well on the radio. Shortly after the education broadcast, he called her into his office and offered her a regular program on Saturday mornings for children. *The Children's Birthday Party* began broadcasting around April 1935, with its host becoming known as the Birthday Lady of CFNB. Disappointed or not by Gertrude's success in gaining a radio show, Mary immediately became involved by contributing stories and sometimes bringing along some of her more talented students to take part in the broadcast. In a letter Gertrude wrote to the Maritime Merchants Alliance on September 23, 1936, she described the contribution Mary made to her show:

Even the stories are sometimes sent in by the children. But for the most part, the stories are those, which in my ten years association with children, I have found to have special appeal. Though I have many children's books to choose from, I am fortunate indeed in having as a friend, Miss Mary Grannan, a most gifted writer of children's stories. On all special occasions, such as Easter, Empire Day ... etc., she has written for me stories which the children love and ask for again and again. Miss Grannan is herself a teacher, and writes with great ease ... often on a few hours notice she will present me with a most interesting story. I have often wished that her stories might be published, and only hope that the children of the birthday hour might have the opportunity of owning them, either singly or in book form.[8]

When King George V died in January 1936, Mary wrote a special piece for *The Children's Birthday Party*, telling the King's life in the form of a child's story. It was this broadcast that caused Stewart Neill to call Mary into his office.

"Young lady, do you realize you can write radio scripts?"[9] Mary recalled Neill said as he asked her to present some program ideas. From her list of suggestions, he chose two: the *Musical Scrapbook*, a program filled with talk and music, "a narrative of history, theatre, travel, art, people,"[10] and *Aggravating Agatha*, a comedy serial centered around the exploits of a maid named Agatha. At that time, Mary was in the midst of rehearsals for the upcoming St. Patrick's Day play, *The Meddlesome Maid*, written by Charles George and published in *Baker's Plays for Amateurs* in 1933. The play may have inspired Mary to develop *Aggravating Agatha*. Around the same time, she and Gertrude broadcast a second educational dialogue, this one on art, for the 1936 Education Week. On April 21, 1936, Mary's new radio programs began broadcasting.

Although both programs were enjoyed by listeners, *Aggravating Agatha* became extremely popular, starting out as a five-minute skit with Mary as the maid and Gertrude as her employer, Mrs. Van Smythe. When a local automobile company, Valley Motors, agreed to sponsor the show, the skit was lengthened to fifteen minutes as the character of the chauffeur was added, played by station announcer Carl Watson. A local newspaper reporter interviewed the cast after three months of successful broadcasts and offered some insight about the real appeal of the chauffeur character: "Since an automobile dealer was backing the programme it was thought that the male voice would 'get the male listeners.' 'But we learned differently,' and Mrs. Van Smythe and her maid Agatha looked meaningly in the direction of the tall, blonde, popular announcer known to everyone as 'Hap' and told me of the female fans that have written in for the free picture."[11]

Mary wrote and typed out the twice-weekly *Agatha* scripts, for which she was paid seventy-five cents, and she earned an equal sum for playing the lead role. The cast had a jovial time performing the show, sometimes rehearsing at the Grannan home and other times at CFNB studios. Mary recalled that one of her frequent typographical errors recorded the word *car* as *cat*, causing the chauffeur to read the line, "Madam, your *cat* is waiting for you outside."[12]

"Yes, we had fun doing that ... I can remember one morning, we laughed," Gertrude said. "Something happened and we laughed, and Don Pringle was the announcer and he started to laugh. He *dissolved* behind the piano. I'll never forget it."[13]

The *Agatha* scripts featured a limited plot, depending largely on silly, humorous dialogue for its audience appeal. While the more cultured Mrs. Van Smythe spoke with proper English, Agatha the maid used poor grammar. The show's underlying themes were Agatha's mischief and her romantic interest in the chauffeur. Promotional bits for the show's sponsor were written directly into the program. The following excerpt comes from one of the few remaining scripts:

> The Valley Motors Company Limited, Westmorland Street Fredericton distributors of Hudson and Terraplane cars, presents the wealthy and discriminating Mrs. Van Smythe, her chauffeur Ignatius and that aggravating maid, Agatha. As the scene opens, a horse and sleigh may be seen coming down the street. When the turn out nears the Van Smythe residence we see Agatha sitting in the sleigh. It is apparent she is not a horsewoman.

Agatha	Stop ... hey ... lookit horse if you don't stop, I'm going to get mad Hey ... wait ... here's the house ... horse ... Poppin' pink parrots he's gone by ... listen if you don't stop. I'll give you a crack with this whip ... (BELLS LOUDER AND FASTER) wait ... wait ... I was only foolin' ... Help ... HELP ... the horse is running away ... HELP Ignatius
Ignatius	Whoa ... whoa ... there
Agatha	Oh Ignatius. You saved my life. You handsome big lifesaver and that ain't peppamint candy I mean with a hole.
Ignatius	(laughing) Holy cats ... I didn't save your life

Agatha	Well somebody musta. I ain't dead.
Ignatius	Well don't get excited about it.
Agatha	I will. Wouldn't you get excited if you found out you wasn't dead.
Ignatius	Oh I don't know
Agatha	Well I would … after I near as killed with a runaway
Ignatius	(still laughing) Runaway … why that horse was merely strolling
Agatha	Strolling? It was liberally galloping … why … why … I could see the half soles on its boots
Ignatius	Well is that a fact?
Agatha	Yes, Ignatius … its feet was liberally in my nostrils
Ignatius	Oh trust you to get your nose into everything
Agatha	Oh … you … you symphonic gem …
Ignatius	(LAUGH)
Agatha	I won't drive another step. I'll take it back
Ignatius	Where'd you get this turnout anyway?
Agatha	Wouldn't you like to know
Ignatius	To be frank I would
Agatha	What do you want to be Frank for. Ignatius is a nice name. And your mother give it to you. You ought to be ashamed wanting to change it, for no other reason than to find out that I got this the lend from Judge Richilieu. And I'm not going to tell you where I got it. So you needn't bother changing your name. I wouldn't change my name.
Ignatius	Wouldn't you Aggie?
Agatha	No I wouldn't
Ignatius	Oh well … (melodrama) I suppose I might as well find it out first as last … but it's quite a blow

Agatha	Ignatius, what have I did?
Ignatius	I thought I'd change your name to Kelley sometime but …
Agatha	Oh Ignatius I …
Ignatius	But you'd sooner keep "O'Shaughnessy" well … I'll get over it …
Agatha	Ignatius I never …
Ignatius	I never expected this
Agatha	Listen Ignatius …
Ignatius	I've never had anything to hit me so hard … to get me down like like this
Agatha	Well don't get down … get up … get up …
[SLEIGH BELLS]	
Agatha	Wait … wait I never meant you horse … wait … Oh Ignatius … stop him … help … help …
Ignatius	(laugh loudly) Whoa …
[BELLS CEASE]	
Agatha	Oh you saved my two lives. I'll change my name to Kelley today
Ignatius	Oh no rush
Agatha	Oh yes they is. I'm a rusher … oh Poppin' pink parrots, I can't I ain't got a veil
Ignatius	Good. Now listen, how did you get this rig from Judge Richilieu
Agatha	How'd you know I got it … I ain't gonna tell you where I got it
Mrs Van	Well where on earth did we get the swell turnout.[14]

If Mary had been well known in the community for her teaching, school plays, and amateur acting, she quickly became a local radio celebrity with the launch of *Aggravating Agatha*. Within a few months, the show became a darling favourite, with fan mail and requests for cast photographs pouring in. Mary probably loved the heady feeling of celebrity, embracing radio with all the fervour she had for the circus and theatre. It became her new circus, with its added advantage of being respectable and likely mother-approved.

As the first season of the successful comedy ended, Carl Watson began to write to the CRBC to see if he could interest them in carrying the show.

An Educational Scientist

On March 3, 1935, less than a month following Mary's first radio broadcast, her father died of stomach cancer at the age of sixty-seven.[15] Since Mr. Grannan had begun receiving care for the illness the previous December, the family likely knew for several months that he was seriously ill. Because of his long association with the Fredericton Fire Department, his casket was carried from his home to the church on a fire truck, with a fireman standing guard on the rear step.[16] Mary, her mother, and her sisters would naturally have felt great sadness at the loss. He was not to learn of Mary's success following that first educational spot on the air.

While Mary was doing her regular radio broadcasts at CFNB, she continued teaching full-time at Devon, which became Devon Graded School in 1935 after losing its superior status when the Devon School Board refused to accept students from outside its territory.[17] The radio work was only an after-school hobby that paid a pittance, while education remained her proud profession. The thirties were difficult years economically, and New Brunswick teachers experienced two salary reductions brought on by the Depression. After seeing her salary gradually rise from $600 annually in 1921 to $750 in 1928, Mary's salary was cut to $700 during the fall term of 1929, and by June 1934 it had been further reduced to $630.[18] However, the salary reductions did not dampen her enthusiasm for teaching, for nearly everyone suffered from the effects of the Depression, and those who had secure jobs felt fortunate indeed. By the fall term of 1935, her salary had risen again to $700, and it increased to $800 during the fall term of 1938, where it remained for the rest of her time at the school. The upward trend of the salaries would have been a relief, since Mary and her sister Ann were likely helping to support their mother and younger sister Helen following their father's death.

The period from 1935 to 1939 were years of tremendous personal growth for Mary, in teaching and beyond. In addition to her pivotal connection with J. Stewart Neill, she met other influential people during this time. One of these was Wilfred Wees, a well-respected school and university teacher who, following the completion of his doctorate in 1935, became editor of W.J. Gage & Company, publishers of school and college text books. During the first half of 1937, Wilfred Wees visited Devon School as part of his promotional travels across the country. Author and publisher Marsh Jeanneret aptly described Wees's activity:

> More than once I tracked Wilf Wees of Gage as he flitted about the country, dazzled by and somewhat jealous of the ease with which he closed in on the top educationists in one province after another. His doctorate in psychology set him apart from other educational "reps", and he had a suavity that made me glad that elementary readers, spellers, and arithmetics kept him too busy to level his artillery at mathematics, modern languages, or senior high school literature.[19]

Mary began to review primary textbooks produced by Gage and also corresponded with at least four other school publishers in Canada and the United States. In addition, she participated in an experimental trial of readers for the Curriculum Committee of the Department of Education during the winter term of 1938. During 1937 and 1938, she exchanged a number of letters with Gage's Frank Strowbridge and Wilfred Wees. Wees wrote eleven letters to Mary, beginning with one on July 5, 1937:

> I should have written you long before to thank you for the hospitality which you and your class showed me when I visited Devon School. I carry the experience with me always, and whenever the visit comes to mind I think particularly of your baptismal service

for slates. I think also, of course, of the perfect co-
ordination of activities in the room. I think I never
saw a room run so smoothly. I remember particularly
that 47 children showed me 47 drawings in about 47
seconds, which suggests to me that they have been
trained in the despatch of visitors. I may add that I
still carry the signed drawing by Turney Manzer in
my pocket and find a great deal of enjoyment in
showing it to people every now and again when they
speak about children's art.[20]

Having been a schoolteacher himself, Wees was apparently
impressed by Mary's skills in the classroom, since she reported later
that he had dubbed her "an educational scientist."[21] During their discussions about school textbooks, Mary and Wees also exchanged some
personal information: Wees learned of her radio broadcasts at CFNB
and her children's stories, while Mary learned that his wife, Frances
Shelley Wees, was a writer. Wees raised the topic of Mary's stories in a
letter he sent her on July 12. By this time, she was in New York attending summer school at Columbia University along with a select group of
New Brunswick teachers.

Will you not send Mrs. Wees the Children's Stories of
which you speak? The editor of the "Country Guide"
in Winnipeg has just written to me asking if I knew of
anyone who was interested in writing children's stories, as she was starting a new page for her magazine. I
don't think they pay very much at the "Country
Guide" — $5.00 to $10.00 a page, or something like
that — but if you have not been able to place them
elsewhere, I am sure that Mrs. Wees would be glad to
look at them to see if she thought Miss [Roe] might
like them. If you have the stories with you, do send
them right along, and if not, perhaps they would forward them on from your home.[22]

Just Mary

After she received his letter, Mary sent a package of stories, which he reviewed because his wife was ill and then busy with another novel. He praised the stories, citing "The Gift of Lady Moon" and describing what he liked. With some advice about the format of the text, he encouraged her to submit them to Amy Roe at the *Country Guide & Nor'-West Farmer*.

> Now that I have read your stories, I understand better than I did before the reason for your success in primary work. I have always been interested in methods of teaching, but have come, in the last few years, to the conclusion that it is not so much the method employed but the teacher who employs it that accounts for successful teaching. When I tell people about your work, they are amazed at your success, but if I were able to show them, on each occasion that I tell the story, the manuscript that you sent me, no other explanation would be required.[23]

Encouraged, Mary submitted stories to Amy Roe, who was interested but needed something shorter, five hundred words only. Within a month, Mary sent three shorter stories, selling two, for which she was paid five dollars each. Her first published stories appeared in the January and February issues of 1938. During the process of working with Amy Roe, Mary learned what the magazine liked and did not like. Roe rejected one story, "Toyland's Gift," because it appeared to reward begging,[24] and another, "Fairy Freckle Nose," because the language was more suited to adults than children.[25] Overall, Roe accepted most of Mary's stories, pleased to find an author who could provide a regular supply. Mary began a long relationship with the magazine, continuing to send monthly stories for years. Her first story, published in January 1938, was "Magic Cookies":

> The heart-shaped cookie that Peter Martin was just going to set his white teeth into, leaped from his hands and ran down the road.

Peter was so surprised that he forgot to shut his mouth and the mischievous snow fairies went in and did a tap dance on his little red tongue. Then he got cross. He liked heart-shaped cookies, and he was hungry too. So he took to his heels down the road after the runaway. He'd three more cookies in his pocket but he never thought of that.

"Hi! ... wait," he called. "Where are you going?"

The cookie stopped on a little mound of sparkling snow, and cocking his sugared face to one side said saucily, "You won't eat me if I tell you?"

"No, I won't," promised the now excited Peter. "Go on, tell me."

"Well," said the cookie. "I'm going home to Valentine Land."[26]

Progressive Education and Drama

Fletcher Peacock, Director of Educational Services in New Brunswick, began plans in 1937 to improve the credentials of New Brunswick teachers, initiating a summer school for teachers in Saint John during 1937 and selecting a number to attend the summer school at Columbia University Teachers' College in New York. Mary, who had almost twenty years of teaching experience by then, was one of those selected to go to New York, studying progressive education, educational dramatics, and fine arts. Hayden Leaman, former professor at Teachers' College in Fredericton, describes Mary's role:

> Mary Grannan broke all the norms for grade one teaching. The standard was drill at that time. Fletcher Peacock, the Superintendent of the time, was set to drag the New Brunswick system into the twentieth century. Part of his method was to find key people, leaders, and send them to Columbia University. The job when Mary Grannan came back was to instruct

teachers in the summer school at Saint John Vocational School. Peacock had a gift for finding talented people and promoting them.[27]

When Mary returned to Devon School that autumn, she was imbued with enthusiasm and new ideas that were not diminished by the delay in the opening of class until October 12 because of an outbreak of infantile paralysis, or poliomyelitis. Scott Webster, who was a student in Katherine MacLaggan's Grade 6 class at Devon that year, recalled some of the activities Mary Grannan introduced. "[Miss Grannan] would take older students down to her class and ask them to sit with the younger students and help the younger ones with their work. The older students were impressed to be involved. I never had paid much attention to the young ones before that."[28]

After school, Mary sometimes took small groups of students into Fredericton by bus to see educational movies. After the movie, she would take the group to her house on Brunswick Street for cake and cookies on the lawn. Webster attended the movie outings a couple of times.

During this same fall term, Mary met the talented and charismatic Elizabeth Sterling Haynes, whom Fletcher Peacock brought from the University of Alberta to lead the drama section of the 1937 Saint John summer school. After the positive response to her teaching, he arranged for her to stay through the 1937–38 school year to assist the New Brunswick Department of Education with a drama-in-education program.

Moira Day and Marilyn Potts have called Elizabeth Sterling Haynes "one of Canada's most influential pioneers of drama."[29] In the five years immediately before coming to New Brunswick, Haynes had been the full-time travelling drama instructor for the Department of Extension at the University of Alberta. She had wide-ranging involvement at the forefront of community drama and drama-in-education in Alberta, including the Edmonton Little Theatre, Chautauqua community theatre, the Alberta Drama League, and the first provincial drama festival, and was co-founder of the Banff School of Fine Arts. In addition, she frequently broadcast drama instruction over CKUA radio, established by the Extension Department at the University of Alberta.

During her busy and productive year in New Brunswick, Haynes made significant contributions to the training of teachers in the dramatic arts, a desired goal of the educational reforms taking place. She gave lectures, issued bulletins, built a large collection of resource books for teachers, and established a series of school festivals in music, speech, art, drama, and physical education across the province. It was in connection with the school festivals that Mary became involved with Haynes. Mary, like everyone else who came into contact with the tall and strong-willed Haynes, was thoroughly impressed with her knowledge, experience, and profusion of ideas.

Exhilarated by her studies in progressive education and her contact with Elizabeth Haynes, Mary wrote to Fletcher Peacock on December 21, 1937: "I want to thank you for the very happy fall term I've had. I've had the freedom of conscience to take time to do things I love to do … things I've always felt instinctively were important. And now you are promoting these very things. I am glad to say that on December 17, fifty one six-year olds and I, all parted reluctantly … good and understanding friends."[30]

With a lengthy quote from her November issue of *Progressive Education*, Mary wrote about the need for teachers to be understanding people capable of eliciting the best from each child:

> These thoughts make me think of what you have done for us in giving us Mrs. Haynes. I taught drawing skills before this year … I was proud of the results always, but this year I have gone in for creative expression and am more than satisfied. I shudder to think of the manner which this work might be evaluated, but it is original work out of the child's own experience. And that is what I saw this summer, and that is what you want, I think. Colors are mad … proportion is utterly disregarded, but the work is interesting … very. Perhaps I am presumptuous in taking up your valuable time to voice my enthusiasm, but I HAVE had such a delightful two months that I couldn't resist telling you as a prelude to my "Merry Christmas."[31]

Peacock responded ardently to this letter, undoubtedly pleased that Mary had gained so much from the Columbia summer school experience and from Mrs. Haynes's contributions. He complimented Mary: "It is this indefinable spiritual insight which you apparently possess in a high degree that all of us engaged in Education must acquire if we are going to accomplish anything that will be creatively progressive."[32] He asked Mary to think creatively about organizing a model progressive school for teachers to observe at the 1938 summer school in Saint John.

Peacock also had a word to say about Mrs. Haynes: "It is a great satisfaction to know that Mrs. Haynes is able to be of service to you. She also, I believe, possesses something of the value referred to above and is causing the teachers whom she meets to think creatively."[33]

During the year that Elizabeth Haynes was in Fredericton, she lived in a house on Charlotte Street with her children, Shirley and Sterling, while her husband, Nelson, remained at home in Alberta. Sterling, who was ten years old at the time, remembered that Mary came to their house frequently for dinner, at least once a week, bringing him treats and always telling him stories. Warm, friendly, and keenly interested in children, she impressed him because her stories related to his interests in chemistry and sports.

"She was tuned in to me,"[34] Sterling said. She would sit by the fireplace in their home, sometimes with Sterling on her lap, and enchant him with tales. It was an experience he could not forget, accentuated by the memory of her lavender perfume.

Mary and Elizabeth Haynes apparently developed a personal friendship that went beyond the drama work they were doing in education. According to Sterling, they remained friends for the rest of their lives. Since Elizabeth was a little over two years older, with a wealth of dramatic and radio experience, she was likely giving Mary some advice and could have been acting as a mentor. The two women shared deep convictions about drama and education, as well as an interest in radio. Both were strong-willed and ambitious women who were fond of hats. Elizabeth's influence on Mary came at a critical time, for as the year passed, plenty was developing on the radio side of Mary's life.

"Born to the Circus"

Invigorated by the sensation *Aggravating Agatha* had caused among CFNB listeners during its initial season, Carl Watson wrote on August 4, 1936, to J. Frank Willis, Director of Broadcasting (Maritimes) for the CRBC. Willis had gained wide attention four months earlier for his live reporting of the mine disaster at Moose River, Nova Scotia, and also produced his own program from Halifax, called *Atlantic Nocturne*. He was noncommittal about *Agatha*, promising only to table the scripts for an upcoming program meeting. Moreover, he indicated that the CRBC was not favorably disposed to programs that had previously received commercial sponsorship, as *Agatha* had. He did, however, hold out one bit of hope.

"However, Miss Grannan shows a decided aptitude in the writing of dialogue, and it is possible that if the 'Agatha' script is not accepted, she will be commissioned to prepare a series along similar lines, using different characters."[35]

As the fall progressed, Watson wrote again to Willis but did not hear anything further until December. During this time, though, many structural changes were taking place; the CRBC was replaced by the Canadian Broadcasting Corporation on November 2, 1936. When Willis wrote finally on December 8, he rejected the series, but again he mentioned Mary Grannan: "It is possible that at some future date, if Miss Grannan writes an original and different type of series, we will be able to produce it, at least regionally."[36]

Since Watson had no success, Stewart Neill decided to take up the cause. Believing he had found some genuine talent in Mary Grannan, he thought the comedy series could do well nationally. On December 11, shortly after Willis's letter had arrived, Neill wrote a long, four-page letter to his friend Major William Gladstone Murray, now head of the new CBC. After reviewing the talent in the Maritimes, he zeroed in on his pet project.

> We have here as well, a very clever script writer and she is equally as clever in acting. The little fifteen minute script which she has been preparing and presenting twice each week since early last spring has created an

immense amount of favorable comment, not only locally, but throughout Nova Scotia and Maine. Up to date, we have not had one unfavorable comment. When they were off the air in July, the Valley Motors had hundreds of requests to put them back on again.

When you were here, you asked me if I could recommend them for the National chain. I hesitated, of course, yet, on thinking it over since, I honestly believe that this skit would be considerably more popular than some of the features which have been carried by the former Commission, under DuPont's direction. ...

I am going to ask a personal favor of you, Bill. Give my little group of three a chance on your Eastern network for a month or two.

You know Amos 'n Andy were on WGN, Chicago, for over a year before they were snapped up. I remember when WGN tried to sell them to other Stations, and even I had some correspondence with them several years ago, shortly before they were taken over by Pepsodent.

You never can tell — we may have an Amos 'n Andy in this little group. I certainly do know that Miss Grannan, the authoress, is extremely clever and I think can produce something which would be pleasing and amusing. However, a chance is all I ask for and, after all, the public would soon be heard from. ...

It is necessary to hear Miss Grannan to appreciate her, and all I ask for is a chance for a month or two.

I would suggest two, fifteen minute periods per week, or, possibly, you could not spare more than one, but I certainly would like to see them tried out.

Yesterday, while talking to Mr. Elliott, of CFCF, Montreal, who has heard them on the air, I asked him if, in his opinion, they were good enough for the Eastern chain. He positively said "Yes, and they are much better than a lot of stuff that they are now using."

This statement is what encouraged me to write you. Well, Bill, I hope I have not bored you with this long letter. …

If you think I am too presumptuous in making the recommendations I do in this letter, tear it up and forget about it, but, if not, give us a try.[37]

In spite of his best efforts, Neill failed to gain the desired opportunity for *Agatha*. By the spring of 1937, Mary had heard through a friend that the CBC did not want this type of show. Confident that she could produce something acceptable if only she knew what they wanted, she wrote to Robert Bowman on May 15.

Quite some time ago, Miss Mary Van Wart of this city, told me that while in conversation with you, my scripts "Aggravating Agatha" were mentioned. She told me that you were of the opinion that this vehicle was not what the CBC wanted in the way of entertainment. May I presume to ask your advice? I would like to present other ideas. Ideas seem to come quickly and easily to me. I presented Agatha, to the CBC on account of its popularity here, but I feel quite certain I could write a series altogether different if I had any inkling of what might be considered the type acceptable. I can write children's stories and plays that children love. They are used over CFNB. I can dramatize history. I have in my possession travel literature from all over the world, from places as remote as the outlying islands of the Netherlands Indies, from Iceland to Indo China. I could dramatize this material into travel programs, sprinkled with humor. I attended Vesper George School of Art, in Boston. I know a great deal about artists, ancient, and modern. I could use this knowledge in a sketch, that would be altogether different from the usual thing. Then, again, I can write them like "Agatha" pure sheer imagination.

I am enclosing a newspaper clipping, that might tell you better than I, that had I the opportunity, I could deliver the material too. I would appreciate greatly Mr. Bowman, hearing from you at your convenience. I would be grateful for any suggestions you might care to offer. Again hoping that I have not presumed too much on your time.[38]

It was a letter full of unbridled enthusiasm and self-confidence — she knew she could do it if she just had the chance. The clipping she had attached to the letter was a review of a concert at which she had recited several pieces, many of them ones she had learned through her elocution lessons with Mrs. Mooers. The Fredericton reviewer dubbed her "one of the most gifted elocutionists of this community."[39] Mary had by this time written and presented another comedy sketch on CFNB for the Maritime Merchant Alliance and was writing a number of radio commercials for two local companies.

Bowman replied two weeks later, on June 1, apologizing for the delay in responding by explaining that he had been away producing broadcasts of *Night Shift*. He insisted that *Aggravating Agatha* was excellent, rejected only because it had already been broadcast in the East. He encouraged Mary to send him a half-hour program that presented New Brunswick to the rest of Canada, saying that he would keep her letter in mind for the upcoming National Programme Conference.[40]

With an escalating enthusiasm that fairly leapt off the page, Mary wrote back promptly on June 5. Energized, her fingers must have flown across the typewriter keys. Errors abounded, but she was likely too excited to notice.

I cannot thank you adequately for your kind interest and prompt reply to my letter. I am very proud of your comment on "Agatha." "She" is, I am glad to say, still on the air, and still popular. Thursday last we presented the eightieth sketch.

I will make an attempt to present something for your approval as soon as I can, I am very anxious to do so, and appreciate your suggestion. The only thing I lack just now is time to get it in shape properly. I think I have a fair idea in mind.

I appreciate too, your saying you would keep my letter in mind for the National Conference. Perhaps it might help me towards a children's program, if I told you that I have been selected by the Department of Education for New Brunswick, to go to Columbia University this summer to specialize in primary work. I expect to derive a great deal from this intensive course, and I believe I could use the material to great advantage in a children's program. The course will include art, reading, story telling from a psychological viewpoint. So I could make a program constructive as well as entertaining.

I am sending you some children's stories that I have written for my school work. Children do like these stories. (I beg you to pardon the shape they are in) I would be pleased if you would look them over sometime at your convenience. I think I can bring almost anything in history or current events down to the child's level. I would be glad of any suggestions you might offer me at anytime. Your own program has such strength, I might be able to absorb a bit of it. Thank you again for your consideration.[41]

In her letter, Mary raised the topic of children's programming once more, backing it up with her credentials and enclosing some samples. She was so eager to please, her joy palpable. When Bowman wrote again on June 12, he returned Mary's stories, confirming that the CBC was indeed eager to improve children's programming, but he said that a national broadcast for children was impossible at that time because of time zone difficulties. He suggested that Mary contact Frank Willis to explore the possibility of a children's program on the eastern network.[42] Bowman also wrote Frank Willis that day, asking him to deal with Mary. Although she appeared qualified because of being selected to attend

Columbia University, Bowman was afraid of being overwhelmed by her eager letters, which had been arriving in quick succession.

"She seems to be bright and ambitious — so much so, that I will be smothered with her letters unless she deals with you in future. For heaven's sake, give Miss Grannan the best possible chance to show what she can do!"[43]

On June 30, Frank Willis wrote to Mary, congratulating her on being selected to attend Columbia University and complimenting her stories. Since the program committee had recently decided to improve children's programming, he asked her to consider developing some dramatized children's work.[44]

Since Willis's letter likely arrived shortly before Mary left for Columbia University, she must have had some hope during the summer of developing stories for the CBC, at least on the eastern network. Nevertheless, Mary applied in August for a position at the Provincial Normal School when an opening was posted, although she missed being considered because her letter arrived one day after the position had been filled. Her application for the position, though, would likely indicate that Mary still considered education to be her main professional field, while any possible radio work would continue to be an extra activity.

When Willis wrote again at the end of the summer, he returned Mary's scripts, saying that he could not use them at that time but would keep her in mind. The attitudes of Bowman and Willis appeared to indicate some skepticism of her abilities, although it may have been difficult to select the best talent from the large number of letters they likely were receiving. However, Mary and Stewart Neill did not give up.

Neill was shrewd enough to understand the problem: the CBC needed a proven winner, something that had been tried out, not a proposal on paper. Not even his personal appeal to Gladstone Murray had convinced the CBC to give Mary a chance. Neill was determined that if the CBC had indicated a need for a children's program, he and Mary would provide one — a good one.

Neill's guidance was most critical at this point because Mary would have been naturally disappointed by the latest rejection. Encouraging her once again, he suggested she develop a storytime for children. Her skill and training as a teacher and all the practice she had had writing children's stories during the past few years made her a natural. With the cunning of a clever broadcaster, Neill positioned Mary's new program to be broadcast on Sunday evenings at 7:45 between two popular programs, a commentary program by Dr. H.L. Stewart, a Halifax philosophy professor, and the star American program *The Jack Benny Show*. This prime-time slot was guaranteed to maximize audience numbers. Mary said she called the program *Just Mary* because it was only she that was doing it, although it may have been a literary allusion to Rudyard Kipling's *Just So Stories*. *Just Mary* went on the air over CFNB in November 1937 and received immediate positive response from listeners.

What was it about *Just Mary* that had special appeal over the other radio shows she had broadcast on CFNB? For a start, it drew on all the best of Mary's abilities — natural talent, education, and learned skills. She had a natural storytelling bent, a gift for drama, and a love of children. After many years of teaching primary school and observing children closely, she had gained an understanding of them. She had watched their behaviour and speech patterns, noticing what type of stories held their interest. Her stories had been honed into shape through the practice of telling them in school and writing school plays. Even the years of participating in the St. Patrick's Day plays and her private elocution studies all became useful training. Through her work at CFNB, she had learned the basics of broadcasting and scriptwriting, handling a microphone, dramatizing a radio reading, and reaching out to the unseen audience. In addition, the program was solid — good stories, well told — and it meshed with a particular need of the CBC. Thus, all factors came into play and converged.

Delighted by *Just Mary*'s success, Stewart Neill wasted little time in making a presentation to the CBC. Within one month of its start, he sent a package of manuscripts to the CBC, this time choosing W.H. Brodie as the recipient. Once again, Mary's sponsor made the pitch himself, from one broadcaster to another. As such, it carried more weight, and Neill wanted Mary to have her best shot at succeeding this time in attracting the CBC's interest. He firmly believed in her abilities and yearned to see her have a wider audience.

After reviewing Mary's manuscripts, Brodie wrote to E.L. (Ernie) Bushnell, General Program Supervisor, on December 2:

Manuscripts of stories suitable for very young children. So far as I can judge, they are very good indeed. Likely to make a real appeal to children of the age of 5, 6 or 7. Their success on the air would depend entirely on the voice, manner and personality of the person who read them.

Apparently Miss Grannan or her station asked children to send in suggestions for stories. Some of the suggestions are enclosed, written in the children's own handwriting. From these suggestions she obviously took out one every week or so and wrote a story based on the chosen suggestion. This strikes me as a good idea for building a local children's audience.[45]

After receiving a positive assessment from Brodie, Bushnell wrote to Neill two weeks later, expressing interest in the program. Neill replied appreciatively, but nevertheless he and Mary sent along an additional letter of recommendation from Elizabeth Sterling Haynes:

I have known Miss Mary Grannan since coming to New Brunswick and have heard of her long before then. It has been my great pleasure this fall to read her stories for children and to hear them over the air.

I have listened to radio announcers, story tellers, and play makers, for the last five years and I have never heard one that appealed to me in subject matter and in manner as much as Miss Grannan.

It seems to me that with her talents she should be reaching a much larger audience than she now has. She understands children thoroughly, her stories are written for them and of them, and are based on incidents given her by the children themselves. Therefore it is no wonder that they hold our attention.

It gives me great pleasure to write this letter for Miss Grannan and I hope that soon she will be much better known to the radio audience of the Dominion.[46]

Alas, things stalled, and by spring, 1938, the CBC had taken no further action. Once more, Mary determined that some prodding was required and sent a letter of reference from Theodore Corday (Cohen), who was in New Brunswick during May 1938 to adjudicate drama in school festivals. Corday, a former drama instructor at the University of Alberta and a close associate of Haynes, worked at Sam Grisman's office in New York. On June 5, Mary sent a strongly self-confident letter to Bushnell, presenting her best case for her work, listing her credentials, offering a slew of references, and mentioning the name of Stewart Neill at the opening and closing of her letter.

Action followed the letters, as Bushnell passed the file to Rupert Lucas in the Department of Drama and Production, who in turn was impressed with the work but wanted to hear Mary's performance abilities. In separate letters to Stewart Neill and Mary, Lucas asked for a private audition through CFNB facilities so that he, Bushnell, and others could listen in their Toronto office. Her ten-minute audition took place on Thursday morning, June 30, just before noon, and elicited a positive reaction. Hugh Morrison in the Programme Department sent a telegram of congratulations to Mary, saying that he had listened with Rupert Lucas and would be writing.

As the audition was held on the last day of school, Mary was scheduled to go to Saint John for the summer school. She was undoubtedly excited and eager to learn if she would get a spot in the network schedule. A few days after the audition, Mary dropped in to see her friend Elizabeth Sterling Haynes, telling her about the audition and the telegram from Morrison. Since Haynes was in the midst of correspondence with him about another matter, she related Mary's excitement in her letter of July 5:

> Mary Grannan was just in to see me for a few minutes. She is quite thrilled because of a telegram of congratulations that she had had from you recently when she had her audition. She is anxious, I know, to find out whether she is to do any work here this summer as she is teaching at the Saint John Summer School.

She told me she mentioned that she knew me and I would like to add to the eulogies you must have had about her from Wilfred Wees. I think she has rare talent for writing children's things. I have worked with her quite closely all winter and I find her always more delightful, always more charming, always more interesting.

She and I are engaged now in writing a series of children's plays and I have come to know her better and better and have come to have more and more respect for her talent.[47]

Morrison, however, did not need the prodding, for he had already written to Mary. "I was very much taken with your sample broadcast,"[48] he wrote, asking her to do six new *Just Mary* stories on Saturday afternoons at four o'clock from July 23 until August 27. Originally, her program was to be broadcast nationally, but in the end it was only for the eastern network with a payment of eighteen dollars a program.

Mary had a busy, happy summer in Saint John. As part of the New Brunswick Summer School of Education and Fine Arts, she taught a demonstration class each weekday at the King George School on Bentley Street, presenting the new educational curriculum. As well, she wrote children's plays with Elizabeth Haynes, who was also involved with the summer school. Best of all, she broadcast her weekly stories for the CBC, using the facilities at CHSJ. The six programs went ahead as planned, except for one show being dropped on August 6 and another added on September 3.

In August, Hugh Morrison and Gladstone Murray both visited New Brunswick and met Mary in person. Morrison, who was in New Brunswick and Nova Scotia on a general talent tour, declared to the local newspapers that Mary Grannan was his outstanding talent find. Gladstone Murray was visiting his friend Stewart Neill.

"Father [Stewart Neill] was tickled with [Mary Grannan's] ability," said Malcolm Neill. "He was entertaining Gladstone Murray in Fredericton — they were good friends. Murray came down for a weekend at Father's lodge, and Father insisted that Murray interview Mary."[49]

After Murray met Mary, he was as taken with her as Stewart Neill was, uttering a phrase she would never forget: "You were born to the circus ... do you want a job?"[50] While Murray was in Halifax on August 17, he broadcast one of his national talks called "Chatting with the Listener," in which he praised Mary Grannan and her *Just Mary* program, calling it a successful experiment that the CBC would carry on an extended network as soon as possible. Newspapers in Fredericton and Saint John carried the news of his praise for the Devon schoolteacher.

Stewart Neill sent a telegram to Mary in Saint John: "Heard Gladstone Murray's tribute to your fine work. No more than you deserve. Best wishes for the future. We are all behind you. Manager and staff CFNB."[51]

Mary wrote at the side of the telegram, "The beginning!"

Although Murray talked to Mary in the summer about joining the CBC, he did not make a definite proposal to her for a while. In the interim, the CBC did not have room in the schedule for any more *Just Mary* stories until a last-minute change at Christmastime gave Mary another opening for ten broadcasts between December 26 and January 6. She did not have much preparation time, since the offer came by telegram on December 14, but she delivered. Unfortunately, her Christmas broadcasts could not be carried on CFNB because of previous broadcast commitments.

In December 1938, Gladstone Murray, Hugh Morrison, and E.L. Bushnell carefully considered the possibility of employing Mary Grannan. Writing to Bushnell on December 6 for a special report on Mary from Morrison, Murray said she was "a highly exceptional prospect for general production and continuity work as well as an unusually capable producer of a certain class of programmes."[52]

Saying that he had just been talking to Morrison about Mary, Bushnell responded, "In [Morrison's] opinion she is quite a capable person but he was not so sure that we should try to entice her away from the Maritimes. I believe Stewart Neill talked to him about her and more or less indicated that if we showed evidence of being interested in her the School Board would increase her salary in an effort to have her remain with them."[53]

This was likely a clever ploy on Neill's part; after promoting Mary relentlessly, he tried to make it appear that it would not be easy for them to hire her.

Bushnell added a cautionary note: "We should be pretty sure about whether we want her or not for if she doesn't work out satisfactorily she might have to go back to the teaching profession at a lower salary than she is getting now."[54] While appearing to give the matter some careful second thought, Bushnell said he would keep her in mind for spring, thinking she might be useful either in Vancouver or Toronto.

Before Christmas, Stewart Neill visited Gladstone Murray in Ottawa to discuss Mary and her possible employment with the CBC. Finally, on January 5, 1939, Gladstone Murray wrote to Mary with the long-awaited offer:

Quite a long time has elapsed since our conversation in Fredericton. Perhaps since then, Mr. Stewart Neill has given you some account of the conversation I had with him during his visit before Christmas. It is only now that I am in a position to discuss a definite proposition with you. I would like you to join the staff of the Corporation on April 1st or May 1st, if mutually agreeable terms can be arranged.

We are not sure yet where your services will be required. This might be in the Maritimes, in British Columbia or in Toronto. May I, first of all, then inquire whether you are still disposed to take up work with the CBC?

What is envisaged for you is that you should join the staff in the capacity of Junior Producer, for which you seem well qualified by previous experience and aptitude. I have no doubt, therefore, that you could sail through the three months' probationary period with flying colours. In this capacity, you would be called upon for a variety of duties, including pro-gramme work — music, drama and talks — script writ-ing, and so on. In this formative stage our departments are not rigidly circumscribed so that there is of necessity some overlapping of duties and functions.[55]

Thrilled as she was to receive an offer in writing at last, Mary was nevertheless unnerved by the possibility of being sent to British Columbia, wishing to remain closer to home. The salary offered must have been quite enticing, being more than double her teaching salary. However, she had a problem starting in April or May, since she was required to teach until the end of June. After discussing the letter with Neill, Mary accepted the job, outlining her exceptions to the details and asking for clarification about the duties. She closed with reference to Stewart Neill: "Mr. Neill has been most interested and helpful to me and my efforts, and with you he feels that I will soon adjust myself to the work."[56]

Neill appeared to be instrumental in helping her make a final decision, reassuring her that she would easily adapt to the work. Last-minute nerves were probably causing her to think it over carefully. He also may have assisted her in approaching the Devon School Board to ask for a leave of absence, which would provide the safety net she needed to move ahead.

Murray changed the start date to July 1, confirming as well that she would not go to British Columbia. "Your success at the microphone is the best guarantee that your broadcasting will continue. You would be expected, however, to do script writing and to help with drama and talks."[57]

Finding the details satisfactory, Mary thanked Murray for his prompt attention and explained why she did not want to go to British Columbia: "I would like to tell you incidentally, that my 'fear' of British Columbia was due only to distance from New Brunswick … having had the responsibility of home for so long, that to put a continent between me and my 77 year old mother just seemed too much at the first break."[58]

On June 8, Murray wrote to tell her to report to E.L. Bushnell, General Supervisor of Programmes, at 341 Church Street, Toronto, on Monday, July 3.[59]

Through the spring, as arrangements were gradually being finalized, Mary's final task was easing the distress of her mother and Helen, who were not happy to see Mary leave Fredericton. She comforted her family by promising that she would be home for the holidays and would write every day.

On Mary's last day at Devon School, the other teachers gave her a farewell gift, accompanied by a little card shaped like a suitcase and decorated by pink roses and blue forget-me-nots. The message read, "A little gift, To let you know, That thoughts go with you, As you go!" It was signed, "the Devon teachers."[60]

In September 1939, a new teacher, Mary Galen, arrived at Devon School to take over the Grade 1 class that had been Mary Grannan's. Galen, who had once been a student in Mary's class, was overwhelmed by the artwork that had been left behind in the room.

"The blackboards were beautifully decorated," Mary Galen Cassidy said. "When the inspector came in, he advised me to remove Mary Grannan's artwork and do my own. He said the new grade one students wouldn't have known Mary Grannan anyway."[61]

Chapter Five
Toronto Beginning, 1939-1940

Arrival in Toronto

Danforth was the last stop before Toronto, and the pool train number five soon passed Leaside and Don, arriving at Toronto's Union Station at 6:15 in the evening on Sunday, July 2. With the *ding-ding* of the train bell, the hissing of steam, and the sound of air escaping from the brakes, the train slowed and came to a rest. A whirlwind of activity surrounded Mary as passengers crowded for the door, and on the platform baggage carts rumbled, with baggage men and porters springing to action. The damp smell of steam and the oily smell of train assailed her nostrils as the push and shove of the crowd created the excitement of arrival.

Emerging into the twenty-year-old station's main concourse, Mary walked across the smooth stone floors. Tall pillars, a high arched window, and an ornate ceiling had an immediate impact, as if to say, "You have arrived in the big city." Probably leaving some heavier luggage checked and taking only her small bags as Hugh Morrison had advised her,[1] Mary headed toward the taxi stand at the west exit. As she passed through the pillars at the entrance on Front Street, the sight of the immense Royal

York Hotel met her eyes. Opened ten years earlier, it was at that time the largest hotel in the British Empire and a major landmark in Toronto. The contrast to her small hometown of Fredericton would have been striking.

At the suggestion of Frances Shelley Wees, Mary booked herself into the red brick, four-storey YWCA on Elm Street near Yonge. She likely found this a welcome suggestion, as the cost was reasonable, and, upon arrival in Toronto that day, she had only seventy-five dollars in her purse on which to live until her first CBC pay.[2] In addition, the YWCA was a short distance from the CBC building at 341 Church Street, where she would begin work the next day. She had just Sunday evening to rest from her journey, but she was undoubtedly eager to begin.

A duality of feelings must have rocked Mary to sleep that first night in Toronto. While she was certainly excited about the start of her new career and being in Toronto, she was also apprehensive about the challenge, probably feeling a bit lonely knowing so few in the large city and being so far away from her family.

Summer Preparation

After a short walk from the YWCA on the morning of Monday, July 3, Mary reported for duty to Ernie Bushnell at the four-storey, yellow brick building that stood on the corner of Church and Gerrard streets — the new job had begun at last. Her first few days were undoubtedly filled with settling in, meeting people, and finding her way around. After having her new duties assigned, she would have met with Bushnell, Morrison, and others in the program department to plan for the fall season. On Tuesday, she wrote a note to Gladstone Murray: "I have just finished my second day with the CBC. Everyone has been most kind and most helpful. I am in rather a daze myself as yet ... but hope to find my way into the things I am so anxious to do, real soon. I resent this awkward stage ... but I suppose I must accept it as part of my new job. I do hope I may be able to please you and I thank you again for letting me become part of this thing."[3]

Enthusiastic and grateful to be there, Mary nevertheless had to go through a period of adjustment. In Fredericton, she had become used to the familiar ease of a long-held teaching position and the comfortable feeling at CFNB where she knew everyone. Usually a confident person, she would not have enjoyed the timid feeling. In a later interview on CFNB, she said Ernie Bushnell had reduced her fear immediately when she first met him that day and he said, "Do the best you can ... right or wrong, I'll stand behind you."[4]

Mary was part of the CBC's effort to improve children's programming. The CBC had a few prior children's programs, among them Greta Masson's *Lamplighter* series, whose cancellation permitted Mary's entry into the schedule, but Murray saw Mary Grannan's arrival as progress. Eager to put forward her name as proof of their increased efforts, he mentioned her not only in his August broadcast but also in his appearance before the House of Commons Special Committee on Radio Broadcasting on March 17 that year: "We have made use of the talents of Miss Mary Grannan, a primary teacher with a very special gift for story telling, and who lives in Fredericton, New Brunswick. Miss Grannan will be joining our staff in July. She broadcasts her stories under the title of 'Just Mary.' She is one of the few 'naturals' in broadcasting, both in script writing and in microphone technique."[5]

Such a compliment from the head of the organization was surely a boost to Mary's confidence. Since she had understood from Murray that she was to lead the new programming trend for children, she adopted the unofficial title "Supervisor of Children's Programmes" or sometimes "Director of Children's Features." These terms were frequently used to describe her in various CBC publications, even though her official title was simply "Junior Producer." No one at the time seemed to notice the discrepancy, but it would surface later as a point of contention. The title suited her, for she liked to be in charge.

Although Mary later asserted that she quickly had lost her fear upon meeting Ernie Bushnell, her lingering uncertainty and worry are evident in a letter she wrote one week after arriving in Toronto. From her new temporary residence at 50 Dundonald Street across from the Ontario Provincial Normal School, she typed a letter to Fletcher Peacock, Director of Educational Services in New Brunswick, apparently intending to write a simple personal greeting, but her thoughts flowed from there:

Although I am on a new line of work this summer, my thoughts were in Saint John today, and I am writing to wish you every success with our summer school. I think the teachers of New Brunswick are very very fortunate to be able at last to get in contact with the best of every line of work. [...] And the new advancement scheme is splendid. I may be back to take advantage of it. I have a year's leave of absence.

I came to write scripts and to broadcast, having been offered the position by Mr. Gladstone Murray, General Manager of the CBC who said I was "born to the circus" That with my psychological twist makes them call me an "expert" and instead of being a script writer, I find myself the Director of Children's Programs, which makes me responsible for entertaining young Canada. I choose or discard presented material ... I choose or denounce people who have auditions. I am worried a bit about the responsibility, but think I can manage when time helps me to fit into the picture.

Strangely enough, the Normal School is just across the way. Today I took myself over there and met ... now I didn't get his name very well but it sounded like McCullough, or McCollum. He was a very nice man and said he had been to Nova Scotia one year and they wanted him again but Toronto would not let him go. I was soliciting the reaction of teachers to the radio, so he said he had great faith in the judgement of a Miss Dick. He took me to her. She had the primary room in the Demonstration School, and was I thrilled. Of course we had so much in common. I talked with the children and asked them things to help me in building a program. I met about ten teachers and we had a grand chat. I am going to dinner with Miss Dick to talk "shop." [...] I am going to see Dr. Blotz [probably Blatz] when it is possible. I understand he is not so much in favor owing to his progressive ideas, but if he had the time I hope to get his slant on things CBC. I called Dr. Corbett today but he is gone until August. The office felt he could help, and I am glad I had the opportunity of meeting him last year. I will be visiting schools during the year … I will be meeting educationalists, so if at any time you want to get the common teacher's slant on anything up here, I'll be so pleased to look after it for you. [...]

I was to dinner at Dr. and Mrs. Wees on Friday. We talked of her books most all of the time. I had been reporting to her all year on the effect of them … I sent her illustrations from the children. She seemed so glad to have someone talk constructively of them with her. And although I'm now a show woman, with a salary that doesn't look like a school ma'am, I'm still the school ma'am at heart, and if I do not find happiness in this work, I'll go back to the work I love.

I hope I've not taken too much of your time. I didn't intend my note of good wishes for a successful summer to stretch to such great proportions.[6]

With only a week of experience at her new work, Mary comforted herself with the idea that she might return to teaching if radio did not make her happy. Her connections to education remained strong, causing her to seek opinions about radio from teachers and schoolchildren. While her initial consultations may have been for the purpose of building her program ideas, she began to investigate school broadcasting later in the summer when the CBC assigned her to look after a BBC expert who was invited by the Ontario Department of Education to give lectures on the topic. Mr. Cons, associated with the London Goldsmiths College of Training, had worked on school broadcasting with the BBC for years. As well as arranging for the technical help Cons needed and taking him to dinner, Mary attended his extensive talks to teachers on August 15 and 16, taking copious notes, primarily for the CBC but also for Fletcher Peacock. He had responded to her first letter that summer by asking for her assistance initiating educational radio programs for schools, saying, "The radio is the great educational agency which we should bring into play as quickly as possible."[7] Eager to benefit New Brunswick education however she could, Mary began a frequent correspondence with Peacock about school broadcasts. "Please ask me to do anything for New Brunswick that you feel I can do ... I am meeting people ... I have access to the ideas of all Canada right here."[8]

Through the summer, as Mary worked on planning and story-writing for the fall season, she met with educational leaders to gather ideas about children's radio. By the time she wrote Peacock in September, her confidence had grown: "I am doing quite well, I think ... they seem to like me, and are all ready to help me out of my darkness. Each day brings more light to me ... there are so many things in a big corporation to learn."[9]

The First Broadcast Season

For her first season of broadcasting, Mary originally planned a forty-five-minute program that would include her "Just Mary" stories, but as September arrived, world events intervened with the long-expected start of the war in Europe. Suddenly, the CBC's focus shifted dramatically.

For the CBC, the year 1939 produced two large challenges that occupied most of the corporation's attention and resources: extensive coverage of the royal tour of the king and queen, which was six weeks long and covered more than seven thousand miles, and the outbreak of war in September. At once, this caused massive reorganization as the corporation dealt with issues of "news, propaganda, maintenance of national morale, censorship, protection, personnel, reorganization, technical development."[10] In comparison to all the serious issues the CBC faced in reporting the news and responding to the war effort, children's programming suddenly paled in importance, and the corporation was pleased to leave it to Mary. With the demands of news broadcasting, the forty-five-minute children's time slot had to change, as Mary explained to Gladstone Murray in a note dated October 23, 1939:

Our first plan was a 45-minute broadcast with my "Just Mary" stories included for the very young listeners. Newscasting at this time made it necessary to cut fifteen minutes from our time. So we decided to put JUST MARY on at noon Sunday. In this way we have two shows for children on the air, at no added expense. JUST MARY is not going out over Toronto, as church services intervene, but to quote Mr. Forsee, JUST MARY is terrific. I have had several wires and letters from the Maritimes about it. For these too, I am duly thankful.[11]

It was probably fortunate for Mary that news requirements forced her *Just Mary* program into its own broadcast time and kept it under its own title. The name recognition that she gained from what became her signature program would not have been the same had the story series been merely part of a longer show. Mary continued with the same format she had developed in New Brunswick, writing and narrating the stories and drawing on the names of family, friends, and children who wrote to her. During her first Toronto season, she broadcast such stories as "Katy Kinsella's Kitty Cat," "Halloween Adventure," "Monkeys and Measles," and "Toyland (Antoinette, Topsy, and Susie)." She began the fall broadcast of *Just Mary* on Sunday, October 15, with the story "The Cowboy and the Pony":

> I'm singing a funny song, I am,
> Of a little boy and a little lamb,
> Of how each of these little ones wanted to be
> Something he wasn't ... so now you'll see
> By turning their wishes into play,
> They were happy ... yes, happy ... the livelong day.

> The little lamb was beautiful. He was just as white as snow and just as soft as down. His little nose, with its shining black tip, was just the kind of nose you'd love on a little white lamb. His tail was short and frisky. His

legs were long and gambolling. Truly, he was a beautiful lamb; and he was happy too, except for one thing — he wanted to be a pony.

The little boy was … well, I can't say the little boy was *beautiful*, for no little boy wants to be beautiful. But this little boy was just the nicest little boy that ever stepped off a back porch of a morning. His eyes were bright and blue, his nose was short and freckled, his teeth were white and wiggly. Truly, he was the best kind of six-year-old boy you could find in a world of boys; and he was happy too, except for one thing — he wanted to be a cowboy.[12]

Mary's second children's program was *The Children's Scrapbook*, a thirty-minute show featuring a lively exchange of dialogue between cast members who introduced the program and provided the connection between the featured stories. The first broadcast was aired on Saturday, October 21, receiving the following introduction in the CBC Programme Schedule:

The "Children's Scrap Book", to be heard on Saturdays at 12.30 p.m., will also be under [Mary Grannan's] direction. This entirely new presentation is designed to appeal to children of a more advanced school age. Along with an orchestra, the highlight of this variety programme will be a serial dramatic sketch, "The Adventures of Don Stephens." This original script, by Harry Junkin, relates the college experiences of a typical Canadian youth. In addition, the "Children's Scrap Book" will feature unusual actuality broadcasts of particular interest to boys and girls. These will be especially prepared by R.T. Bowman, Director of the Special Events of the CBC. At various times, young listeners will also hear interviews with interesting personalities.[13]

The first broadcast was a special occasion with a group of local Toronto schoolchildren brought in by chartered bus. Photographs and a front-page story gave prominence to *The Children's Scrapbook* in the November 11 to 18 issue of *Radio Flashes*, a radio guide from Edmonton, and also appeared in the Ontario Regional Programme Schedule. The top photograph showed a wide-eyed and smiling Mary Grannan, smartly dressed with a perky hat, holding the script before the microphone, while Stanley Maxted, the master of ceremonies, looked on. Next to them stood Sydney Brown, the producer, and cast members Lloyd Bochner and Murray Davis. The bottom photograph, taken outside the CBC building, showed Mary and Stanley Maxted in front of a microphone with the crowd of children standing around them.

Austin Willis, a staff announcer from Halifax who had arrived at the CBC in Toronto around the same time as Mary, soon became involved with both of her broadcasts. At the age of twenty-two, Austin Willis was handsome, cocky, eager, and the younger brother of CBC producer J. Frank Willis. As Austin and Mary fell into a friendly working relationship, he saw that she was somewhat nervous that first fall season, taking a little longer than he to overcome her "Maritime-ness."

"Mary was very, very sort of tentative," Austin said, "wondering if she was going to work in this new environment. See, I guess it was a big leap for her. … Perhaps a lot of people didn't know that, of course. … She didn't show it, but I knew she was [nervous] because we talked. … [For her,] it was like starting over. And I said, 'Why did you do it?' She said, 'Oh, I'd always wanted to.'"[14]

Sydney Brown, who produced Mary's shows, found that she had much to learn. "I [produced] practically everything Mary Grannan did [in the beginning]," Brown said. "And I had to because she was pretty green at that time at writing radio scripts. She'd say some outrageous things without knowing that she was saying them. We had a lot of laughs."[15]

Syd Brown played a large role in the development of the program, writing several of the feature stories. He taught Mary a great deal about scriptwriting and radio production in spite of a slight tug of war between their strong personalities. Austin describes their relationship:

Syd actually was wonderful for Mary. He scolded her a lot and taught her a lot about radio dramas and things. But Mary remained very, very innocent in the most peculiar way. She would write absolutely hideous double entendre things in the script which you could take in hideous other ways and was absolutely oblivious to it. We'd be absolutely cringing and she couldn't understand why. You see, she didn't mean it that way. ... She would get mad and say "It's not dirty at all. It's you. It's you and Syd," she would say to me. "You two have minds like that."[16]

New faces appeared among the *Scrapbook* cast regulars, including Byng Whitteker, Peggi Loder, Bud Knapp, and musician Isidor (Paul) Scherman. For a short time, young Frank Perry was on the cast, but he was unable to decide whose directions he should take — those of the producer, Syd Brown, or the contrary ones given by the writer, Mary Grannan. Tongue-tied and confused when his lines came up, Perry dropped out of the show, feeling like a basket of nerves.[17] Austin explains the show:

> [*The Children's Scrapbook* was] all little bits and pieces that occurred to her — sometimes poetry, sometimes acted-out little shows, and kids. "Where are we going today, Austin?" And I would say, "Well, I'm going to take you to a barn to see a lovely bunch of cows." And off we'd go. We'd be on a farm. Things would happen to me on the farm when I was showing them around. I'd fall down or something. I'd get into terrible trouble with a bull. This was to illustrate farming to kids. And other kids would be with me and I'd have to shuffle them away out of harm's way or something. But it changed every week. Whatever occurred to her and she had a vivid, vivid imagination. She would go off in flights of fancy like you would never know. And off she'd take us. That's why they loved her.[18]

The "actuality" broadcasts in the *Children's Scrapbook* involved field visits to places in the community, such as the Riverdale Zoo, the car shops of the Toronto Transportation Commission, a bird store in the Toronto Arcade, the CNR Roundhouse, a chick hatchery in Ottawa, a bakery, and the RCMP dog kennels at Rockcliffe Barracks, Ottawa. On April 20, 1940, the *Scrapbook* visited the newspaper the *Daily Star*:

Snoopy Views Star in its Own Boudoir
"Children's Scrapbook" Hears How Newspaper Dons Every Day Best

Every week on the Canadian Broadcasting Corporation's Saturday "Children's Scrapbook", Announcer Austin Willis goes exploring with Snoopy, his pet microphone. Finding himself at The Star on Saturday Willis told Snoopy — and thousands of young listeners on the C.B.C.'s national network and the Mutual Broadcasting system across the border — all about how a newspaper is made.

Snoopy picked up a busy linotype machine, one of a battery of 50, and after following the mechanical process from beginning to end, the broadcast concluded in the swelling roar of giant presses.

Youngsters and adults of the radio audience were told how the reporter's stories are set in type, how "proofs" are taken of stories before they go in the paper, and how the galleys of type are fitted into the page-size forms. The method by which "mats" are made of these forms and semi-circular plates cast, for use on the rotary presses, was described.

Special attention was paid to the process by which The Star's comic strips get in the paper, with the announcer laughingly explaining the composing room men sometimes have trouble with Popeye. "After eating his spinach he gets feeling so tough that he's likely to start punching away and break the very plate in which he's cast," the young listeners were told.[19]

The playfulness of the dialogue in the *Scrapbook* was a major feature:

ANN: With Paul and his musicians ... with Mister Wister and his rhymes ... with the bookman and all the books that he's browsing ... with our weekly newsreel ... with Peggy ... with Percy ... and with Austin Willis, your master of ceremonies ... this is Byng Whitteker bringing you the seventeenth chapter in the seventh volume of The Children's Scrapbook.

MUSIC:THEME:

AUSTIN: Again it's hello ... to the north ... to the south ... to the east ... to the west ... to Canada and to all our friends in the United States, a very merry hello ... eh Peggy.

PEGGY: Yes ... a very merry hello ... and hurry up ... hurry up ... hurry up with everything, Percy and I have a secret. (CHANT) Percy and I have a secret ...

AUSTIN: But where's Percy ...

PEGGY: He's with the secret ... and neither one of them are here yet ...

PAUL: (COUGH) But I am Miss Peggy ...

PEGGY: Oh ... OH ... I beg your pardon Paul ... I should have asked you to say hello ...

PAUL: Yes Miss Peggy ... you should have ... that is you should have asked me to say "How do you do," as that is my

preferred salutation, so How do you do
everyone.

AUSTIN: Feel better now Paul?

PAUL: Decidedly ...

BYNG: Well then we can go ahead with a little sleuthing ... Feel like a sleuth
Austin?

AUSTIN: Never felt sleuthier.

BYNG: Well then ... sleuth ...

AUSTIN: Right ... Peggy ... what is the secret
you and Percy have?[20]

Friends and Family

During her first year in Toronto, Mary moved several times as she adjust-
ed to her new city: after Dundonald, her various addresses included 67
Heath, 354 Walmer Road, 361 Spadina Road, and 1560 Bathurst Street.
Most were located in and around the Forest Hill area of Toronto, and,
with the exception of the Bathurst Street apartment building, they were
three-storey, red brick homes in which she boarded.

One of Mary's Bathurst Street neighbours and friends was fellow
CBC staffer Georgina Murray, daughter of George and Margaret (Ma)
Murray of British Columbia, who owned the *Bridge River-Lillooet News*
and later the *Alaska Highway News*. Before coming to the CBC,
Georgina had worked briefly for the *Toronto Star*. Thirteen years
younger than Mary, Georgina was a publicity director in the talks and
public relations department at the CBC, staying there until 1943,
when she joined the Women's Royal Canadian Naval Service
(WRCNS). In a later letter to Georgina, Mary related a story of having supper with Georgina and her mother, Ma Murray:

Your mother's out-going personality got her national
commendation and rightly so. She's made a lot of people feel better just through meeting her. But I remember an incident when I was "agin" her philosophy. I

had a brand new georgette dress — blue skirt — red white & blue top. I was in your apartment at 1554 Bathurst — had gone for supper. You came out of that tiny kitchen door — carrying a bowl of canned peaches — you hit your arm on door frame & most of the peach juice flew up and landed on my new dress. I was aghast and your mother said "Think of what the boys overseas are going through." I couldn't have cared right then if the Germans had every one of the boys in a prison camp. If a person could just think that ten years from now, it won't matter. But we go through life worrying and afraid.[21]

In the same letter, Mary's memories offer a glimpse of the fun and laughter they shared with another staffer, Lois Pope:

What of Lois? Did she ever marry? Her mother was so anxious that she would. Remember the fellow in the drugstore that her mother picked out for her? [...] And remember the day I made up like a madame — mascara, gobs of rouge & lipstick & eye shadow, and draped in your bedspread? After the fun, I took off the bedspread dress, but left the makeup, and your parish priest called? And I, unconscious of my "whore" looks, sat & talked to the priest while you & Lois were bursting with "inside" laughter. We did have some experiences. I could go on & on.[22]

Outgoing and friendly by nature, Mary quickly made herself known in the relatively small family that was the CBC in those early years — approximately six hundred employees altogether. However, of all the friendships Mary developed during her years in Toronto, none were as close as those she shared with J. Frank Willis, his wife, Gladys, and Frank's able assistant, Grace Athersich.

Frank Willis spent the first part of 1939 in Australia on an exchange with the Australian Broadcasting Commission and returned to Canada in the spring to be the commentator for the royal tour. Following the tour, he was transferred by the CBC from Halifax to Toronto, where he assumed responsibility for feature broadcasts. An accomplished artist, painter, actor, producer, and writer, Frank was a capable and well-respected senior producer at the CBC. He brought his *Atlantic Nocturne* radio program to Toronto, dropping the "Atlantic" from the title but continuing the format of poetry reading accompanied by organ music, provided in the Toronto broadcasts by Quentin Maclean. Aired in the late evening, *Nocturne* opened with Frank reading a poem he had written:

> As music builds a bright impermanent tower
> High in the sunlight, wild with birds
> And banners, so this chosen hour
> Will take you,
> So these chiming words
> Will wake you
> Briefly from the world.[23]

New friends and work did not keep Mary from her promise to write home every day. Although she may have written from a sense of duty, her letters to family also allowed her to complain and relieve frustrations. Of all the letters she wrote to her mother, only one has survived the years. In it, Mary demonstrated her concern for her mother's welfare, as well as providing her with all the details of what was happening in her new life.

> Dear Mum,
> Just a little "howdy." I hope your Americans are come and gone and that you are not any more weary than is possible.
> I was out with two teachers last night. They took me to dinner at "Windsor Arms," a very lovely small hotel with a British castle atmosphere. The place was pretty but the food rotten. We went to my room afterwards. They stayed till 9.30 and I just had time to hear Cleve say, "This is C.B.C." so Barry's off the air waves.

Had a letter from Saint John from a Mrs. Horton, Duke St. She wants on the air, she has culture, many admirers, she had an audition but her voice "played tricks" She is not young she says and she needs the money. Mrs. Haynes suggested she write me. I am writing her we can't use her. She just reads. I'm getting pretty good at saying no. I called up Estelle Fox this morning & told her I couldn't go to lunch as someone had come into town for the Exhibition. She is just trying to peddle her stuff and as it stands it's no good.

I'll try at noon again for Ann's dress. I saw some marked down away down near the station. I'll go down there if I can get time. No pay yet. I wish they paid on 15th so you could have money twice a month, but they don't. But Mama anytime you're stuck you use what I have in the bank. You can check it out. Please don't be without a cent while its there. Did you get the glass fixed? And the radio. I wish some honest fixer would tell you if it's worth it. If it isn't maybe we could get a smaller one with 7 tubes — I don't mean like mine. They are $19.75 here. I get Buffalo, Hamilton, Toronto's stations, N.Y., Rochester, St. Catherines, etc. Don't get Chicago. […] Did I tell you Martin Fox told Harry [Grant] that my leaving N.B. was a big loss to the province. I'll get Harry to tell me what he said. I'll write Martin too someday. I suppose he's home by now.

Willard Kitchens will be here on Monday. I'll be glad to see them. I haven't been to the Ex. Haven't anyone to go with until next week. Gladys [Willis] will be back & she said she'd go. […] [section missing] town I ever saw. There [are] about 5 high buildings and rest are just 5 or six stories. Forest Hill Village has beautiful houses — they're like movies. I haven't looked for a coat yet. I wish I'd bought a cheap fur one in the spring. I like to have some one to tell me how it

looks. Elizabeth [Long] is no good. She's no style at all.
[…] No sign of Mr. Neill yet. Kitty didn't know when
he was coming.[24]

Mary's mother and sister Helen found the first year of Mary's
absence to be difficult, so Mary's frequent letters were important to
them. "It was the year that the war broke out," said Helen, "which left
my Mother and me alone and unhappy. Ann was teaching in Moncton.
It was a very bleak time, with blackouts and so on. You had to get
drapes that shut out every crumb of light … it was an unhappy time."[25]

As eager as she had been to go to Toronto, dutiful Mary nevertheless worried about leaving her family behind. "She felt very conscious
of the fact that she had left her sisters there [in New Brunswick],"
Austin said. "I used to say to her, 'You know, they have to create their
own life, dear. They can't depend on you.' But she wouldn't accept
that. So, she was a very sad person that way."[26]

Probation Passed

Mary's first season unfolded successfully with strong favourable
response from listeners, both adults and children. "It didn't take very
long. Very quickly her stories caught on," Austin said. "And with
grown-ups! An awful lot of grown-up people listened to these stories on
Sunday. I would say, I always thought that the greater part of her audience were not children at all, but grown-ups."[27]

Soon fan mail began to arrive at her desk with many requests for
printed copies of the broadcast stories. As Mary commented in a letter
to Fletcher Peacock, children were not the only ones writing to her. "I
have been getting letters from the west, from the east, asking for my
stories … they come in great numbers from Primary teachers. That
really adds to the value of my stories to me, for when the teachers are
writing in asking for them, I know they must have a bit of something
deeper than entertainment."[28]

Seeking to write without interruption, Mary received permission
from Ernie Bushnell to work at home during the mornings. In the after-

noons, she went to her office to polish her work and answer mail. On some of the walks between the CBC and home, Austin accompanied her:

> [Mary] was very, very observant. We would sometimes walk from CBC College Street — we did the *Scrapbook* from there — and we would walk to her apartment. On the street, she'd see a group of kids playing and ... I'd be talking to her and she'd say, "Shush." So, I'd stop talking and she would watch the kids; stand there for five minutes. Watch them and hear what they were saying. Then, of course, I heard every damn work she wrote either listening to *Just Mary* or doing the *Scrapbook*. And, by George, that little scene would come up somehow in a story. And I got to recognize the times I was with her when she would glean some material.[29]

Since Mary's original appointment was probationary, Hugh Morrison, Supervisor of Talks, prepared a review of her work for Ernie Bushnell, General Supervisor of Programmes, on October 26:

> Miss Mary Grannan's services have been most satisfactory. She has brought to the CBC not only a specialized knowledge of the psychological and educational needs of children, but also a talent for showmanship.
>
> She has been devoting all her energies to the success of both her programmes: the Children's Scrapbook, 12.30-1.00 PM on Saturdays for children of all ages, and "Just Mary" 12.00-12.15 PM on Sundays for the very young children.
>
> I feel confident that both these programmes will reflect credit to the CBC as soon as they begin to be widely known to listeners.
>
> I have no hesitation in recommending that Miss Grannan's appointment be confirmed.[30]

"Agreed," noted Ernie Bushnell in the margin. After the positive report made its way through the chain of command, Mary received the official notice of her permanent appointment as junior producer near the end of December. Managing to get excused from the usual medical examination, she finally received a welcome increase in pay after writing to Gladstone Murray to complain that the increase had failed to materialize in the January pay.

Surprisingly, even as her appointment was being confirmed and her fall season declared a success, Mary expressed the last remnants of uncertainty to Fletcher Peacock in a letter on December 18, 1939:

> I find myself still saying what I am going to do "after school." They all laugh at me here when it comes out so easily. I have been very fortunate in pleasing all "the powers that be" to date. They have been very complimentary about my efforts. I do get frightened at odd times when I feel myself getting piled with work, but I generally manage to get out. [...] It is all very different. I meet lots of interesting people. [...]
>
> The other day I was talking with the Director of Women's talks. She was asking me something and I replied "Well, I haven't made up my mind ... I may go back teaching." Mr. Morrison, TALKS came down on me from his office ... He said "Don't let me hear you say that again ... ANYONE can teach school." Isn't it odd, the value some people put on teaching ... ANY-ONE ... I differed with him quite strenuously. [...]
>
> I would be interested to know if I took courses here at the University of Toronto (night courses) if they would be of any credit to me in New Brunswick.[31]

Detecting the mixed tone of her letter, Peacock offered encouragement in his reply. "I cannot but notice that you are toying with the idea of being permanently out of the teaching field and that you are not quite reconciled to this as yet. May it not be that you could contribute to education directly very effectively through the medium of radio so that in that case you could still be associated with both the schools and the talkies."[32]

So, gradually through the early months at the CBC, Mary's excitement and pleasure in her new work won over her insecurities. The wonder she felt at her new situation sometimes crept to the surface when she was back in the privacy of her room. Instead of the simple name and date she used to write in books she owned, she began to put a new type of inscription in books acquired in Toronto: "Mary E. Grannan, CBC – TORONTO,"[33] and "Mary Grannan, TORONTO ~."[34]

Chapter Six
Making the Grade, 1940

The "Just Mary" Style

As Mary continued to write her *Just Mary* stories, she gradually shaped and evolved her characteristic style of storytelling. Making frequent use of rhyme, alliteration, and repetition, Mary also invented words that reflected the type of words that children made up, or "coined," as she called it. Invented words used for rhyme and effect, such as "roughy," "weenty," "doggiest," "standy-out," and "awakiest," seemed to be more prevalent in early stories.[1]

The sound of the story was an important element because these stories were written for broadcast — designed to be heard performed: "Katy Kinsella's kitty cat caught cold,"[2] "Greeny Grub and the Grasshopper,"[3] "Laughing Leander of Landeroo,"[4] "Princess Elmira Eldena Eldona Eldoo."[5] And for a pleasing rhythm and rhyme, nothing beats the fourteen r jingle from the "Fourteenth Letter," which sounds like a child's skipping rhyme:

> Sure and this is Tanyss MallabaR ... Who hops because she has no caR ... ARE you happy? ... ARE

you glad? … ARE you merry? … ARE you mad? … ARE you going? … ARE you here? … ARE you staying all the year? … ARE you blue-eyed? … ARE you brown? … ARE you living in the town? … ARE you feeling pretty fine? … ARE you coming, Caroline?[6]

When child characters spoke, Mary had them speak in the manner of young children, something she heard a great deal in the classroom: "Mum, guess what … guess what'"[7]; "'Cause … 'cause … it was a magic hood, Mummy'"[8]; "My name is Sylvia, just so's you'll know, and this is my cat."[9]

Humour was frequent, but of a particular type. It was not humour that ridiculed, not adult humour, but humour that was gentle, direct, honest, and readily appreciated by children:

"Well, if saying 'Oh, fudge!' can hurt your feelings, all I can say is you're … you're … you're just pernickety. I always say 'Fudge!'"

"And I always want fudge," sobbed Tommy Turtle. And the creek came up almost three feet higher, for you know turtles when they start to cry![10]

The time had come. Peter Watson must go to school. He didn't much want to go to school, but he was seventeen bricks high. I know, for I'm the one that measured him on the red wall. And when you're seventeen bricks … well.[11]

"Anthony Alexander Alfredo Fred Pig," a name chosen to bring a smile immediately, was the story of a pig who thought he was a prince because he had a princely name.[12] At the beginning of her stories, Mary as the narrator frequently addressed the audience directly, often building a bit of suspense by referring to something that happened later in the story: "Perhaps you'll smile into your blue checkered handkerchief when I tell you this, but I don't care, because it's true"[13] or "I'm not asking you to believe this, mind you. All I know about it is what Jimmy told me, and you know Jimmy. He's the little red-head who lives at the corner in the blue-shuttered house beneath the big oak tree. Jimmy has a way of finding adventure."[14] Sometimes small moral lessons were included, such as the importance of going to school, getting enough sleep, being considerate of others, and listening to your mother, but they were not the main purpose of the story. Mary's main purpose always was to entertain.

From the start of *Just Mary* at CFNB, Mary drew upon story ideas from children, including her students and young fans who wrote letters. W.H. Brodie had cited this as an audience-building technique in his December 1937 correspondence, written when the executives were first considering her.[15] Her use of children's real names and kernels of their suggestions for stories had a strong bonding influence on her young listeners. Broadcasting from Toronto, Mary continued to draw ideas from her fans, but she also began to incorporate the names of her CBC colleagues. This had the effect of making her stories a topic of conversation at the corporation.

As a cornerstone in her personal philosophy of storywriting, Mary professed her firm belief that as a writer, she had to believe in her stories, be honest in her dealings with children, and never talk down to them. From years of working with children in school, she knew how quickly they could sniff out a fake.

"Sincerity is important in story telling," Mary was quoted as saying in a 1951 article in the *Daily Gleaner*. "If you are sincere with the youngsters they in return will be sincere and appreciative with you."[16]

Close to the end of her first year at the CBC, Mary contributed an article to the *C.W.P.C. Newspacket*, having joined the Canadian Women's Press Club in 1938. "Radio Artist Must Have Something Good to Satisfy Juniors"[17] summarized many of her thoughts on writing for children's radio. Citing entertainment and education as the two main ingredients in programs for the young, she stressed that children are our most important radio listeners, with intelligence equal to that of most adults. In spite of all the great care taken in planning programming for them, children will turn the dial to other stations if the programs are not something they want to hear.

With Irish folklore, fairy tales, and the circus as continuing themes, Mary's writing improved with practice so that she was producing fairly consistent, good quality scripts. Above all, her stories were firmly set in their time period — before, during, and after the war. It was a time of nurturing children and placing great value on hearth and home.

"It has now been conceded," noted the CBC Ontario Programme Schedule on December 1, 1941, "that for whimsicality, for tenderness and charm, for clear, lucid narration and for originality, her [Mary Grannan's] delightful little broadcast fairy tales are unsurpassed and unrivalled."[18]

In the Studio with "Just Mary"

With Syd Brown as producer, Austin Willis as announcer, and Lou Snider as musician, Mary and her *Just Mary* broadcast settled into a familiar format. Since he was the show's announcer for the first couple of years, Austin was able to provide detail on the broadcast setting: "I did *Just Mary* certainly until I went into the navy, which was two or three years," he said. "Now, it was [broadcast] in a little talk booth, and the engineer was in another little [control] booth there … And the two of us would be at the table."[19]

A single microphone hung suspended over the rectangular table, with Mary sitting at one end with the control booth window on her left and Austin sitting at the other end, the window on his right. Over the window was a big clock that provided the exact time, while underneath the window was a red "on air" light. Lou Snider was nearby at his keyboards.

Mary, Austin, and Lou would arrive about five minutes early and would chat. As the last thirty seconds to broadcast approached, they would grow quiet. The producer could talk to them from his control booth by pressing a key and would at this time check the sound levels by asking, "Are you ready, Miss Grannan?" and then, "Level," or "Let's have a level, please." Quickly, Mary would speak a few lines of script to test the microphone, and then Austin would do the same.

When broadcast time arrived, the red light came on and the producer signalled with his finger — "gave the big finger" — and Lou began playing the theme, "In a Clock Shop," on the novachord and celesta. Austin would then introduce "Just Mary," his resonant voice rising and falling in a gentle cadence: "For our very young listeners and others, too, the Canadian Broadcasting Corporation presents 'Just Mary,' with her own stories, written and told by herself. And now, here's 'Just Mary' to tell you about."[20]

"I would introduce her and she would start," said Austin. "The name of her story, this would be 'Frankie Frankfurter' — [that] would be her story today. That would be about my brother Frank. She used all her friends, the names, and some of their character, which she put in the little stories she told. And then, I would get out my fingernail file, and I started to file my nails."[21]

With his role as announcer over until the closing of the fifteen-minute program, Austin would settle back in his chair, hunting in the breast pocket of his jacket for his fingernail file because he had developed a habit of filing his fingernails while he listened to Mary's broadcast.

"In the studio, you had to contain yourself," Austin said. "The microphone was very sensitive. When I first used the fingernail file in the studio, the microphone picked it up. The engineer didn't know what it was. After that, I turned sideways so the file would be out of the direct line of the microphone and I had my hands down on my lap."[22]

Once Mary had the story underway, she would be in position before the microphone, bringing to life the voices of the various characters as well as the sound effects. Raising and lowering her eyebrows and shifting her facial expressions to suit the mood of the tale, she nevertheless kept her head steady in front of the microphone and only moved when she needed a loud voice. By moving her head back a few inches for louder sounds, she prevented the microphone from bleating. A warm glow would beam from her face as she performed for her unseen radio audience and for her live audience in the person of her announcer.

"Mary bounced a lot off me," said Austin. "If she had something in the script that amused her, as she read it, she would look at me, and our eyes would connect. I would smile at her."[23]

Syd Brown was the first producer of the show, but another person replaced him partway through the year. Austin explains that the new producer reacted badly to his filing ritual:

> So, we got a new producer when we were doing it about
> six months, and we started off this Sunday and she

began, and, of course, I got my file — couldn't find my file — and fiddled around, and got my file out and started to file my nails. Well, when the program was over, this guy — I thought he was going to have a heart attack — and he turned to me and he tore a strip off me that lasted twenty minutes, about had I no respect whatever for artistry and that some other performer was doing something, that I had the absolute just hideousness to take out a fingernail file and clean my nails. And Mary is sitting there looking at this guy like this. And the fellow finishes and I'm cringing more and more. And this is a young producer. … Anyway, when he finished this, which is very warranted ordinarily, right? Mary tore a strip off him that lasted a long [time]. She said, "How *dare* you speak to Mr. Willis like that. If he didn't file his fingernails, he would not be listening and I would be very upset. I love him filing his fingernails. It is wonderful and it inspires me." I thought it was so marvelous — little things that happened between she and I. And it was a little secret thing, obviously, [that] everyone else thought was really strange.[24]

A few months later, Mary wrote a reference to the fingernail file in a script for a new program, *For the Children*, tucking it into the dialogue as a little joke between them. It was broadcast on Saturday, May 11, 1940, with Austin in the cast:

WILLIS:	Listen boys and girls … We're bringing you a very special broadcast made at Sunnyside Park in Toronto. You see last Wednesday we went down to Sunnyside.
PEGGY:	Sunnyside's an amusement park.
WILLIS:	A big amusement park at that … right on the shores of Lake Ontario.
PEGGY:	And did we have fun?

WILLIS: We rode on everything from the rolly
             to the wooden ponies.
JOHNNY: And we ate everything from … from
             …

And the broadcast launched into the visit of little Peggy, Johnny, and Austin the grown-up, telling the highlights of sights, rides, food, and games. Near the middle of the broadcast, the story finds them at the shooting gallery.

WILLIS: Give me another … I'll try it again …
             I'm not going to let a thing like this
             beat me.
PEGGY: Oh, so here you are. We've been look-
             ing everywhere for you … thought
             maybe you'd gone over to the Whip.
             What are you doing?" ([Sound of]
             POP POP)
JOHNNY: He's filing his fingernails, can't you
             see?[25]

"Now, I'm sitting there this day doing my fingernails," Austin said, "after I've said, 'Now, ladies and gentlemen, Just Mary.' And I settled back and [got] the file out and started to go like this, and she started. This day, she said 'Today, I'm going to tell you the story about Austy the Alligator.' Well, I put down the fingernail file and that upset her. She didn't know what to think of that. Well, she didn't know whether I was going to be upset or not. It was a terrible story about this awful alligator that was so mean."[26]

In this story, Annie is searching for a young alligator from which she could make an alligator bag as a Christmas present for her mother. Then, Annie heard somebody "singing happily, but not very well."[27]

And Annie gulped … "You're an alligator, aren't you?"
"Yes … I'm an alligator. My name's Austy …

What's your name?"

"My name's Annie," said Annie.

"Quite a lot like my name, isn't it, Annie? … Austy and Annie …"

"Yes, they are quite a lot alike. Austy, how old are you?" asked Annie.

"I'm fifteen years old," said Austy.

Annie gasped. He was just the right age! Austy laughed. "I'm fifteen years. That's young for an alligator … and I'm two feet long."

He was just the right length.

"…But that's short for an alligator … but I'm pretty, eh? They do say that I'm the prettiest little alligator in this swamp … they do…"

"Do they, Austy?" said Annie.

"Yes … You're a pretty little girl, Annie. I bet you're the prettiest little girl in the world, I do…" and Austy smiled at Annie.

"Oh thank you, Austy." And then she looked at what he was doing. "Austy, what are you making?" she said, looking at a bunch of palm leaves that were in front of the little alligator.

"I'm making a straw bonnet for my mamma for Christmas."[28]

After Annie had talked with Austy, she decided she could not make an alligator bag out of him after all, because it would spoil his Christmas. So, she decided to give her mother a pin cushion instead.

"And afterward, I said, 'What the hell was that all about?'" Austin said. "And she said, 'Well, I thought I'd brighten you up a bit.'"[29]

Radio Educational Service

Continuing with her efforts to help New Brunswick develop school broadcasts, Mary attended an informal planning meeting on January 5,

1940, at the home of Wilfred Wees. In attendance besides Mary and Wees were Hugh Morrison from the CBC, Stanley Watson, and Dr. E. Corbett, the last two from the field of education. Their discussions ranged from possible content and resource people to practical aspects of setting up the service, including selecting appropriate radio receiving sets for schools, discussing which radio stations and networks to utilize, costs, and the best broadcast times. Mary prepared a detailed report of the meeting for Fletcher Peacock and continued to offer assistance in subsequent letters. Peacock was appreciative, responding promptly to her letters with further questions and telling her of plans to establish a Maritime school broadcasting committee with Nova Scotia and Prince Edward Island.

Educational radio had been in existence in Canada as early as the 1920s, when Vancouver radio station CNRV began a regular series in 1927 that continued for several years. Nova Scotia began the first continuous system of local school broadcasting in the country with its first experimental program on March 19, 1928.[30] At the CBC, school broadcasts began on an experimental basis in British Columbia in 1938, and by 1940–41, regular programs were taking place in British Columbia, Nova Scotia, and Quebec. While Mary did what she could to encourage and help New Brunswick with its plans, she was not involved in the school broadcasts department, although she thought she might like to be at one point when she was writing Peacock. In the fall of 1940, Peacock asked her if she might consider writing some dramatizations on democracy and citizenship for primary grades, but Mary was too busy with her regular work to accomplish this.

The CBC school broadcasts department, established in 1943 with Richard S. Lambert as its head,[31] aired its first national school broadcast, called "Heroes of Canada," in the 1942–43 season.[32] Finally, in 1943–44, the Maritime School Broadcasts began. While the correspondence between Mary and Peacock during Mary's first years in Toronto demonstrated the interest and assistance she offered to New Brunswick on this topic, the letters were just as insightful for the reports Mary wrote of her activities.

A Difficult Birthday

With her CBC appointment now confirmed, Mary should have been feeling on top of the world, but February 11 brought her birthday, and in 1940, it was her fortieth. The milestone birthday probably left her suddenly feeling alone and unmarried, with the realization that she was likely to remain so. She went out for a weepy winter's walk in the city to think things over. Perhaps rejecting the long-time relationship with Bill Shea in Fredericton had seemed at the time to be not a permanent rejection of the possibility of marriage but merely a postponement, a matter of putting behind her a less ambitious life and seeking the satisfaction of her career. Someone else might come along. But by this time, it was clear that she had made a life's decision to pass up marriage and children for her career.

"Turning forty was a hard time for her," said her friend Donald Roberts. "Alone, unmarried at forty. … When she began thinking of her career, she felt better."[33]

Her métier had blossomed into something far beyond what she had envisioned in Fredericton. She had escaped the confined life of teaching in a small town and achieved more than she had dared to imagine. This was her fulfillment — developing her talents and being paid for it. With all this to weigh in the balance, she returned to her apartment with her misery soothed.

In a Class by Herself

Pleased with what he saw, Hugh Morrison, Supervisor of Talks, was paying careful attention to Mary's broadcasts and fan mail. As early as February 1940, he was showing preference for Mary's program over other possible new shows for young children, while at the same time looking at possible interest from American radio networks. On February 21, 1940, Morrison wrote Walter and Robert Anderson, rejecting a proposal for another children's program:

We have listened to the recording of "The Tale of Peter

Peregrine Patch" as read by Joan Warren (Mrs. L.P. Sherwood) for her programme "Tell Me a Story-Time."

Our feeling is that "Just Mary" is in a class by herself as a story-teller for young children. Her stories are original; they are written for the ear and thus adapted for broadcast presentation. "Just Mary" herself has the dramatic ability to portray the various characters which she creates.

The audience mail which "Just Mary" receives is distinctive and is evidence of true appreciation of the programme by listeners, young and old, in all parts of Canada.

This had led us to change the time of the programme "Just Mary", which is at present at 12.00 Noon, EST, Sundays; to 1.15 to 1.30 PM, EST Sundays beginning March 10th.

Also, the Mutual Broadcasting System are aware of this unique programme and are currently engaged in an attempt to find time at which they can also carry it from us.

Under these circumstances, I do not think we could consider another monologue for young children.[34]

The Mutual Broadcasting System did indeed begin to carry both *Just Mary* and *The Children's Scrapbook* in the spring of 1940. In addition to the American interest, however, Morrison was most enthused by the audience mail Mary received, especially the letters from children. Their persuasive requests for written copies of the stories caused Morrison to begin to think of publishing her stories in book form, as he explained to C.R. Delafield on March 19, 1940:

You were kind enough to pass on to this office, the audience mail file of "Tell Me A Story Time."

The file on "Tell Me A Story Time" is being passed on to those interested at the National Programme Office.

I am sure that you in turn will be interested in noting the audience mail file on "Just Mary". I am particularly impressed by the letters from child listeners, which total about half the number.

I think that the Programme Liaison Officer and the Public Relations Officer would be interested in seeing this file.

I am hopeful that NBC will take the programme.

The insistent requests for publication of the "Just Mary" stories in book form leads me to believe that we should consider seriously some such undertaking as soon as feasible.

Would you be good enough to return the "Just Mary" audience mail file at your convenience.[35]

Letters of appreciation flowed into Mary's mailbox, particularly from those in the Maritimes who were proud of one of their own. One such letter came from the Moncton Local Council of Women, who wrote in praise of Mary to Gladstone Murray on April 27, 1940, noting that "'Just Mary' deserves particular credit, since she is not only the author of these delightful and highly imaginative stories, but also has the ability to present them in such a charming manner."[36]

As her first season drew to a close in June 1940, Mary knew she had succeeded. Beyond just the fact that her appointment had been confirmed, she had achieved praise from Morrison and other CBC executives and the support of radio listeners. During this year, her fame as a broadcaster had spread from New Brunswick to the whole of the country and even across the border into the United States. There was no question of going back to New Brunswick to teach. Since the leave of absence from the Devon School Board was coming to an end, she needed to resign officially from her position, and she did so with a bit of nostalgia but a lot of satisfaction. The school board reply from Fred Mawer was prompt and congratulatory:

The Devon School Board in accepting your resignation are as reluctant as you in tendering the same. They recall your many years of arduous, sincere, and faithful service, and esteem with pride the honor you have brought to the Devon School from time to time. They are very pleased to hear of your successful year with the C.B.C., however, nevertheless, the same was never in doubt when they granted you a leave of absence a year ago. They [unclear] felt the break had come in association with the Devon School. We shall be pleased to welcome you in Devon at any time, and wish you continued success.[37]

Mary's train trip back to Fredericton in the summer of 1940 was a different experience from the one she had taken to Toronto the previous July. Confident and buoyed up, Mary returned home triumphantly. She would have had a joyful reunion with her mother and sisters and quickly made the rounds to visit J. Stewart Neill, the staff of CFNB, her friends Gertrude Davis and Muriel Burtt Walker, and former education colleagues, including Fletcher Peacock. If she had been a local celebrity when she left, she returned as an even bigger star.

Frank and Gladys

Before returning home to Fredericton for her summer holiday one of those first years in Toronto, and most likely it was June 1940, Mary was invited to visit Frank and Gladys Willis at the summer place they had rented on an island near Pointe au Baril on the eastern shore of Georgian Bay, north of Parry Sound, in an area called Thirty Thousand Islands. The friendship developing between Frank and Mary was affectionate, characterized by many jests and teases. Frank felt he would be labelled forever as the man who turned down Mary Grannan.

"I was not infallible as a great judge of potential talent," Frank later wrote. "I turned down one of our greatest talents, a lady named Mary Grannan … when she first auditioned for me. Mary doesn't hold it against me, because her audition was a fearful sketch, called *Aggravatin' Agatha*, which nearly drove me up the transmitter tower."[38]

Besides the broadcasting interests they had in common, Frank and

Mary were fellow Maritimers who shared a passion for painting. In fact, Frank was a fairly good painter, even if he was not often much help as a teacher.

"There would be Grannan on the floor," said Austin, "with one of Frank's books, trying to draw and asking him, 'Now, Frank, what can I do? Is this any better?' And he wouldn't even look at it. He does that. He would say, 'No.'"[39]

There were times when Frank cheered Mary up and encouraged her, and there were times when she drove him crazy. Austin describes one of Mary's summer visits:

[Frank and Gladys] took an island for one summer near Pointe au Baril — that's way, way north of Toronto. And you drive up all that way, which was two hours and a half drive. Get there, get out of the car, get on a boat with all your gear and stuff for *them*, because they would have come ashore and phoned and said please bring this and this and this. You get in the boat and you have an hour's boat ride out to this island. Well, you were really in the wilderness when you got there. And, so we went, Mary and I drove up. Stopped and had *three* lunches on the way. She loved lunch, ice cream. And we got to the boat, and we went out to the island. And just as the boat slowed down, I heard her say — now, I'm in the front of the boat looking to see if I can spy them on the island or something. In the back, I heard Mary say to the boat-man, "Can you slow down a little bit. I'm having an awful time with this hat." She could have been going to church. She went out to this wilderness island all dressed up. And Frank came down to the dock and he looked at her and he said, "In God's name, *where* do you think you're going?" And that's the best thing to explain their relationship right there.[40]

Chapter Seven
First Books, 1941-1943

> "Vacation is over and Just Mary tells of an adventure she had with a mouse one vacation time long ago, when she was no bigger than a ladybird herself."[1]
> — CBC *Programme Schedule*, September 1, 1940

The Second Year

By the end of the summer in 1940, Mary was back in Toronto for her second broadcasting season as Canada headed into its second year at war. At the CBC, wartime broadcasting had expanded to keep Canadians informed of news developments, leaders' speeches, and commentary, while promoting morale and keeping citizens feeling involved in the war effort at home with such features as *Carry on Canada*. Audiences tuned in to hear programs highlighting the armed forces, such as *L for Lanky*, *Fighting Navy*, and *Comrades in Arms*. Normal broadcasts of entertainment, sports, and music, considered essential to the well-being of the nation by providing relaxation, had by then settled into a balance with the war programming.

In contrast to the First World War, when the population at home felt distantly removed from the theatre of war in Europe, radio broadcasts from overseas brought a closer connection to Canadian troops, just as the rebroadcast of CBC programs over the BBC kept Canadian troops connected with the happenings at home. Some of the most popular programs produced by the overseas unit were *With the Troops in England, Sandy's Canadian Half-hour,* and *Quiz for the Forces.*

Children's programming remained limited, with Mary's two regular shows providing the mainstay. As much as the CBC might have liked to do more for the children's section, few resources and personnel were available given the enormous war effort. One other CBC effort aimed at older children was *And It Came to Pass,* which featured dramatizations of Bible stories. School broadcasting slowly expanded, while two selections from the CBS School of the Air of the Americas were carried weekly — *Wellsprings of Music* and *Tales from Far and Near.* Occasional special broadcasts were also heard, such as a Christmas radio play from Vancouver, written by Christie Harris and directed by Andrew Allan.

Re-energized by her summer at home and enthused by the successful first year, Mary launched into the new fall session, beginning *Just Mary* on Sunday, September 1, with a story called "Adventure on a Star," and *The Children's Scrapbook* a month later on Saturday, October 5.

"My 'Children's Scrapbook' is beginning tomorrow," Mary wrote on October 4 in her continuing correspondence with Fletcher Peacock. "I am spotting a couple of educational bits. I'm having a more flexible orchestra (last year I had strings — this year I am hiring musicians week by week). I am using a little English guest who will solicit information from her new friends in this new-to-her land that she may write it to her father back home."[2]

Mary told Peacock that she had been in charge of the Talks department during September while Reid Forsee was on vacation, meeting many interesting people, including Dr. Blatz. "He and I had quite a chat about progressive education and when he 'poohed' the idea that I was a progressive teacher from N.B., I told him that Toronto city was not any more progressive than we were — that the teachers here had inspector-fright. And he agreed."[3] Having met Dr. Blatz, Mary went on to take a course from him that fall at the Institute of Child Study, which was affiliated at the time with the University of Toronto.

In the same letter, Mary related meeting another radio guest. "Dr. Wingfield, psychologist of McMasters and U. of T., was also interesting and interested. He took me out to dinner to see what made me 'tick.' I could feel myself being 'psyched.' I helped him with his reading. He must have had a poor teacher — his reading had a rhythmic roll that couldn't be broken down."[4]

Outside of regular duties, Mary gave occasional talks to school and church groups, speaking to the Oriole Park Home and School Association in November on the topic of children's radio. "I talked a half hour, and because I was half teacher, I seemed to go over very well. I really did clarify a lot of things for them. They didn't dream that anybody gave any constructive thought to children's programmes."[5] These talks appeared to be part community service and part public relations for the CBC.

By her second year, Mary's official status had been upgraded to program assistant grade three, while she continued to use the unofficial title Supervisor of Children's Programmes. After the frequent changes of residence during her first year, she settled into a new room at 55 Oriole Gardens, once again a red-brick home in the Forest Hill area, where she would continue to live until 1944.

As her circle of contacts continued to expand, Mary became friendly with CBC staffer Harriett Ball, better known to all as Henri. Harriett M. Ball was a press and information representative who had been with the CBC since its beginning and previously with its forerunner, the Canadian Radio Broadcasting Commission. Before she got into public relations, she had been a newspaper reporter and film continuity and scriptwriter. Apparently a woman of considerable influence, Henri held Sunday afternoon tea parties for the who's who of the corporation. Austin Willis explains:

> Henri Ball was the head of publicity at CBC for years and years. Married Ken Edey. Ken Edey was the managing editor of *The Star*, the *Toronto Star* for years. Henri Ball was a *remarkable* woman. She held Sunday soirees at her apartment in Rosedale, and you were *really not* in the CBC properly unless you were invit-

ed to one of these things on Sunday. And if you *were* invited, you'd better show up because that was another no-no not to go. So, they were all a little afraid of Henri Ball, who was a big, tall lady — handsome was the word, not pretty, handsome. When you went to these tea parties, that were *interminable*, there was never a drop of anything like alcohol. It was *frowned* upon. So, guys like Percy Faith would bring a twenty-six ouncer of rye. He and Maxted, Stanley Maxted, would smuggle it in and lift the top of the toilet off and put it in the toilet tank. And then they'd all get up from their *ninth* cup of tea and say, 'Well, I have to go to the bathroom because of all this.' So, they'd head off and have a good sip out of it in the bathroom. And of course, some of them would get very merry by the end of the tea party. She could never figure out where they got the booze from. So Mary became a disciple of Henri's.[6]

Her first name is Henri …that's for her grandfather …her last name is Ball … that's for bouncing, because Henri bounces everywhere! And she has the most magic things happen to her. If you'd like to hear of this little girl, Henri Ball, I'll tell you about her.
    — "The Chinese Bracelet," *New Just Mary Stories*[7]

The First Book

When I was so little that I just reached that second freckle on the end of your nose, the most exciting thing happened to me. An angel looked into God's pantry, and finding there one of His most beautiful of days, he took it from its place on the shelf and sent it to earth. And because I was so little (just to the second freckle, remember) I thought the day was all for me, so

I set out with my little dog to use every bit of it, before
came bedtime.
— "Blue Breeches," *Just Mary*[8]

Following Hugh Morrison's memo of March 1940 suggesting that
the CBC consider publishing some of Mary's stories, the Publications
Department began to look for possible publishers. By the end of
October 1940, they had received a favourable offer from W.J. Gage &
Co., the textbook publisher directed by Dr. Wilfred Wees. In a letter
on October 26, E. Austin Weir, Supervisor of Press and Information,
wrote to the general manager, Gladstone Murray, outlining the offer
and requesting permission to proceed. Weir noted that "Dr. Wilfred
Wees, in charge of this organization, after careful study of the manuscripts involved, has been so impressed with Miss Grannan's work that
he has offered the following tie-up with the CBC."[9]

Gage offered to produce four thousand copies at a cost of thirty-
two cents each. Of these, the CBC would contract to purchase fifteen
hundred at cost for a total commitment of five hundred dollars. Weir
estimated that by selling the copies for fifty cents each, the corporation
would realize a profit of ten cents a book after mailing and handling
costs. Nowhere in the memo was there any consideration of royalties
for the author. Since Mary was a salaried employee, the executives considered that the CBC owned the intellectual property. Gladstone
Murray sent his approval by teletype two days later limiting CBC commitment to a maximum of five hundred dollars.

In January 1941, Mary's first book rolled off the press, "published
for the Canadian Broadcasting Corporation by W.J. Gage & Co.
Limited." *Just Mary*, with twelve stories, was a hardcover book illustrated by Gage staff artist Georgette Berckmans. The tan cover sported a red and black drawing of a girl riding a rocking horse and carrying
a banner that displayed the title. Opposite the table of contents was a
letter of tribute from Mary to her former students:

Dear Boys and Girls of New Brunswick:
    This is truly your book. All these Just Mary stories
were written in New Brunswick when I lived there, for

New Brunswick is my home. I was a teacher, and it was my boys and girls in the Devon School who told me the things to write about … who told me the things they wanted to hear. And these are the stories they liked the best.

I hope you will have as much fun reading this book as I have had writing it.

My very best wishes to you all!

Just Mary[10]

In the end, Gage printed forty-five hundred copies, which would retail in bookstores at sixty-five cents, while the CBC would sell their copies for the planned fifty cents. In his January 23 note to the general manager, Weir described how Dr. Wees had canvassed the Department of Education, obtaining advance orders for the book. Weir also explained that the book dated back to "discussions by Mr. Blangsted, Mr. Morrison and myself with Dr. Wees of the W.J. Gage Co., over a year ago. Mr. Blangsted has been following through ever since."[11] If "over a year ago" is accurate, it would appear that discussions for the book were underway a couple of months prior to Morrison's March 1940 memo, and that Dr. Wees and Gage were involved from the beginning. This is perhaps an indication of the sincere interest Dr. Wees had in Mary's writing.

Whether or not she was perturbed at losing any share of the royalties, Mary was thrilled by the publication of her first book. She immediately sent an autographed copy to Gladstone Murray, as well as many others such as DeB. Holly, her first announcer when she broadcast from CHSJ in Saint John. When Murray wrote back to thank her, he added, "Incidentally, I more than appreciate the wonderful work you have done and are doing in radio."[12] Book reviews were generally full of praise, citing the stories' charm and language that children could understand, but there were some contrary opinions, such as those expressed by Gwenyth Grube, writing in the *Canadian Forum* in May 1941. Grube felt that while the imaginative and interesting stories with skillful alliteration passed the critical test of appealing to her five-year-old, some produced too much anxiety, particularly the harrowing "story of a cat who, having lost one eye, is too ugly for anyone to want," which reduced her child to tears.[13]

As her second season in Toronto drew to a close in the spring of 1941, Mary's happiness over the continued success of her programs and the publication of her first book was enhanced by the welcome news of a considerable increase in salary. She immediately wrote Gladstone Murray to thank him:

> This is two "thank yous." First for inviting me to your party on Thursday last. I enjoyed and benefited. I was wishing you'd asked me to speak. Then the "GM" would have had a bit of a "plug" too.
>
> Secondly — Thank you for the increase in my salary. I appreciate it very much, and it's an incentive to go on — and up!! But even without it I'll confess ... I love my job.[14]

The Second Book

Six months later, as the *Just Mary* book was almost sold out, S.A. Blangsted and E.A. Weir were busy planning a second one. On July 2, 1941, Weir wrote to Dr. Frigon and Gladstone Murray outlining plans for the second book, a larger edition with eighteen stories and more illustrations. Weir proposed to bring out the new book by October 15, with the CBC purchasing two thousand copies from Gage. By advertising the books on the air at the selling price of one dollar each, he calculated a profit of twenty-four cents a book. Weir concluded the memo by noting, "It should be of very real prestige value to the CBC, a permanent contribution to bookdom. It has had wide commendation among educational authorities."[15] While nothing had been mentioned in writing thus far of sharing compensation with the author, Weir addressed this issue in a letter on July 18 to the general manager that included the memorandum of agreement between the CBC and W.J. Gage:

Herewith a memorandum of agreement in triplicate between the CBC and the Educational Book Company of Toronto, Limited, for W.J. Gage & Co. Limited.

The agreement, I believe, is in line with that usually made in such cases. The main point I am sending it to you for is in connection with Miss Grannan's receiving 5 cents honorarium. I do not know whether there is anything standing in the way of her receiving an honorarium or not. Except for the matter of protecting her, I do not think any agreement is really necessary.

Will you please indicate as quickly as you can your wishes in this connection, in order that the matter may be put in hand. If the agreement is O.K., perhaps you would be good enough to sign and return to me.[16]

In the margin of this memo, Murray wrote by hand: "Sorry can't pay Mary 5¢ a copy — She's a staff member." On July 26, W.O. Findlay replied to Weir, returning the agreement unsigned and explaining the situation about honorariums. "Administrative regulations do not permit payment of bonus or honorarium to full time members of the staff and I have no power of discretion to vary these regulations in the absence of a definite pre-engagement understanding. These scripts would appear to belong to us and the honorarium should be made payable to the Canadian Broadcasting Corporation."[17]

As the new book, *Just Mary Again*, was about to be released, Gladstone Murray wrote to Weir on October 30. "As I mentioned to you hurriedly this morning on my way out of the office, Miss Grannan is concerned about retaining some of her rights in the book about to go to press. It is understood that you will look into this on her behalf and see what can be done to protect her interests, particularly in films, but also in re-publication in other countries, particularly in England."[18]

Just Mary Again, containing sixteen stories and once again illustrated by Georgette Berckmans, appeared in late fall 1941, with its tan cover graced with a green and black drawing of a girl being lifted into the air by an umbrella that bore the title. The "published for" and "by" line had been dropped, and the CBC and Gage were listed with equal billing on the title page. These stories contained the first characters named after CBC colleagues.

Frustrated in her efforts to retain any royalties on the book sales, Mary was attempting to keep at least some additional rights and took her concerns to the top person in the organization, Gladstone Murray. It is evident that both Murray and Weir were trying to be fair in looking after Mary's interests with regard to the books.

Following the release of her second book, Reid Forsee interviewed Mary on December 4 in a fifteen-minute CBC Radio special called "Just Mary Again." During her talk about her programs and books, Mary spoke about her "great benefactor," J. Stewart Neill of CFNB. In Mary's own estimation, she owed her whole new career to him, and she was loyal in remembering her debt to him. Whenever she wrote Neill from Toronto, she began her letters with the greeting, "Dear Man who did all this for me."[19] Neill was thoroughly pleased by Mary's success and proud of her, knowing that his assessment of her talent had been fully proven. In response to her flattering comments about him, Neill sent a telegram on December 5: "Enjoyed your program. You did a swell job. Thanks for the plug. It is a wonder that CBC would allow it. You have all that I said you had. This should be a great help for your book. I am going to order five tomorrow. Best regards and more success to you. J. Stewart Neill."[20]

"You have all that I said you had," Neill said. Truly, this was a special statement that would have stayed in both their memories for quite some time. Even Mary herself had some doubt about success when she first left Fredericton. It was a tender moment between mentor and protégé. Mary kept the telegram for the rest of her life.

Books Go to War

> Once there was a little bug. Once there was a little boy. Once there was a little box. And somehow the three of them got together. The little box was paper. The little boy was nice. And the little bug was Orville.
> — "Orville Bug," *Just Mary Again*[21]

Somewhere in Canada, a box of *Just Mary Again* books accidentally made its way onto an army truck servicing the Canadian military and subsequently onto the base. The soldiers were surprised to find that the box contained children's stories. While some of the soldiers looked at them with just mild interest, a few became interested enough to take them to their huts and were later caught reading them after hours. From the army camp, some of the books migrated to a nearby Ferry Command base, where some of the airmen took a liking to them. Some of the men gave an airplane the name "Orville Bug" after a story character named in honour of Orville Shugg who did the CBC farm broadcasts. Others gave an anti-tank gun the nickname "Georgie the Rat" after another character that Mary had named after CBC staffer George Taggart. Taggart had forgotten to listen to the broadcast of a story Mary had written for his boys. So, "Georgie the Rat" was a story about a little rat who didn't listen. When some of the men were shipped overseas, some of the books travelled with them. This story made its way back home after the war when one of the men from the army camp, Bob McPherson, an army sergeant-major during the war, joined the CBC station relations department in Toronto and related the tale.[22]

The apparent fondness of the servicemen for the children's stories could not have come from growing up hearing them, for *Just Mary* had been broadcast across the country for only two years at that point. So, why would Canadian soldiers enjoy these children's stories? Perhaps they were simply a little part of home.

In a later interview with Bill McNeil on his CBC program, *Voice of the Pioneer*, Mary told how she had received letters from the Coast Guard at Fort George Main in Maryland and from servicemen at Camp Shilo in northern Manitoba. One colonel wrote her to say that he liked to listen because it was nostalgic and relaxing. A soldier from Prince Rupert, British Columbia, telephoned her to pass along the message of how much the boys enjoyed her stories. When the war was over, a veteran who worked at the CBC brought his copy of a *Just Mary* book to her for an autograph and told her how the books had travelled with servicemen all over the world.[23]

This is a very sad story. It's about Georgie, the little rat who didn't listen. And if you haven't got your own handkerchief, and your mother's handkerchief, and your father's handkerchief, and your sister's handkerchief, and your brother's handkerchief, all ready and waiting, you'd best run and get them right now, for you're going to need them. I'll wait for you … one, two, three, four, five, six, seven, eight, nine, ten! Are you back? Well, then, it was like this…

  — "Georgie the Little Rat Who Didn't Listen,"
Just Mary Again[24]

The Third Book

Largely as a public service, the CBC's Publications Branch produced books, booklets, and pamphlets that were based on broadcast talks. Mary's two books were among approximately eleven other publications the CBC released between 1939 and 1942, either directly or through other publishers. An overall picture of the variety being issued was detailed by S.W. Griffiths in a summary report sent to W.O. Findlay on March 18, 1942: *This Canada*; *Enquiry into Co-operation*; *Old Country Mail*, numbers one, two and three; *Canadian Literature Today*; and *We Have Been There*, numbers one and two. *Old Country Mail*, drawn from broadcasts by R.S. Lambert, consisted of letters about life in Great Britain during the war. While the two issues of *We Have Been There* had the highest combined sales at almost twenty-five thousand, Mary's two books ranked next with total CBC and retail sales of approximately four thousand each.[25] However, Mary's books sold out with such speed, within six months each, that more was definitely in order.

  On March 23, 1942, Weir wrote to the general manager to outline the proposal for the third book. The new book, Weir said, would be a combination of the first two books, and the print run would be ten thousand, with the CBC taking half. "The astonishing sale of the books, 'Just Mary' and 'Just Mary Again,' has been something very unusual in children's books in Canada. I understand that the combined sale of these 2,500 copies @ 50¢ and 2,000 copies @ $1.00 through the CBC Publications Branch, and an equal number through the printers, is the largest sale of a Canadian book of its kind. Both editions are now sold out, or practically so."[26] Astonishing and unusual, yes, because for the first time in Canada, the far-reaching influence of broadcast media was fuelling the sale of children's books in the country. The books were, in effect, spin-offs from the broadcasts.

Murray wrote back, "This is a highly gratifying state of affairs and all those concerned deserve great credit."[27]

In the spring of 1942, *Just Mary Stories: Combining Just Mary and Just Mary Again* was published with a new plain tan cover and simply the title. Once again, the CBC and Gage were listed on the title page as apparent co-publishers.

Concern for properly compensating Mary for the sale of the books persisted in the minds of several executives, in spite of the restrictions imposed by CBC regulations. In his annual personnel report for 1942, Ernie Bushnell addressed the matter: "Miss Grannan has done excellent work. I believe we receive royalties on the sale of her books and I think she should get added compensation because of this. She is really more than a Programme Assistant and should be reclassified to a Producer, Grade 1."[28]

With Bushnell's recommendation, Mary gained that and a little more in June 1942, when she was reclassified as producer, grade two, with the accompanying increase in salary.

The Scrapbook Goes to the Circus

During its third year, 1941–42, *The Children's Scrapbook* did a live broadcast from the Maple Leaf Gardens featuring Bob Morton's Circus. Actuality broadcasts had always been a regular part of the show, but this one was a special effort. Producer Sydney Brown, Mary, and the cast, including Austin Willis, Peggi Loder, Paul Scherman, and his musicians, were all on site — and Mary couldn't have been happier.

Syd Brown said the broadcast was "quite an event. ... Mary was a circus fan. She loved the circus. So, we put on the circus. We recorded some shows from the Maple Leaf Gardens with the circus master and all that. And we put the thing on live, cutting from one thing to the other."[29]

The circus episode was notable enough to win an honourable mention from the Institute for Education by Radio in Columbus, Ohio, in May 1942. Mary was present at the conference to hear the announcement:

> Mary Grannan accepted the invitation to speak on her job as CBC's Supervisor of Children's Programmes before the 13th Institute for Education by Radio held in Columbus, Ohio, this month. Mary took her brief-case along because one of her associates on The Children's Scrapbook had given it to her for Christmas. Mary speaks without notes, so she puts little vanities of all sorts like paper hankies and fresh gloves in her brief-case. Mary bowed when she finished her speech, bowed again when she was given an award for the circus episode in one of her Scrapbook broadcasts.[30]

Mary wrote about her excitement in a June 10 letter to Beatrice Belcourt, Pubic Relations Officer of the CBC in Ottawa: "I was indeed glad ... I should say thrilled, to hear my programme read out as a winner down in Columbus. One of the judges on the panel told me that they were a bit weary with listening and when the Canadian recordings came in they sat up again, because our approach was fresh and new."[31]

Bob Morton, owner of the circus, was also pleased with the news and sent a telegram of congratulations on May 11, 1942: "Received enclosure from Columbus Ohio. I was so overjoyed that I felt like shouting out loud. All performers felt the same way. Congratulations to you, also Sydney Brown and the entire staff. I am writing special story for the Billboard, and will also carry special display space in the Billboard. It was a great piece of work on your part and thanks a million."[32]

The Ohio distinction brought some further opportunities Mary's way, as she described in her July 1942 letter to Gladstone Murray:

This is to thank you for my increase in salary. I appreciate it very much.

I'm going home Wednesday — for a whole month. Then I'm going to the National Music Camp at Interlochen Michigan. I've been invited to speak there in August ... it's from being heard in Columbus. I'm also invited to attend the Radio Council in Cleveland in the Fall. I made some very fine contacts in my short stay in Ohio, and I learned a great deal. Now I feel I'd like to look in on New York and see what makes them "tick" ... I came back from Ohio feeling that we really had something here — we're sincere in what we do — They felt that too and liked what we had to offer.

Thank you again and if and when you get a vacation I hope it'll be a pleasant one.[33]

Murray wrote back, "You have become a distinguished ambassador of Canada as well as a distinguished broadcaster."[34]

The circus episode had proven to be so successful and popular that Mary and Syd Brown decided that it was worth doing again. For the opening program in the fourth season of the *Scrapbook*, Saturday, October 24, 1942, the program once again presented the Bob Morton Circus live from the Maple Leaf Gardens in Toronto. Austin Willis, DeB. Holly, and Byng Whitteker took turns announcing and interviewing performers. They talked with Dolly the lion trainer, young Kay Frances Hanneford who rode horses bareback, and singer Bubbles Ricardo who performed "There'll Always Be an England." Bubbles had been an acrobat until she lost an arm in an accident.

To provide a visual image of the circus over the radio, the announcers described events with the actual sounds in the background — bears walking on a tightrope, the antics of clown Slivers Johnson, and Captain Roland and his trained seals. Since the circus had long been so special for Mary, she would have been thoroughly thrilled to be in the midst of it and talking to the performers. Bob Morton even asked Mary if she wanted to be a promoter for his circus.

Gladstone Murray's Exit

In November 1942, Gladstone Murray was removed as general manager of the CBC after years of difficulties with Alan Plaunt and the CBC board, which began in the fall of 1939. Philosophically opposed in politics and radio, Plaunt had cited Murray's expense account irregularities and drunkenness as well as his administrative weaknesses as reasons for wanting him dismissed from the senior position. The Board of Governors dismissed Murray as general manager and gave him a position as "director general of broadcasting," with responsibility only for programming ideas. Murray resigned from the CBC three months later. From the autumn of 1939 until his dismissal as general manager in November 1942, Gladstone Murray had been under his own great difficulties as Mary Grannan turned to him from time to time for advice and help with administrative matters, including issues surrounding her books.

Knowlton Nash, in his book *The Microphone Wars*, described Gladstone Murray and Ernie Bushnell as believing in radio primarily as entertainment rather than as education as others, including Alan Plaunt, believed. Nash also cited Bushnell as maintaining to the end that Murray had great programming strengths that far outweighed his weaknesses.[35] Mary saw her radio work as predominantly entertainment in spite of her own background in education. Thus, her attitude toward radio was very much in line with the sentiments of Murray and Bushnell. She felt great loyalty to Gladstone Murray, probably because he was the one who offered her the job, but also because of his continued support and appreciation of her work. She frequently corresponded with him, and whenever she received a salary increase during his time as general manager, it was he she thanked.

On December 31, 1942, one month after his removal as general manager, Murray sent a handwritten letter to Mary:

> Dear Miss Grannan:
> My many thanks for your greetings, which are heartily reciprocated.

You have the balance wrong. It is the CBC that should be grateful for your enrichment of the service. But whether the CBC is grateful, is another matter![36]

Publication Blues

"That's all," said the story-teller.

"All!" said the king. "That's all? I've a good mind to throw you into prison for telling such a yarn. Why, that's the silliest story I've ever heard."

"And you're the silliest king I've ever met to sit there and listen to it."

— "A Silly Tale," *Just Mary*[37]

The otherwise happy situation with regard to the successful publication and sale of the *Just Mary* books was not without its headaches. It is amazing how much trouble a single person can cause. Mr. A.H. Jarvis, an Ottawa bookseller, was absolutely livid that the CBC was publishing and selling books. He began his complaints in 1939, protesting that the sale of war maps by the CBC interfered with bookstore sales. When the *Just Mary* and *Just Mary Again* books were released in January and November 1941 respectively, he kicked up a considerable storm, writing letters of grievance to the CBC. Jarvis began his complaints about the sale of the *Just Mary* books with a letter written on November 3, 1941. He said the CBC was selling the books directly to the public instead of advising people to go to their local booksellers. The frequent letters that followed declared that this was unfair competition to the booksellers and that the CBC should not be a managed bookstore.

Jarvis also took his complaints to a wider circle, soliciting support from his member of Parliament, George J. McIlraith, MP for Ottawa West, from Dr. McCann, MP, Chairman of the Committee on Radio Broadcasting, and from the Book Publishers' Branch of the Board of Trade of the City of Toronto, all of whom wrote their own letters to the CBC. The CBC responded that it was providing a public service by issuing printed copies of broadcasts, and, in addition, the books were available for bookstores to sell. As the third book was about to come out in the spring of 1942, Jarvis asked that only booksellers be allowed to sell the new edition. Correspondence continued back and forth with Jarvis throughout 1942. As well, a Montreal lawyer by the name of E.C. Monk wrote to express his concern about the possibility of the author receiving profit from the open promotion of the book on the air.

While the corporation was still struggling throughout 1943 to settle the whole issue of copyright and the author's rights, this thorn of annoyance in the form of Mr. Jarvis kept festering. E.A. Weir wrote to Dr. Augustin Frigon, the new general manager, on October 2, 1943, to give the history of the corporation's correspondence with Mr. Jarvis:

> This has extended over several years during which Mr. Jarvis has exhibited a degree of pertinacity only to be found in a bookseller and, incidentally, in my opinion, more than a little unfairness in his correspondence.
>
> He has maintained a perpetual grouse at the CBC regarding the printing and offering of books for sale; he has contended that we have no right to do this; that the author receives a bonus; that the business is carried on at the expense of the Corporation; and that we are merely competitors of the bookstores.
>
> In April 1939, while broadcasting his "book sales" over CKCO, he asked for the privilege of price mention. In November of the same year he complained about our offer of a war map, contending that we were interfering with legitimate sales of maps through bookstores. In November 1941 he again complained about our interfering with business and inquired why we did not sell "boots" as well as "books". At the same time, a complaint was made to the Minister that the Corporation was unfairly competing with book stores.[38]

Meanwhile, the CBC was still busy answering the complaints of the Board of Trade of the City of Toronto. Earlier that year, in January 1943, the Book Publishers' Branch began again to write to the general manager, then Dr. James Thomson, complaining in a more formal and polite manner than Mr. Jarvis about the direct publication and sale of *Just Mary* and *Just Mary Again* on the grounds that it was "outside of the proper sphere of operations of the Corporation" and was "an encroachment upon the functions of book publishers and booksellers."[39]

On January 29, Dr. Thomson wrote to J. F. MacNeill, law clerk and parliamentary counsel in the Senate, to inquire if the CBC was "keeping within the provisions of Section 8(b) and (j) of the Canadian Broadcasting Act."[40] While dutifully checking to be certain of their position, the early sentiments in the corporation can be summed up well by E.A. Weir's comments in his February 3 memorandum to the general manager: "In the meantime, I might say in my opinion it is no business of the Toronto Board of Trade whatsoever as to what the CBC does. They have their own place but in this case they are poking their noses into other people's business."[41]

MacNeill replied to Dr. Thomson on February 16, outlining the three objections put forth by the Book Publishers' Branch of the Toronto Board of Trade in accordance with its interpretation of the Canadian Broadcasting Act. Firstly, the Board contended that the CBC was not authorized to publish books of any kind, and further, these particular books were not seen as furthering the objectives of the CBC. Secondly, the CBC was not authorized to announce the prices of the books because this was not part of its information services. And thirdly, the CBC was not authorized to make private arrangements with privately owned companies for the joint publication of books. In his estimate, Mr. MacNeill offered the opinion that the Broadcasting Act did permit the CBC to publish and distribute papers and literary matter that it felt were conducive to the objects of the corporation, and that it was up to management to interpret what items it felt were in keeping with its objectives. Similarly, MacNeill felt that decisions about announcing the price of books were also a matter for the judgment of the management. As for the third objection, MacNeill felt that the CBC did have the authority to make suitable business arrangement for the publication of materials rather than having to establish its own separate printing establishment.[42]

Around the same time, H.H. Love of W.J. Gage advised Weir to assure the Board of Trade that it was not entering the publishing field with a view of directly competing with publishers but merely making available to the public copies of broadcasts at a reasonable price. Love felt that the complaint was likely caused by one or a few members and that booksellers were lucky to have such a readily saleable book.[43]

However, this was not the only issue. Several matters were coming to a head in the publication of the books, and Weir outlined these in his memorandum of March 15 to Dr. Thomson. Gage was proposing to make arrangements to publish the books in other countries and had a letter of interest from Thomas Nelson & Sons in Edinburgh. In his letter, H.H. Love stated that Gage owned the Canadian copyright. Weir felt this was open to discussion and that the CBC should be investigating its rights regarding publication of the books in other countries. Was Gage the publisher, or was it merely the printer for the CBC? But beyond this, there was a larger question that Weir raised with Dr. Thomson.

> All of this however merely opens a still greater issue, and that is the copyright question in its relation to not only Mary Grannan's material but the material of all other performers on CBC networks or stations, and especially in relation to the question of a publication. I think it is something which should be clarified as definitely as can be done because it applies not only to the English Network but also to the French Network. Books and pamphlets are being printed by the CBC and some by outsiders. Some of these we may know about before publication and some we do not know about. I think it might well be the subject of discussion at an Administrative Conference, and that the Department of Justice should be asked to clarify a number of issues associated therewith, such as mentioned above.[44]

Dr. Thomson agreed to refer the matter to the next administrative conference. It was the beginning of discussion on a complex issue that would touch many more than Mary Grannan. Her books were merely the first to raise the issue of copyright. This question, part of the growing pains of the corporation, would take over two more years to resolve.

Effect of the War on Children

Behind their merry and entertaining radio stories for children, broadcasters shared a deep concern for children suffering along with adults from the effects of war. While certainly not as severe as those hardships suffered by children in the direct theatre of war, children at home had needs to consider in broadcasting. "Radio in the War and After" was the topic of the fourteenth annual conference of the Institute for Education by Radio in Columbus, Ohio, from April 30 to May 3, 1943. In addition to sessions dealing with school and educational broadcasting, the conference conducted two sessions on children's programs. Topics for the first included "children's special war and post-war needs, potentialities of radio in meeting wartime needs, what is now being done with programs specifically designed for children," and "program needs for the future." The second session, which featured both youth and adult panels, addressed the question of how radio writers could serve the needs and interests of youth in wartime.[45] On the two adult panels for these sessions, Mary was the only Canadian.

In preparation for the conference, Mary gathered opinions from a selection of Canadian children on how the war affected them. Her sister, Ann, collected responses from three schools in Moncton, New Brunswick, while the director of school broadcasts in British Columbia solicited thoughts from children in four communities in his province. The remaining answers came from a couple of schools in Ontario and Manitoba. Mary's resulting fourteen-page document, featuring comments of children ages eleven to fourteen, evoked a poignant view of the war by the youth in Canada, with quotations ranging from sad tales of losing loved ones in the war and suffering economic hardships to expressions of compassion, surprisingly mature thoughts, and humorous suggestions about dealing with the enemy after the war. The following excerpts have been selected from the document:

The war has affected me because we have to have our ration books when we go to the store and we can't have all the things we like. It has brought us sorrow too because my cousin was killed in England.

The war has affected me plenty because my brother was killed flying over Germany and my dad can't get enough help now to run the orchard.

After the war I would like to see the Japanese that lived here and that were loyal and took good care of their crops come back again.

Has the war affected you? Yes, it has. How? Well, you can't even listen to a quiet radio programme without some news coming on about every fifteen minutes telling that a ship was sunk with all the crew drownded or that many people were killed in a daylight raid on London, or that you are going to be cut in your butter or sugar again. Do you listen to any radio programmes on the war? I do not understand some of it so therefore do not listen to any regularly.

This war has affected me, but when you get to thinking, we're lucky we live in Canada and are free. I was listening to a program the other night about a soldier who was in the raid on Dieppe. They say he lost his legs; we know that he didn't lose his legs, he gave them to keep us free. When this world is free again I bet that soldier will be proud to think that he gave his legs to keep this world free.

I feel down right discouraged. If our men could only get their hands on the one who started it what wouldn't happen to him wouldn't be worth telling. Two of my uncles have enlisted in the Army so now Merrit has to stay home to help around the farm instead of finishing his course at Training School. I'll be glad when the war's over so that Miriam can get her ice skates and we can build a house somewhere. I do not listen to any radio plays on the war as I can hear all I want to from the folks talking, and I can see all I want at the movies and a person can sure read enough in the newspaper to keep you reading for a month. I'd like to see Canada and the United States join into one country.

After the war we should braid Hitler, Mussolini and Hirohito, then choke them, then run the steamroller over them and make a mat out of them for the king.

I wish they would bring Hitler to every city in Canada and America to let every boy and girl spank him for starting this war.

I would like to see all the little English children that are over here to go back to England and see their mother's and father's safe.

I especially like the "Fighting Navy" every Thursday night and "The Soldiers Hour" on Sunday. It was very interesting listening to the refugees on Sunday morning. There is another program called "You Can't Do Business with Hitler" that is very interesting.

The European children really know what war is because they are in the thick of it. They have been driven out of their homes many a night waiting with anxiety of what will happen any minute while we are sleeping and dreaming at home without any care in the world. Many night[s] I lay and [think] of how children may be lying and crying for want of hunger. Many little children haven't seen their parents for days and many have lost them too. There are boys and girls too who haven't seen daylight for hours. That is why the children of Canada should be happy that they live here.[46]

In the difficult and serious war years, Mary's gentle and wholesome stories for young children were undoubtedly welcomed as entertainment with an appropriate tone. Programs for older children, such as the *Scrapbook*, attempted to provide thrills without the usual blood and thunder. In addition to the care given to the style of her regular programs, Mary made some more direct contributions to the war effort at home. Her children's program on rubber conservation, presented in June 1942, was eagerly noted by the National Salvage Campaign. For the Second Victory Loan campaign of 1942, she wrote two school plays, *Blue Boots* and *Builders of Canada*, both "written under terrific telephone pressure" in a single day without benefit of research materials.[47] She wrote an additional play, *The War Wolf's Waterloo*, for the Sixth Victory Loan of 1944. Designed to be performed with minimal costumes and properties, the plays concluded with encouraging messages: "So this is the moral of our little tale — Chins up, thumbs UP, and we cannot fail";[48] "Come on, you Canadians — we've work to do."[49]

Letter Home to Sisters

With thoughts written as they came, Mary's chatty but hurriedly typed letter to Ann and Helen in the spring of 1943 described some experiences of Canada in wartime mixed in with details of Mary's preparation for a CBC publicity tour — an odd conjunction of the serious beside the frivolous. At the end of the letter, she added a recipe for hops yeast, possibly a tip for dealing with war shortages.

> Dear Girls ... Not much to add to yesterday's letter. Last night I went home at five ... got my supper and worked on a Victory Loan show. I wrote another corny bit for the Dept. of Education ... I told them if they didn't like it they didn't have to use it ... I meet them tomorrow for

lunch at the hotel. One thing about Victory Loans ... you eat well when you work for them. I called Gladys [Willis] ... she is considering taking a Grade 6. She has Gr 4 now. I guess the schools are terribly upset ... teachers coming in that haven't taught for years and don't know how to get going. I called up Ruby Cook's about a hat. She's the one who made the white one. I'm going tomorrow. I'm going to get a plain black one. I still have seven of my American dollars ... I think I'll get a purse for myself. I am afraid to try bringing anything over the line out west ... and so I won't be buying presents. If I get a chance to get off by myself in Chicago I might take in a five and ten ... with my seven. I did think of a housecoat again but I guess I don't need to look so grand all by myself ... I'll wash it again and do with it. I have everything now but a slip, gloves and stockings. I'll get those at the end of the week. I'm not touching the $89 now ... I'll have a hundred about when Ann gets hers to it ... no hurry for that and then the two V-bonds ... I haven't got the other one yet but I'll send it to you when it comes from Ottawa. It was paid for there you know. Got a letter from Ann yesterday too. She's got a dandy little bunch ... CHEE it ain't much like Devon eh? I often wish I could look in on it and see my room ... I can feel myself there now ... see the stove and the dust. Elizabeth [Long] has written to Winnipeg to line up some people to do for me when I am there. I'm writing Amy Roe. I have to get at my JM now so until tomorrow this is Just Mary saying goodbye and happy playtime if any.[50]

Goodwill Tours

While her first three books were being published, Mary expanded her regular radio programming with the addition of week-long Christmas and Easter specials. *The Magic Chord* and *Magic in Spring*, which first appeared in the 1941–42 season and continued for several years, presented the adventures of Billy and Bunty, who discovered that a particular chord on their toy piano unlocked magical worlds. But Mary had been spreading her wings beyond the studios as well during this period. By the end of the spring season of 1943, she had attended two conferences of the Institute for Education by Radio in Columbus, Ohio, spoke at a music camp at Interlochen, Michigan, and at the Radio Council in Cleveland, and at the end of May 1943 she embarked upon a CBC goodwill tour to several cities in the Canadian West.

On May 31, 1943, Mary left Toronto by train and travelled to Vancouver, visiting the West Coast for the first time. During the week she spent in British Columbia, she broadcast her regular *Just Mary* show from the Vancouver studios on June 6 and visited Victoria before continuing on to visit Edmonton, Calgary, Saskatoon, and Winnipeg. In each city, she made appearances, visited schools, spoke to groups such as the home and school associations, and gave interviews. A clipping from a Moncton newspaper later in the summer described some of her visit in the West:

> While in Western Canada she [Miss Grannan] visited Victoria, Vancouver, Edmonton, Calgary, Saskatoon, and Winnipeg and talked to Home and School Associations, Canadian Authors in Victoria and visited the children in the schools. From these schools as well as on the trains she gathered many of her stories. For instance a small dog on the train which was taken out at every stop made an interesting story, also while in Capilano Canyon, a wild duck that settled in a garden and was given the name Jimmy, supplied the material for another story.[51]

During her travels, she was busy preparing for a tour in the Maritimes later in the summer, which she would fit around some vacation time at home in Fredericton. As she shaped her plans, she wrote several times to George Young, CBC's regional representative in the Maritimes.

Just prior to leaving Toronto, Mary wrote to Young: "Mr. Bushnell advises no definite planning due to the scarcity of producers, announcers, in fact, staff. He suggests rather an investigation tour. I'd appreciate any suggestions from you as to where I should stop off and whom I should contact and how long I should make my stay."[52]

Young responded, outlining two good talent prospects whom he wished Mary to interview — Marian Cox in Saint John and Stan Chapman in Campbellton. From Winnipeg, Mary wrote George again, requesting help with hotel reservations and guidance on her Maritime visits. This letter provided some of the flavour of her trip.

> You may have no patience with me for leaving this so long but ... I wired Nova Scotian for a reservation on Sat night for July 5 6 7 they wire today ... they cannot confirm. ... What shall I do next ... please or ... do you think it better for me to go home first ... and then come to Halifax ... I can do that. I thought I'd go to Halifax on Monday ... stay the three days ... then go home. I considered going CN [Canadian National Railway] and coming back CP [Canadian Pacific] ... thus dropping in on Campbellton. I couldn't get anything but two one way tickets ... so thought perhaps it would be more economical if you wished it ... that I go to Campbellton from home as a side trip. I've been doing so many things and meeting so many people that I've not gotten any business letters written at all ... I'm too tuckered at the end of the day ... today I've been to three schools ... spoke and told a story at each. I'll speak to anyone you wish me to in Halifax ... and I'll see Miss Cox in Saint John. ... Perhaps Joan Marshall could interview me ... Miss Heming did in Vancouver ... Miss Mjoldnes in Edmonton. I've a public meeting tomorrow night ... I sort of wish it weren't public but I guess that's the way Mr. L'Ami likes it. I'll have to work in the morning at it. I've learned a lot ... especially about regional feelings which is good.

But to get back to my problem … Can you find me someplace to stay … a YW [YWCA] … a rooming house … a hotel … anything but the YM [YMCA]. That's not scruples … it's the policy of the CBC…

I'll be "home" Friday to Toronto … I hope you are still there … if not will you leave me a note advising me the best procedure. I made reservations as far as Saint John … leaving Toronto June 30…

Sincerely,

Mary

P.S. Don't advise me NOT to come. I got the check & I'm aching to see me own provinces. M.[53]

As events unfolded, Mary took the train home to Fredericton on June 30 and took her holidays until August 13, postponing her travel to Campbellton until the end of July and her trips to Moncton, Saint John, and Halifax until the second half of August. For her Maritime visits, Mary was not able to make any appearances at schools or home and school associations since they were not in session, and so her duties centred around auditioning two people for George Young, giving a radio interview to Joan Marshall in Moncton, making an appearance at the New Brunswick Summer School to promote school broadcasts, and sending her *Just Mary* program over the national airwaves from the Halifax studios on August 22. Young had also requested that she promote school broadcasting to a couple of key people: "It would be a good thing when you are in Moncton or Fredericton if you could contact Dr. Blakeney; or Fletcher Peacock in Saint John or Fredericton. Both of these men need a little pepping up regarding Maritime School Broadcasting. They are very luke warm at the present."[54]

One of Young's main interests was the audition of Stan Chapman in Campbellton: "The fellow in Campbellton I thought should be visited. He has an interesting little show, possibly a little amateurish but still he doesn't talk down to the kiddies. I am seriously considering him for a series this fall. It will be a split between he and Marion Cox. These shows, I don't think, will interfere in any way with your projects."[55]

Mary sent Young a report about Stan Chapman following her visit to Campbellton:

> About the show ... I liked the elf Hoppy. I thought the story teller made this imaginative creature very real indeed and very appealing and very amusing.
>
> I made two suggestions in my criticism of the programme. The first was regarding the shape of the show. The second ... the pace. The shape used was thus
>
> THEME * HOPPY * POEM * STORY * MUSIC * THEME
>
> (Hoppy was scattered in a bit between this routine) The music was definitely used to fill out the time. I suggested the show would have a better shape thus...
>
> THEME * HOPPY * POEM * MUSIC * STORY * HOPPY * THEME
>
> To my mind there is better balance in this programme picture and the music takes an important place ... I can see Mr. Chapman's point ... up to now he's not bothered with a before-show timing. I'd like him to have the show positively shaped and timed before hitting the air.
>
> The pace of the story and poem for my listening was a bit slow. I felt the need of a little lift. I didn't demonstrate what I meant because then I'd be putting "me" in ... and this storyteller is himself as much as I'm myself and I might ruin the whole thing if I tried to project me. He sounds a thoroughly nice person on the air ... he sounds sincere and he likes the elf.[56]

A few years later, the CBC began to carry Stan Chapman's program, *Sleepytime Storyteller*. In her analysis of Chapman's show, Mary demonstrated the experience she had gained from radio production in the previous few years.

While Mary's spring and summer tours were largely meant for public relations, they also offered her an opportunity for discussion, shar-

From left: Mary, Ann, and Helen Grannan, 1906.

Mary (second row, third from right), age ten, with her St. Dunstan's class, 1910.

Above: Grannan family, 1912: William, Ann, Catherine, Mary (in back), and Helen.

Left: Mary, 1914.

Mary as she completed high school, 1917.

Haney-Grannan home, 325 Brunswick Street, as it appeared in 1898.
From left: Catherine Grannan and baby Ann, Catherine's sisters
Margaret Flanagan and Mary Haney.

325 Brunswick Street as it appeared when Mary lived there.

Left: Mary with unknown man, possibly Bill Shea, circa 1925. "Ain't he nice?" Mary wrote on back of photo.

Below: At Palmer's Point, Grand Lake, July 19, 1931. Front row from left: Mary Grannan, Joe O'Connor, Mabel Burtt (Muriel's mother), Nancy Kitchen, unknown man, William Burtt (Muriel's father), unknown man. Back row from left: Gwen Kitchen, Gladys Hall, Lois MacLaggan, unknown man, Bill Walker, Muriel Burtt.

At Palmer's Point, Grand Lake. From left: Mary Grannan, Muriel Burtt, Bill Walker, and Josephine Burtt.

Muriel Burtt and Mary Grannan with two unknown gentlemen.

Courtesy of Mary Hayes

Grades 1 and 2 students dressed for Mary Grannan's 1935 school play. From left: Louise Pringle, Elizabeth Jewett, Annie Stirling, Margaret MacLaggan, and Catherine McGinley.

Courtesy Eleanor Monteith Stillwell

Left: Seven-year-old Eleanor Monteith dressed as the honeymooning bride in Mary Grannan's 1935 play at Devon School.

Below: Devon Superior School, circa 1920.

Courtesy Walter Long

Teachers of Devon School circa June 1937. From left: Harry Grant, Katherine MacLaggan, Kelsie Gregory, Leah Stickles, Mabel MacDonald, Muriel Blair, Mary Grannan, and Charles Murray. Possibly year-end gathering at the summer home of Leah Stickles at The Pines, Douglas. Mary wrote on the photo, "In this it can be clearly seen that I lead a double life."

Cast of *The Meddlesome Maid* at St. Dunstan's Hall, Fredericton, March 19, 1936. From left: Matthew Dobbelsteyn, Helen Grannan, Walter Myshrall, Ms. Hughes, Ed Quinn, Mary Grannan, Mae Savage (front), Gregory Rowan, Mary Foster, Joe Dobbelsteyn, Dorothy Hughes, and Ed Carten.

Cast of CFNB's *Aggravating Agatha*, 1936. From left: Gertrude Davis, Mary Grannan, and Carl (Hap) Watson.

Carl (Hap) Watson in CFNB studio, Fredericton.

One of several political cartoons Mary drew for the *Daily Gleaner* for the June 1930 provincial election. This one appeared in the *Daily Gleaner* on June 17, 1930, page 12.

Catherine Grannan with her broom outside 325 Brunswick Street, circa 1941.

Mary, 1937, as she appeared during summer school at Columbia University and when *Just Mary* began on CFNB.

The Children's Scrapbook broadcasting from Bob Morton's Circus, Maple Leaf Gardens, 1941–42. In front from left: Austin Willis, circus girl (possibly Kay Frances Hanneford), Mary Grannan, and Sydney Brown.

Gladys and Frank
Willis with their dog,
circa 1940s.

Austin Willis. "Hello
Mary Dear. This is 1947
and they are getting
more touched-up all the
time. Austin."

CBC meeting, early 1940s. Clockwise from bottom left: Taggart, Brodie, Lucas (hidden), Baker (hidden), Mary Grannan, Wicklund, Hamilton, Bushnell, Miss Appleby (his secretary), Delafield, Radford, Neil Morrison, Hugh Morrison, and Beardlet. A photograph of Gladstone Murray can be seen on the wall.

Mary posing with her second book, *Just Mary Again*, and a stack of scripts, December 1941. She inscribed the photograph to "James," one of many pet names for her sister Helen.

Mary reading to some young listeners, 1941, at Mary's residence, 55 Oriole Gardens.

"Author Mary Grannan, alias 'Maggie Muggins,' at a book signing, 1947." Accompanied by Beryl Braithwaite dressed as Maggie.

From left: unknown man, Mary, Beryl Braithwaite, and Harry Adelman, a Reliable Toy representative, at the launch of Reliable Toy's Maggie Muggins doll, 1948.

Mary and Beryl Braithwaite with children at the launch of *Happy Playtime*, 1948.

Mary Grannan receiving the key to the City of Fredericton from Mayor Ray Forbes on the occasion of her tenth anniversary of broadcasting with the CBC and Fredericton's one-hundredth birthday, July 30, 1948. CFNB owner J. Stewart Neill is observing the ceremony.

Above: Noel Langley, circa 1949.

Left: Mary and Andrew Cowan in front of the BBC, London, 1949.

ing ideas, and making plans with the corporation's regional people. She mentioned to Young that Ira Dilworth in Vancouver had "some very ambitious plans for the fall. He wants me to go out there for three months."[57] The cross-country networking and planning would have pleased Mary because she was keenly interested in helping to develop a national children's programming department.

With the summer over, Mary went back to Toronto for the fall 1943 season, writing her sisters after her arrival:

> I wrote mum on Saturday … and nothing MUCH has happened since except I saw Bill Walker last night. He came up for an hour or so. […] Gladys was up Saturday night. Austin was in for a while on Sat afternoon. He is all NAVY now … I hope he makes good. He's got a lot to learn. […] Oh yes … they didn't put my picture in New World … consequently I think it's a very poor set up […] it's not interesting at all … I didn't even buy a copy. They were to have had an eight page spread. It's not CBC's fault … it's the magazines … I don't care really a bit. Going to the circus this afternoon … letters may be scarcer this week.[58]

Chapter Eight
The Birth of *Maggie Muggins,*
1944–1945

Dud Allen & Thomas Allen Company

With sales of the three *Just Mary* books reaching twenty-three thousand by spring 1943,[1] Forbes Duncan (Dud) Allen approached Mary on behalf of Toronto publisher Thomas Allen Limited about the possibility of distributing her third book in the United States. Son of company founder Thomas Allen, Dud had joined the firm as vice-president that year after leaving the army. In early January 1944 he visited E.A. Weir at the CBC to discuss the matter.

Following the meeting, Weir reported to the general manager, Dr. Augustin Frigon, noting in particular, "Miss Grannan is naturally anxious to see some such arrangement proceeded with, because her Just Mary stories are her chief literary asset at present and can be the means of making something which will be of very great importance to her financially."[2] On January 13, Frigon gave Mary his permission to proceed with the American publication as well as to receive a royalty, although he cautioned that this was not to be taken as a precedent since the issue of copyright was still under study. Later that year, in the fall of 1944, G.P Putnam's Sons released the American edition of the combined volume of *Just Mary Stories*, the first of Mary's books to appear in the United States.

Sometime in 1944, while further Canadian editions of *Just Mary* stories remained on hold, Mary chanced to show Dud Allen the story she had written for Harry Halperin, owner of an educational comics business in Montreal, who wanted to use the story in a colouring or paint book for children. Mary called the story *Maggie Muggins*, selecting "Maggie" because it was a happy-sounding name she liked and "Muggins" because its double letter *g*s complemented those in "Maggie," producing a pleasing visual effect on the cover.[3]

Recognizing that *Maggie Muggins* was entirely new material not previously broadcast by the CBC, astute Dud seized an opportunity that was free and clear of the copyright stalemate. Convincing Mary that it was too good for a paint book, Dud published *Maggie Muggins* in the fall of 1944 as a slim, oversize book, eleven by nine inches, with red and black illustrations by Nancy Caudle. Mary later wrote that the book "was large and flat because of the paper shortage" during wartime.[4] On the cover underneath Mary's name was the phrase, "author of 'Just Mary,'" with "Just Mary" in bold black type that was twice as big — Dud knew the selling point.

In ten short, simple stories that began and ended with "tra la la" songs, Mary introduced six-year-old Maggie, with red pigtails and freckles on her turned-up nose, and her gardener friend, Mr. McGarrity, who helped solve problems. The small beginning was destined to lead to much greater things.

> "Tra la la la la la lee
> I was to Spinella's Party in the Red Pine tree.
> I don't know where I'll go tomorrow!"[5]

Capturing some of the excitement that Mary must have felt with the fall publication of two books that paid royalties, Kay McMullen, who had written an article about Mary, "Just Mary, Herself," for *Catholic Youth* magazine in June 1944, wrote to Mary on Sunday, October 15, about the new book:

I intended to wait until I had read your new book before I sent you my congratulations, but after listening to you just now & hearing that priceless rendition of "Three Blind Mice", I felt I better let you know right now how very glad I am to hear that "Maggie Muggins" is off the press.

I sincerely hope that all the luck of the Irish will go into its reception & sale.

Knowing the "Just Mary" & "Just Mary Again" stories & then knowing Just Mary herself, I feel fully convinced that "Maggie Muggins" need have no fear of the future.

May you both live forever![6]

In addition to her first book royalties in 1944, Mary received some extra money that year when she was offered a commercial spot. All of her CBC programs until 1944 had been regular or sustaining features free of commercial sponsorship. There had been an attempt in 1940 to commercialize one of her shows when an advertiser approached the CBC about sponsoring the *Children's Scrapbook*. However, the CBC declined the offer so that the goodwill the program had developed with parents would not be disrupted. "So the money bags once more disappear beyond the horizon," Mary had written to Fletcher Peacock when she told him of that development.[7]

During 1944, the Robert Simpson Company, a national department store chain, asked her to develop a sponsored children's program. The resulting fifteen-minute show, *Sonnie and Susie*, aired later in the 1944–45 season, broadcast Monday through Friday, first on CJBC and then on CFRB. It was Mary's first sponsored program since *Aggravating Agatha* at CFNB.

In spring 1944, while waiting for confirmation of the Simpson program, Mary wrote a letter home. She had recently met Noel Langley and his wife, Tillie (Naomi). Langley, a novelist, playwright, and screenwriter originally from South Africa but whose work was carried out largely in Great Britain and the United States, was looking for work in Toronto, arriving from New York City sometime following the birth of his son, Garrick, in May 1943. He had become something of a legend in Hollywood when, at the age of twenty-six, he wrote the script for the 1939 motion picture *The Wizard of Oz* in only eleven days.[8] Whether or not he found any work at the CBC, he likely became known among the CBC crowd, where he soon attracted Mary's friendship.

> Dear Girls, the first nice day of the season, and I see clouds creeping up even now. It's Friday tomorrow and mind you, I've no Just Mary done and I have to go do that recording in the morning. I hope I heard right. I hope he said FIFTY and not fifteen. I've been wondering since about it. I'm being very lazy. First of week I'll get at the Foster layout. Tillie Langley goes to NS [Nova Scotia] tonight. She's been here three weeks. I've liked knowing her. He [Noel Langley] goes to Hollywood on Sunday if nothing happens. I'm going to tell him to see if he can see [Walt] Disney. He doesn't know him. I wish he did. He's the only one that could use me stuff. […] I am not telling you when I'm coming because I want to wait till I see this Simpson thing through. I'd like to know before I leave what's what. If it's a NO, I should try to get something else. Mary Gurney got a letter from a French girl today. She used to write to her years ago in some sort of a Letter writing club. The things she told made your blood run cold. Her little sister 8 years old died of starvation. They have no stockings at all and she herself got chilblains in her legs very bad. She said that the Germans buried 17 young men alive one night. They could hear them screaming but could do nothing to help. She saw mechanical saws used on children. A student was put in prison, a girl of fifteen, because she happened to go into a professor's room for something when some of the professors were listening to English radio. Of course, the professors were shot. It's so hard to believe. I didn't know I could be so moved. Reading

it in papers is different. She told about how she had no clothes and some people sold some rags for cleaning to a store. You were allowed only one rag, but because she knew the clerk, she managed to get two or three and made herself a dress. And I talk of commercial programmes. The letter was written in French and Mary got Mr. Brodie to translate it for her. [9]

Before going to Fredericton for her vacation, Mary moved from 55 Oriole Gardens to an apartment at 89 Breadalbane, near Wellesley and Yonge streets, close to the University of Toronto and within a short walking distance of work and the church she attended, St. Basil's Roman Catholic. This apartment building remained her home during the rest of the time she lived in Toronto, although she switched apartments within it once, upgrading to a larger one at a later time. For Mary, this was a positive upward move.

Resolving the Copyright Dragon

While Mary made some progress with her publications during the fall of 1944, publishing *Maggie Muggins* and releasing the first American edition of *Just Mary*, she continued to wait for the CBC and its legal counsel, F. Willard Savignac, to make a decision on the issue of copyright. Much discussion on the topic had been taking place during 1943 and 1944.

In 1943, the CBC Board of Governors had requested an opinion from the Department of Justice. With W.J. Gage & Company claiming it owned the Canadian copyright, General Manager James Thomson wrote the deputy minister: "The question on which the Canadian Broadcasting Corporation would like to have an opinion is concerned with the ownership of the copyright, whether this ownership resides in the Messrs. Gage & Company, in the author, Miss Mary Grannan, or in the Corporation."[10] The deputy minister, F.P. Varcoe, replied that in his opinion copyright was vested in the corporation, while Gage & Company held a licence to print, publish, and sell the books in Canada.[11] The author apparently did not figure into his opinion at all.

Meanwhile, Savignac noted that there were diversified views on copyright, performing, and publishing rights, urging that any proper protection for the CBC could be acquired only through written documentation. He suggested a roundtable conference to discuss the issues of copyright proper, publishing rights, assignment of copyright, Canadian Performing Rights Society, fan mail, CBC Programme Productions, and CBC Copyright Repertoire. He then suggested that the CBC develop a long-range plan for dealing with this issue as it pertained to: "(1) CBC Personnel who produce dramas, musical settings, etc., e.g., Miss Mary Grannan. (2) Free lancers outside of permanent staff."[12] The issue grew more complex all the time.

Savignac had noted in a letter of May 1943 that while Gage & Company had grown more aggressive in claiming copyright over the works, "Miss Grannan, it would appear … has acquiesced throughout."[13] Mary, however, was not willing to sit back indefinitely. While preparing for the American publication, Dud Allen and Mary consulted G.M. Kelley, a lawyer at Cassels, Brock & Kelley, to inquire about the legalities of the situation. In a letter to Dud on April 14, 1944, Kelley offered the opinion that the CBC was the owner of the copyright in the stories Mary wrote during her employment, but that copyright might be limited to publication by broadcasting with any further publication requiring her consent. He further stated that the CBC had no right over the title *Just Mary*, since Mary previously had broadcast stories under this name in New Brunswick. In conclusion, Kelley said that Mary was at liberty to proceed with the American publication.[14]

With a legal consultation for Thomas Allen Limited concluded, Mary sought another for herself, retaining the services of law firm Messrs. White, Ruel & Bristol. On her behalf, Gerard Ruel wrote to Ernie Bushnell on May 8, 1944, outlining a number of points respecting Mary's rights as author under the Copyright Act. Even while defending her rights, she was anxious not to appear difficult. Ruel prefaced his comments with a congenial introduction:

> Her [Mary Grannan's] reason in consulting us was not with the view of occasioning any trouble to the Canadian Broadcasting Corporation since her relations

with your concern have been most agreeable. What she wished to know was to what extent is she the owner of the copyright in her stories, and how far is she restricted by her arrangements with the Corporation in dealing with publishers and others, in Canada and elsewhere, in the reproduction in any form of her works. Publishers and others naturally insist on a clarification of her present position with the Corporation before they will even consider having anything to do with her little stories.[15]

Citing section twelve of the Copyright Act, Ruel stated that his advice to Miss Grannan was that she was the first owner of the copyright in the works, and further, according to section three, had the sole right of production and reproduction and could part with these rights only through definite arrangement, acquiescence, or assignment. With a long and nuanced interpretation, Ruel focused on the distinction between a contract of service and a contract for services, concluding that Mary's contract for services was for the broadcasting of her stories, while the written form of these stories was outside its scope. He asked for a clarification of the situation as well as a recognition and observation of her rights to all her stories and dramatizations. Declaring an end to her acquiescence in the matter, Ruel asked that publication without compensation to the author be replaced with an equitable adjustment:

> As to publication, it would seem fair that your Corporation should have the right to publish or have published in Canada any stories prepared by the author, and broadcast over your System within the limit of six months from the first broadcast of any such story, and subject to the payment of a royalty to the author on each copy sold, to be arranged, definitely from time to time between the author, the publisher and yourself.[16]

The next month, Bushnell and Weir reached an agreement in discussions with Mary. In his letter of June 26, Weir outlined the agreed-upon issues: (1) the CBC would have first broadcasting rights while

Mary remained a salaried employee; (2) Mary would have subsequent broadcasting rights six months after the original date of broadcast; (3) the CBC would pay Mary a royalty for any stories the corporation published and must decide within six months of broadcast whether or not to publish; (4) royalties on stories published by outside publishers would be a matter for negotiation between Mary and the publisher; (5) while Mary remained a CBC employee, any stories published by an outside publisher would carry the credit line "with the permission of the CBC"; (6) all other rights were the property of Mary. In closing, Weir noted that Mary urged "that something definite should be done to clear the matter as soon as possible as she is going away and her publishers are pursuing her rather relentlessly."[17]

In response, Savignac, while recognizing that Mary was the author of her works with all rights attached, suggested revisions that were more favourable to the CBC. On July 26, he prepared a document for Mary's signature that was an absolute assignment to the CBC of all her broadcasting and publishing rights within six months from the first broadcast. In return, Mary would be able to rebroadcast material after six months with previous written notice, would receive a royalty for publications, and could publish through outside publishers after six months with written notice and the credit line "Courtesy and Permission of the Canadian Broadcasting Corporation."[18] Practically speaking, the end results of the two approaches may appear to be similar, but the overall tone and intent of the revisions gave more power to the CBC over Mary's rights.

Weir wrote back to Savignac on July 27: "I do not think that it follows out the spirit of the arrangement agreed to in the discussions between Mr. Bushnell, Miss Grannan and myself."[19]

After receiving the letter of assignment that Savignac had prepared for her signature, Mary turned once more to her lawyer for a response. On October 19, Mary sent a letter prepared by Ruel to Dr. Frigon, advising him that the assignment letter was unsatisfactory "in that it does not sufficiently recognize my absolute rights, as author, to the production or reproduction in any form of my work under The Copyright Act."[20] The letter outlined a licence with terms more acceptable to protecting Mary's rights, omitting the absolute assignment in Savignac's letter.

Still, Savignac was not satisfied, finding many of the points objectionable. He suggested meeting Ruel in person to settle the issue, but Frigon had decided to get an additional legal opinion to resolve the complicated issue, to be followed by a conference on the matter. Realizing in December that this would take some time to resolve, Frigon asked Mary to carry on for the time being, saying that it was CBC policy to deal as liberally as possible in such cases as long as CBC broadcasting rights were protected.[21] On December 14, he gave her provisional permission to receive royalties from her publisher, with further permission on January 31, 1945, to go ahead with a new *Just Mary* book. These two decisions, of course, were made with the stipulation that they would not set a precedent. So the legal wrangling continued into 1945.

Sometime between January and April of 1945, the copyright matter was at last resolved. While the final text of the agreement between Mary and the CBC has proven elusive, the resulting actions were clear: the CBC never again published any of Mary Grannan's books. In April, she signed a contract with Thomas Allen Limited, and from that point retained the copyright of her books and received her full share of royalties. None of her subsequent books carried a statement of permission from the CBC.

What is not known here is just how much help and advice Dud Allen gave Mary in recognizing and standing up for her rights as author. He may have been instrumental in this and may have advised her to get a lawyer. However, he was definitely eager to become involved in publishing her books. As noted in one of Weir's letters, Mary had reported that Thomas Allen was relentlessly pursuing her.[22] Thus, directly or indirectly, Allen was applying pressure to the CBC to resolve the issue as he sought permission to release an American edition and publish a new *Just Mary* book.

In spite of what might have appeared to be conflicting and adversarial positions throughout the lengthy negotiations, the relationship between Mary and Dr. Frigon, F. Willard Savignac, Bushnell, and Weir remained friendly and respectful. The executives had sympathy for Mary's situation and her rights, while everyone involved was aware that the complex issues being considered were not just for Mary Grannan but for all other employees and freelancers.

In his personnel report on Mary for spring 1944, Ernie Bushnell tried to rectify the financial unfairness caused by the delay by recommending an increase in salary. He wrote in his report: "Miss Grannan has done most distinguished work and is deserving of greater remuneration. This should either be done in the way of a straight salary increase … or she should be allowed to participate in the royalties received on the sale of her books. If something is not done soon there is little doubt in my mind but what we will lose her as I know that she has had many tempting offers both here and in the United States."[23] Mary received the salary increase.

Savignac later wrote to Mary in a letter dated January 24, 1958: "You have many, many friends and I may add that the late Dr. Frigon was also an admirer of your creative spirit and I can now say that his personal feelings were that your salary did not by any measurement reach anywhere near your talents. Unfortunately, he was not demonstrative and hence you were unaware of his sentiments."[24]

For her part, Mary was grateful to Dr. Frigon for his help in resolving the issue and sent him an autographed copy of her new book. She also had warm feelings for E.A. Weir for his help with the early publications and copyright issues and continued to send him autographed books for several years inscribed, "For Mr. Weir who has been so kind, so often."[25]

Sad News from Home

Sitting in her office on Friday afternoon, March 23, 1945, Mary typed a letter on a blue airmail form to her friend Georgina Murray, who was on leave from the CBC serving in London with the Women's Royal Naval Service (WRNS):

> Dear George … I got your books … and I loved them … as you knew I would … they were both so different … thank you for them and for your thought in sending them. I have sad news which I want to get down right now … Mum died … on February 28 She

was well … up and about all day … had listened to the 10 o'clock news and went to bed. She said to Helen that she felt sick … She got up … had a hemorrhage and died … Helen got the doctor … a nurse and a priest all in a short space, Fr. Boyd says he really doesn't know if she was alive or not when he got there. But she was a good woman … and I'm glad she didn't live to see her power slipping from her. The news came to me at midnight. … I was asleep … I called Gladys Holley … she came over … she packed for me … I called Frank Willis … he did my cancelling of Just Mary, etc. Syd Brown took me to the station The trip home is now sort of like a dream … I can hardly remember it … but I was glad of my commercial money for sure. There have been times, as you well know when I would not have been ready for an emergency. I hope that the commercial is renewed … It'll be hellish to go back to poverty cove, after once having had me feet wet … I got Dr. Frigon's permission to go ahead with a new book. I've been so busy that I've not had a chance to edit for it yet, but if it has even half the success of the old one, I'll do OK. We're at the Jarvis street place now. I've a nice office between Ernie Morgan and Frank Willis … Lambert is across the hall. He has an educational conference in progress just now. This place is just about three blocks from my apt. which makes it very nice indeed for me. I've enjoyed the apt. It's warm … and compact … I'd like to have a bedroom instead of bringing down the bed … but I'm lucky. SO lucky to have found what I have. You have to have a permit now to move into a place. I was evicted the right year. […] I heard from Bill [Shea] in February by mail … I answered it … but no answer back. Mary Shea Jones [his sister] was over from St. Catharines yesterday […] I keep wondering when you'll be coming home … I thought maybe before this. […] Bill Walker whom your "Bill" knew is coming to Toronto this week end and I'm seeing him … nice break. I'm too busy to be sociable this winter … and I get lonesome sometimes … and wonder what I want. Once I thought if I could be on a national network nothing else would matter. […] Bob [Bowman] as you know is in Washington. He was here in the spring … tried to locate me to take me out … but of course I would be unavailable … just around somewhere doing not much of anything. I'd like to have a NY trip to see publishers … I thought that Victory Bond was going to cancel a show … but now I don't believe it is. I could record Just Mary if the big one were shoved off. George Taggart got $2500 for getting the four red cross shows on the air … just managing them … not producing or anything and ten dollars for every meeting he called. There's easy money if you know how. I'm restless today. I think I'll go home … Wish you could come … I've beer in me icebox. I wish I liked beer better. […] I know there must be better things to tell you than what I have but I'm not thinking so good. Nine scripts this week. Love, Mary[26]

Reaching out to a friend, Mary shared the sad news of losing her mother but did not tell how she had to borrow the funds for the train ticket from Frank because she had been caught short without enough cash on hand. It was naturally a time of deep grief with signs of Mary being knocked off her usual course: "I'm restless today"; "I'm not thinking so good." Certainly, much of the undercurrent of distress in the letter can be attributed to grief.

In a subsequent letter written to her parents, Georgina described her thoughts on Mary: "I had a letter from Mary Grannan the other day, the first for ages. Her mother died suddenly, but I must say Mary took it in her stride. I was surprised. 'Mom' was just everything to Mary, and her two spinster sisters. Mom ruled with an iron hand. Mary is doing very well, and I enjoyed all the news of everyone. She can be very amusing when she wants to be."[27]

The death may have hit Mary harder than Georgina realized. However, Georgina did note accurately how devoted Mary was to her family.

"Bonnie, Kate and Ellen"

In the fall of 1948, Mary's latest book, *Happy Playtime: More Just Mary Stories*, was released by Thomas Allen, illustrated by none other than Frank Willis. Elmore Philpott reviewed the book in the *Vancouver Sun* on October 15, 1948: "There is one story in this book that stamps Mrs. Grannan as one of the world's greatest writers of Children's stories. I doubt if there is any other living writer who can get so much action in so few words as Just Mary does in 'Bonnie, Kate and Ellen'."[28]

The "Bonnie, Kate and Ellen" story does indeed stand out with unusual passion. But there was a reason. Instead of turning to child fans, colleagues, or friends for fodder for a gentle story, Mary had turned to herself, bringing out in this story the passion and guilt she experienced when she headed for Toronto and left behind her mother, Kate, and sister, Helen. While the broadcast date for this story is uncertain, it would certainly have been prior to the publication date of the book in 1948, and thus could possibly have been written during the time Mary was grappling with her grief over her mother's death and her guilt over leaving home.

In the story, the little girl, Ellen, is going away to school because her parents recognize that she has musical talent that needs better teaching than is available at home. Ellen has the sad task of explaining the situation to her two horses.

> Ellen went to the barn very slowly. This was a hard thing to do. She sat down on the floor in front of their stalls, she swallowed hard and then she said, "Bonnie! Kate! I've something to tell you. I'm going away."

"Oh, no!" whinnied Bonnie.

Big Kate smiled and tossed her mane. "You wouldn't go away, Ellen. You wouldn't do this to Bonnie and me."

"But I have to Kate," said Ellen. "I'm going to learn to make music."

"But you make beautiful music now," said Kate, "doesn't she Bonnie?"

Bonnie nodded a sad brown head. "She makes the most beautiful music in the world."

"No," laughed Ellen. "I really don't. I'm going to learn to make wonderful music, and besides, I won't be far away. The boarding school is just down the road no more than ten miles. I won't be so far away."

"But you won't be waiting in the oak tree in the evening," said Bonnie.

"No ... but ... well," said Ellen, "it's the best thing for me, Bonnie. My mother and father say so and they know. And you want the best things for me, don't you?"[29]

So, Ellen left for the boarding school, but the two horses ran away to follow her. When the school principal saw Ellen riding bareback on the horses, one foot on each back, he decided Ellen and the horses could represent the school in an upcoming regional school festival. Of course, Bonnie, Kate, and Ellen won the prize, and the story concluded happily.

The cheers could be heard at Copplands farm ten miles away. Alma School had won! Bonnie and Kate were very proud and went happily home. Holidays were now not far away when Ellen would be back at the farm waiting for them in the old oak tree.[30]

It was a tidy, happy ending to a child's story, but woven into it was Mary's personal story. It was painful for her to leave her mother and sister behind in Fredericton. They certainly did not want her to leave; they felt she was already doing well enough and was famous enough on the radio right at home. Why was it necessary to leave? But it was the best thing for Mary. Stewart Neill and Elizabeth Sterling Haynes had said so, encouraging her to leave so that she could develop her skills in Toronto, where the best people in radio in the country were gathering. The guilt, nevertheless, bothered Mary, and upon her mother's death she would have felt it more than ever. The happy ending reflected Mary's hopes of what had happened in the end — that her success in Toronto had made her mother proud and more content to wait at home and see Mary during the holidays. Perhaps writing the story and putting down in a disguised fashion a story from her own life allowed Mary to purge some of her grief.

Supervisory Tussle

On December 5, 1945, Charles Jennings, General Supervisor of Programmes, sent a private internal CBC memorandum to Ernie Bushnell, Director General of Programmes, on the topic of "Production Personnel — Miss Mary Grannan":

> We now come to the question of Mary Grannan. Sometime ago she wrote me a rather perturbed note in which she said she was concerned because she thought people were no longer regarding her as a Supervisor. In return I tried to explain the matter to her fairly frankly — that we never thought of her as a Supervisor; that we felt that her greatest value to us was at the microphone and in her creative work; and that if she had any sense she would realize that a person such as herself would be unhappy in an administrative or planning job which is essentially what a Supervisor is.
>
> She is listed on our establishment as a Producer and with the present re-organization, where we are trying to fix the areas of responsibility and the lines of authority, I do not see how we can let her continue to

circulate as a sort of free lance individual. I therefore plan to write her, reiterating the whole situation so far as she is concerned and telling her that as of receipt of the letter she will be responsible in her work to the Supervisor of Presentation, Kannawin.

While when all is said and done she should probably be working as a free lance and we should be buying her services in the open market — (maybe it would be more expensive than our present setup) — she is a valuable and imaginative employee and therefore I think that within reason we should handle this situation in a kind and tactful fashion.

I think I should brief Kannawin carefully on the fact that when she shifts into the Production Pool he treat her tactfully. Within reasonable limits, of course, it usually pays dividends to feed the egos of such people, and if and when we raise the Production Group to the level we contemplate the job of Supervisor of Presentation should be somewhat similar to that of a lion tamer. I am confident that if Mary is properly handled and directed she might even perhaps happily and contentedly increase the volume of work she does for us now.

I want to keep you informed of my actions in these things and get your blessing so that we see eye to eye on these changes.[31]

In the margin, Bushnell noted: "Quite acceptable to me. M.G. is in a bad frame of mind at the moment. She feels she has not had a fair deal so considerate handling will be necessary. EB You might ask her who gave her permission to write for Sven Blangeliads' publication."[32]

Mary had been informally using the title "Supervisor of Children's Programmes" from her start at the CBC in 1939. With the influx of returning personnel and the blossoming of new programs following the end of the war, Mary faced competition in the children's department, causing her frustration at the loss of a primary role. Perhaps it had been easy for her to feel that she was in fact director of children's programs during the war when she was the only one doing them outside of school broadcasts. But she had always longed to be truly in charge of a national children's department.

"She wanted to do the country and so on," Austin Willis said, "and really be head of the children's department … Do the country — that was an ambition of hers." He further noted, "Frank told her she was silly and was far better off without the administration hassles — this would usually quiet her down for a while."[33]

Nevertheless, Mary's longing to be in charge of a children's department was one desire that was not fulfilled at the CBC.

Jennings mentioned in his memorandum to Bushnell that the CBC ought to be buying Mary's services on a freelance basis, although it might cost more. A number of colleagues had urged Mary through the years to work freelance, telling her that she would earn more money that way, but Mary liked the security of being an employee. She reasoned that if her current programs were ever cancelled, she, as a permanent employee, would simply be asked to design new ones.

The year 1945, then, was proving to be a trying year for Mary in a couple of matters. Her mother had died, she was not happy with her situation at the CBC, and, according to Ernie Bushnell, felt she had not had a fair deal. Undoubtedly, the protracted debate over her books added to this discontent. Jennings clearly considered her to be a valuable employee, but just not an administrator or supervisor.

On December 15, Ernie Bushnell followed his handwritten note with a memorandum to Jennings and Kannawin:

> If for no other reason than to straighten out studio bookings and other correlated matters it would seem desirable, indeed essential, that Mary Grannan should work through the Supervisor of Presentation. I think the time has come for her to be told very plainly that she is a producer, and not a supervisor, and that as such she should operate on the same basis as any other producer. Will you please take this in hand at once.[34]

In writing to Kannawin, Supervisor of Presentation, Jennings urged tact and understanding:

> In Miss Grannan we have a very valuable employee and I think that now we are getting her settled in a proper new slot in our setup she will be happier than when she was floating around as a sort of solo effort, and we will be [able] to examine ways of increasing her value to us. She has lots of imagination and ideas and I told her that is what we are looking for. I know that I don't need to suggest to you that in order to get the best results from a girl like Mary she needs to be [handled] with a good deal of tact and understanding and being given this, I am sure we can expect the best from her.[35]

The same day, Jennings also wrote Mary a tactful note, confirming their conversation concerning "the new administrative setup here and our creation of a producers' group under the administration of John Kannawin."[36]

So, that should have been the end of the matter concerning Mary's job title, except that Mary had been using the supervisor title for so long, with its repetition in so many past CBC publications, that it occasionally surfaced again. One such occasion was in May 1947, when Jennings had to write the Prairie regional representative about the use of the title in their regional schedule. J.R. Finlay replied, "The identification of Mary Grannan as 'CBC Supervisor of Children's Broadcasts' in our regional schedule of May 25th was the result of the longstanding misconception which apparently is still retained by some members of our staff, as well as by many listeners. The story dies hard."[37]

Noel Langley

During 1944 through 1945, Mary's friendship with Noel Langley continued to grow. Believing she had talents beyond what she was doing at the time, he wrote the following inscription inside a book he gave her (*Lust for Life: A Novel of Vincent Van Gogh* by Irving Stone): "Noel Langley to Mary Grannon [sic], Toronto 1945. A goldfish among the minnows, who has yet to scratch the surface of her inestimable talents in the line of theatrical writing."[38]

From 1943 until 1945, Langley served as a lieutenant in the Royal Canadian Navy, in charge of entertainment. With his work based in Digby, he moved in 1944 with his wife, Tillie, and family to a farm in Barton, Nova Scotia, but likely made appearances in Toronto now and then. Mary visited the Langley family at their Nova Scotia farm in July 1945. That spring, on May 20, she had broadcast a *Just Mary* story written for young Christopher, "Christopher Langley and the Wolf," which also featured his sister, Jackie, and "Captain Noel" as characters.

In the fall of 1945, with the war over and out of the navy, Noel returned to the United Kingdom, while his family followed later that December. It was at this point that Noel and Mary began their long correspondence.

Surrey Lodge, Thames Ditton, Surrey, Nov.6 [1945]

My dear Mary,

Your letter finally caught up with me, plus news from Tillie that you'd been burgled, & denied paper for your new book, and everything is sour for Mary Grannon [sic], so you're probably sitting on the back perch of the henroost with your head under your wing, waiting for the sky to fall in. However, it won't, & life is merely limbering you up & turning you into shape for what she is going to throw you in the way of a bonus later; in the same way that an athlete being limbered up to get into training again has a hell of a time with stiffness & cramps before being ready for the job. If I were a doctor, I'd say that the CBC is the moral & mental poison in your system that acts as a sort of magnet for other minor misfortunes, & that you ought to get the hell out. Why can't you make a deal into Pollocks & go to CFRB, & then build up from there:

Colgates would move over to you when their deal came up for renewal if you were really doing a job for them. You are still sitting about waiting for these things to happen of their own accord, perhaps? — and not going out with cool, calm, determination to see that they <u>do</u> happen?

Also, I would work in Montreal, if I were you, & get out of the constipated back-eddy of Toronto. Did you follow up the idea of going to New York? No, I bet you didn't. Do I have to prod you from here? Get the lead out of your pants, forget you've had the bottle of gin stolen, tell the [CBC] to go to hell, & things will start going right for you: but not till you help by giving the first push or 2.

I am working at Sound City at my old Hollywood salary on a picture for Syd Field; I have written a play with Robert Morley, & all things are bright & beautiful except that I can't find a house for the family.

With all its rigours, England is the only place for me & I feel alive again & in my own element i.e. there is enough oxygen in the tent for me to keep alive now. I feel as if I've never been away, & all my old friends were in wonderful shape. The people of Toronto all seem like dark green vegetable-life on the bottom of a dirty aquarium, from this distance. I frankly don't know how you <u>expect</u> to survive in that stagnant environment, <u>unless</u> you fight like a she-bitch — if you lie back passively & moan "Eli-Eli" against your weeping wall, the goblins 'll getcha!

If you want to get the full value out of your abilities, go either to New York or set up with an independent unit like CFRB — but <u>act</u>, Mary, <u>do</u> it for <u>yourself</u>.

Best love,
As ever,
Noel[39]

With a strongly worded letter of encouragement, Noel tried valiantly to urge Mary to leave the CBC and Toronto and go where he thought she could best develop her talents. Undoubtedly frustrated at the time, Mary would have been cheered by the letter. However, she did not have the nerve to launch out on her own. Even with all the irritations at times, the CBC offered security, and her affection and loyalty to it were deep-seated.

As the year 1945 came to a close, Mary noted at the back of her agenda, on a page entitled "MEMORANDUM FROM 1945," events from the year that were significant to her:

> Mother died February 28.
> VE DAY   May 7
> VJ Day   August 15.
> Nova Scotia to Langley's
> July 22, 1945-
> Tillie to England Dec:
> Burglarized – [40]

It is curious to note what she listed and what she did not. For Mary, the most meaningful events of the year had been the death of her mother, the end of the war, her visit to the Langleys, and being robbed. She did not mention the conclusion of the copyright issue with the CBC, the contract with Thomas Allen, or any radio broadcasts.

She further wrote that her sister Helen began a new job in November. Helen, who had previously remained at home looking after their mother, began teaching children recovering from polio at the Fredericton hospital. Mother Grannan's death brought about one other major change in the pattern of the sisters' lives: Ann and Helen began to travel to Toronto to join Mary for the Christmas holidays. Since Mary's broadcasts prevented her from going to Fredericton, she was always thrilled by the annual reunion at her usually lonely apartment. Dud and May Allen began a tradition of inviting the three women to the Allen home for dinner on Christmas Eve, while other dinners and parties with CBC friends kept them busy socially. New Year's Eve for 1946 saw the women attend a dinner hosted by Frank and Gladys

Willis, followed by two parties, one at the home of actor John Drainie. In amongst these activities, Mary did her Christmas broadcast of *Just Mary*, followed by a visit to the Hospital for Sick Children to read to the children.

Chapter Nine
Advent of *Maggie Muggins* on the Radio, 1946-1948

New Stories

With the CBC barriers on Mary's books lifted, Mary and her new publisher, friendly and cheerful Dud Allen, moved ahead with her publications. First, Dud re-released Mary's third CBC/Gage book, which noted inside that all broadcasting rights were reserved by the Canadian Broadcasting Corporation. Then Mary and Dud proceeded in the fall of 1946 to publish a new collection of stories, *New Just Mary Stories*, containing twenty-two new tales illustrated once again by Georgette Berckmans. About this time, Dud developed Allen's Popular Library for Boys and Girls, of which Mary's books became part, with the price at that time set at $1.25. Having an affordable price was an important element in sales.

"It was a merchandizing idea," said Dud's son, John, "so children could collect the books."[1]

As *New Just Mary Stories* was about to be released, Wells Ritchie, Supervisor of Press & Information Service at the CBC, issued an internal notice about the book: "We decided that we would not handle the book at all because of the internal bookkeeping complications and also because of the difficulties we have run into from time to time in this connection with booksellers, publishers and private stations."[2]

In spite of its hands-off approach to the new publication, the CBC agreed at Dud's urging to announce in the couple of weeks prior to Christmas that Mary's new book of stories was available without mentioning price, publisher, or bookstore names. Book reviewers welcomed the stories, saying they were "rollicking and readable-aloud."[3] The *Globe and Mail* review glowed: "Miss Grannan has a charm and a very real genius for entertaining the young. That she loves her work sticks out all over it."[4]

One story in the new book was about Willie Wee Rabbit, who wanted to be more fashionable:

> The crow was laughing so hard that he couldn't tell her, so Willie said, "There's no joke, Mrs. Squirrel ... no joke at all ... He asked me what was the matter with me, and why I was sighing, and I said I wasn't fashionable. I was going to tell him that I want to be a purple rabbit with a yellow bow on my neck so I could get my picture on the Easter cards. Mrs. Squirrel, do you know how I could get to be a purple rabbit?"
>
> "Yes," said Mrs. Squirrel...
>
> "Uh," said Willie ... "Uh ... you do know, Mrs. Squirrel? You do?"
>
> "Yes," said Mrs. Squirrel. "I do know ... but it's as good as not knowing as far as you are concerned, Willie."
>
> "Why?"
>
> "Because, the only one I know that could make you into a purple rabbit is Francois."
>
> "Francois? The Fox who keeps the beauty parlour on the other side of the woods?" asked Willie.
>
> "Yes, the Fox who keeps the beauty parlour. He dyes hair. Old Granny Fox who was getting as white as snow is red again, and looks twenty years younger. He's very clever."

"Yes," said Willie … "but … a … he doesn't like rabbits…"

Mrs. Squirrel laughed … "You mean he DOES like rabbits, don't you, Willie … Isn't that what you mean?"[5]

Another Letter from Noel

Letters from Noel Langley arrived regularly in Mary's mailbox, delivering his undiluted opinions with a wallop. This letter of March 16, 1946, contained an offer of help with her publications:

> Dear Buttercup — (& where do you get that Lana Turner crap?),
>
> Thank you for your letter & all the news that fit to squint. I suppose you're blissfully unaware of the fact that you could make <u>big</u> money writing a short story or two about Austin in the vein that you write of his playful gambols to me? I laugh like a drain, you catty old thing, you; you literary rose born to blush unseen; oh, thou soul of Dorothy Parker, thou.
>
> Now, the point of this letter is to send me copies of all your books, plus dates as to numbers printed typed & inserted into fly leafs; as I'm going to go about getting you an English publisher, tragic tho' paper conditions are — even the presses are collapsing now for want of repair — however, a brighter day will dawn. Also, are you getting on with a 3 act play on the side, or just moping on your arse & listening to hard luck stories from bums to make you feel superior in comparison. More, you could easily write a bloody good novel; all of which I'd begged to help you with; but I can't lean over from this distance & take a shoe horn & shunt you to work; you've got to do it yourself.

I've been in bed 3 weeks with flu & a return bout of the bronchial pneumonia I got in Nova Scotia, but I'm feeling faintly human again, tho' only just. Have I described our home? — Six rooms in the wing of a farmhouse 7 hours from London; no bath, bloody little furniture; however, a roof, tho' the place is sloppy as Macawber's kitchen, & the electricity 50 volt, which is a bugger. If you would send us fine gifts, dear, we would go for Kleenex like hungry wolves. I miss oranges most, however, & there's nowt you can do about that. These poor bloody people are rotted with lack of decent food – they're physical & moral wrecks, held together with spit & string: how they keep going I dunno — & on top of that, they elect a government of disgruntled taxi drivers, who appear to be going backwards & sideways but not forwards.

We still can't get a theatre for 'Cage Me A Peacock', but I'm quite content to wait. Do you want a copy of Hocus Pocus? I remember yours was stolen? Writing is really an effort after flu, so it shows how much I love my little Mary. Write & tell me more lovely chronicles in the glorious adventures of Aristide Snotpot Willis the Irresistible.

You <u>like</u> sitting there on your fanny in C.B.C., being martyred. Saint Mary of Isinglass-cum-Twombley, shot through & through the bladder with hummingbirds' priapi.

You'd be a more honest girl if you were whoring down where the Norwegian Flying field used to be.

Nice spread in S.E.P., eh? The old Langley is not without honour save in the Canadian Navy & environs.

Tillie & the kids all thrive, & I bumble about. It'll spring soon, which'll be worth waiting for.

Best love, As ever is,
Noel.

P.S. Send me a carbon of your next book and I'll do the illustrations free, gratis & for nothing on the one proviso that the CBC don't take a pirate cut of the royalties.[6]

With affection and droll humour, Noel delivered his serious message of urging Mary onward in literary efforts. He had seen possibilities for her career that lay beyond her own more limited vision. In addition to offering to find an English publisher for her, he was trying his best to spur her on to new types of writing — a play or a novel. Did she perhaps dream of doing some writing for adults? She had written broadcasts for adults at CFNB, and a decade earlier Mary would have jumped at any suggestion made to her. Those were the years of developing her art and seeking an opening — high energy years, when she wrote to Robert Bowman that she felt she could do just about anything if someone would simply tell her what was wanted.

Noel was not the only one who believed Mary could write for adults. The next year, Charles Jennings also made this suggestion in a memo sent to Harry J. Boyle, the Programme Director of the Trans-Canada Network, and Frank Willis, the Supervisor of Feature Broadcasts, dated September 26, 1947: "I would like to suggest to you next time you have occasion to commission a script for a special show that you might consider asking Mary Grannan to do it. I have the highest regard for her ability as a script writer and have the feeling she would make a great success of writing scripts for special shows for adult listeners. Please let me know when an opportunity arises to do this."[7]

How was Mary responding to these suggestions? Did she secretly long to write for adults and to try other types of writing, or was she growing comfortable and secure in her position in the CBC's children's department? According to Helen, Mary always wanted to write for adults but was too busy with her children's writing and promotional functions to find enough time.[8] However, her present position was more guaranteed of success; she had proven herself there. It was safer to stay put and go with what she knew worked. Besides, there was no urgency or necessity pushing her on, and she was quite busy with the tasks at hand. Why venture out into the unknown when she had a sure thing?

Mary's letter to Noel, now lost, had obviously been full of gossip about the latest exploits of Austin Willis. Much as Noel chided her for remaining at the CBC, Mary was happy there and content with the progress she was making in her own special field, even if it differed from the directions that Noel saw for her. Moreover, some significant children's program development was soon to happen.

New Programs Emerge in the Postwar Era

With the end of the war and wartime broadcasting needs, the CBC was able to exert new efforts on program development. Many personnel who had been away either in the armed forces or as overseas correspondents returned. The CBC by then had two networks, the Trans-Canada Network, whose focus was largely on the "sustaining" or commercial-free programs, and the Dominion Network, which broadcast most of the big commercial shows. New shows and talent blossomed in this era, which writers such as Austin Weir, Sandy Stewart, and Knowlton Nash have called "the golden age of radio." Continuing favourites such as *The Happy Gang* were joined by Andrew Allan's *Stage*, begun in 1944; Esse Ljungh's drama documentaries, such as *In Search of Ourselves*; Johnny Wayne and Frank Shuster in *The Johnny Home Show* in 1945 and later *The Wayne and Shuster Show*; and W.O. Mitchell's *Jake and the Kid*. In 1947, the CBC launched its celebrated *Wednesday Night*, a program devoted to the presentation of longer drama, opera, and music.

With determined effort planned and co-ordinated by a committee of five, the children's department also experienced the energy of new programming. In 1945–46, *Cuckoo Clock House*, a variety show written by Babs Brown, and *Stories for You*, prepared by the Boys and Girls House of the Toronto Public Library, joined the schedule. The next year, 1947, Dorothy Jane Goulding began *Kindergarten of the Air*. Other new programs came along from different parts of the country: *Sleepytime Storyteller* from Campbellton, *Storytime* from Vancouver, *James and John* from Winnipeg, and *Here, Pooch!* from Toronto. Regional programs on Saturday mornings included *Music Makers*, *Magic Adventures*, and

Microphone Moppets. Magic Adventures, written by Kitty Marcuse and produced by Peter McDonald, won Ohio awards in 1946 and 1947.[9] The aim in children's programming was to present a broad range, including "the classics, adventure and animal stories, original fairy stories and variety shows."[10]

Mary's programs, as well, began to branch out. In the spring of 1945, Charles Jennings encouraged Mary to develop a second broadcast of *The Children's Scrapbook*, which he saw as "one of the most consistently good shows we put out, not only in the writing and production but the music and so on."[11] Reworking some sections and adding new ones, the *Evening Scrapbook* began to air on Thursday evenings in the fall season of 1945.

In the spring of 1946, however, the seven-year run of *The Children's Scrapbook* came to an end. To replace it, Mary prepared a new program, called *The Land of Supposing*, which consisted of half-hour-long dramatized stories based on fairy tales and folk tales from around the world. Scripts included some of Mary's original stories as well as adaptations of famous tales, such as "The Tinder Box" by Hans Christian Andersen, "Young Lochinvar" by Sir Walter Scott, and "Desbarollda the Waltzing Mouse" by Noel Langley. The show, which aired April through June from 1946 to 1950 (except for 1949), was narrated by Mary in the early years, produced by her good friend Frank Willis, and featured a full cast of actors and music by Lou Snider. Undoubtedly, Mary would have enjoyed working on the production with Frank. The cast was drawn from the talented CBC pool developed largely by Andrew Allan and Esse Ljungh for their dramas: Alan King, Don Harron, Warren Wilson, Bud Knapp, Syd Brown, Doug Master, Arden Keay, Peggi Loder, Bill Needles, Murray Westgate, Alice Hill, Grace Webster, Bob Christie, Al Pearce, Frank Peddie, Tommy Tweed, and Ruth Springford.

With a half-hour to develop a plot rather than the fifteen minutes of the *Just Mary* series, the stories were more complex, although Mary subsequently selected a few and shortened them for the *Just Mary* slot. Probably targeting a slightly older audience of children in the range of eight to twelve, she used a more boisterous style of language. As with her other programs, she composed a standard opening for the show.

In the following episode, "The Gypsy's Prediction," broadcast on May 7, 1950, Mary named one of the characters "Carroty Kate" after her mother:

NARR: Far over the whispering treetops … behind the stars … back of the moon … is the wonderful Land of Supposing … and there in that land, many things happen … strange things … beautiful things … unearthly things….

ANN: And now, from that Land, comes the bizarre and romantic story of The Gypsy's Prediction.

NARR: It so happened that in the year of sixteen hundred and thirty nine, the Kingdom of Uzengia was ravaged by a company of brigands led by a red headed giantess named Carroty Kate. On the twenty fifth day of July in that year, Kate led her ruffians in attack on the castle … there to sack and pillage. The suddenness of the onslaught found his majesty's guards quite unprepared. The castle was ransacked from cellar to turret, and much in jewels and gold was seized. (BABY CRIES) As the abandoned marauders were about to leave with their loot, the cries of a babe reached the ears of Carroty Kate…

KATE: Hold … wait … Get that bawling brat … (LAUGH — RAUCOUS). We'll hold his little royal highness for ransom … This, men, is our lucky day.[12]

Maggie Muggins Takes to the Airwaves

No matter how popular the continuing *Just Mary* stories or creative the *Land of Supposing* series, no program had as significant an effect upon Mary's popularity with listeners as *The Adventures of Maggie Muggins*. After her *Maggie Muggins* book was published by Thomas Allen in the fall of 1944, Mary had suggested it as a radio show. Unable to stir any interest, Mary had given up on the idea until she got into a conversation with Harry J. Boyle, Programme Director of the Trans-Canada Network, at a Christmas party in December 1946. On the hunt for a new children's program to begin New Year's Day, he decided during the conversation that *Maggie Muggins* would be the one. Mary described the beginning to Beth Morris, who would later play Maggie:

> I had just a week ... and had to write a script, find a MAGGIE, a Mr. McG, and besides that I had my sisters visiting me from New Brunswick, and I didn't want to be working at something new. But I did. I knew Mr. James Annand would make a good Mr McGarrity. He had a nice merry laugh. Some one told me about little Beryl Braithwaite, who had just come from Saskatoon, Sask. I auditioned her, and knew she was the one. She was nine* at the time, blonde and full of fun and hops and skips. We had Lou Snider play the music. It was a nice combination of people. We got along fine and worked together for seven years. I did all the animal voices ... Petunia Possum ... Frog ... Grunter Pig ... Fitz ... Harry Rabbit ... Newcome kitten ... Mr. Goat ... etc. One year we suggested that listeners draw a picture of Maggie ... I wish you could have seen them ... we got hundreds ... another year we suggested Fitz would like a Valentine ... He got 1620.[13]

---

* *Beryl Braithwaite was ten, not nine, when she auditioned for the role of Maggie Muggins.*

Beryl, coached by her father, Max Braithwaite, had begun acting on radio a year earlier on a program he had written. In late December 1946, she returned home to Streetsville from an acting role in Quebec to find a message from Mary Grannan. Beryl knew who Mary was, having been fond of listening to *Just Mary* since she was three. When the Braithwaite family moved from Saskatchewan to Toronto during the war, the familiar program had brought comfort to young Beryl in her new surroundings:

> As long as I was able to listen to Mary, I was alright. Still might be moving around, but she was my touchstone. So, meeting her was just amazing. ... I had done a film of *Maria Chapdelaine*, playing young Maria. Had my hair dyed dark and the whole thing. ... And got back, and there was this message that when I got back, Mary Grannan wanted to see me. That was like being summoned ... I was totally in awe. So, mother and I went down ... and here we were with this wonderful woman. ... I was so taken with her beaten silver bracelets. ... and these incredible earrings, and her hats ... I guess she gave me this book [*Maggie Muggins*] to look at, the first one, which I didn't realize was 1944, and said they were going to do a radio series and she was going to do all the parts, except for the gardener and Maggie. Seemed like a piece of cake to me. ... Anyway, we started and in those days, radio was really relaxed, really relaxed.[14]

After a successful first broadcast of *Maggie Muggins* on New Year's Day, 1947, the series continued on Wednesday afternoons, quickly becoming popular. The show routine began mid-afternoon on Wednesdays, when Beryl arrived at the Jarvis Street studio to do a couple of script readings with Mary and James Annand, followed by a dress rehearsal complete with musician Lou Snider on the celesta and novachord and the producer, often Elsa Franklin and later Kay Stevenson, timing the performance in the control room. After a short break, the program was broadcast live at five-thirty.

During the first year of broadcast, Mary gradually developed the *Maggie* stories, which at the beginning closely followed the early style of the first *Maggie* book, with Maggie meeting new woodland creatures on each adventure. But partway through the first season, Mary introduced the characters of Grandmother Frog and Fitzgerald Fieldmouse. By the second season they were continuing characters, and Mary added other creatures to the group as time went on, thus providing a continuing cast for listeners to follow, which was a marked difference from the *Just Mary* stories. Beryl shared some memories of working on the show:

> Mary was an incredibly inventive person, which is obvious from what she did. She'd do all those characters so well. She, as I say, slipped from one to the other. … She never made you think that there was anything but a bunch of characters talking to you. … She and Jim Annand and I really liked each other, and neither of them treated me like a child — which suited me just fine. … I remember once Lou, who was the soul of professionalism, put his elbow down on the celeste, which was what he played for the show and had a little musical. But it was so short, I gather any but us realized it. It seemed enormously funny to me because he just put his elbow down. I really don't remember any glitches. We just churned them out.[15]

With the new radio series providing more stories to publish, Dud Allen wasted little time. *The New Maggie Muggins Stories: A Recent Selection of the Famous Radio Stories* appeared late in 1947, illustrated by Nancy Caudle.

While the early stories were more elementary than the later ones, they featured the characteristic opening, with Maggie dancing and singing as she arrived to greet Mr. McGarrity. The following excerpt is from "Maggie and the Porcupine":

> Maggie Muggins had had a busy morning! She'd told time by the dandelion, she'd been to see the deermice

in their nests, she'd been down to hear the sandpiper singing his funny little sandpiper song, and now she was out of things to do, so she went dancing to the cucumber bed to see Mr. McGarrity, and she sang as she danced.

"Tra la la la la la lee,
Here comes Maggie Muggins, me,
And I have something to tell you,
Mr. McGarrity, I've nothing to do."[16]

In 1947–48, Mary took the idea of a Maggie Muggins doll to the Reliable Toy Company, whose executive decided to proceed after an informal questioning of people in the street proved that Maggie was a well-known name. In November 1948, the Maggie Muggins doll arrived on toy shelves. Mary continued relating the *Maggie* history to Beth:

> The first year, they sold 11,000 of them. We had a DOLL party at Eatons in Montreal, Beryl and I went down … They brushed her blonde hair a fiery red … She loved it and didn't want to wash it off at all … She held on to it about a week or more. We went to Hamilton together several times … She wore her dress like yours, except it was green material like on the doll … the factory gave us the material. Her apron had MAGGIE MUGGINS embroidered on it. Once when we were having a Christmas party in Simpsons Arcadian Court, Maggie had a broken leg. She went in her cast, and all the children wanted to autograph it.[17]

With books and a doll to promote, Mary and Beryl made many publicity appearances in southern Ontario and Montreal, often appearing before large crowds in the auditoriums of Simpson's and Eaton's department stores.

"We did start these tours," Beryl said. "Mary made them very exciting. We went out to dinner. She always made them special. And she must have ... been extremely busy, but ... we were a pair and we had our meals always together. And she took very good care of me. ... [There were] crowds and crowds and crowds. [I] loved it. Sometimes there were too many children for one group, so there'd be a second and a third group. The kids just loved it."[18]

Playing the role of Maggie from the time she was ten until she was seventeen — all the way through high school — Beryl found Mary, along with Beryl's own working mother, to be good role models. "It's a lot of years to spend with somebody once a week and never remember any sharp remarks, any," Beryl said. "We were glad to see each other every Wednesday ... but she was also very business-like. This was a job."[19]

One other aspect of Mary that was remarkable was the great care she took with her public image:

> Mary had most of her clothing made and she knew exactly how to dress for Mary — exactly. The jewellery was all handmade for her and she had a milliner who made those hats. Her image was something she took very seriously. And I don't ever remember running out to breakfast or anything on these trips without everything being on because people would recognize her. Room service we would have sometimes. That was wonderful when you're the oldest of five kids and both your parents are working authors. Room service was a treat.[20]

For Beryl, who had decided to become an actress at the age of three after seeing her first movie, *The Wizard of Oz*, playing the role of Maggie was a natural evolution of what she expected in her young life. She saved all her earnings from the show and used the money to travel to London to study acting when she completed high school in 1953. For Mary, the excitement that surrounded *Maggie Muggins* cemented her public role as a star.

The Beaver Award

Popularity, fan mail, bestselling books, and dolls formed one type of reward to Mary for her work, but receiving a certificate of distinction represented a special honour. On March 17, 1947, after eight years of broadcasting with the CBC, Mary received the Beaver Award for distinguished service to Canadian radio for her program *Just Mary*. The newspaper the *Canadian Broadcaster* and its editor, Richard G. Lewis, established the award in 1945 to acknowledge exceptional radio service with the hope that honouring great radio talent would encourage the individuals to stay in Canada.

Broadcast by the CBC on *Canadian Cavalcade*, the award ceremony took place at a dinner at the Radio Executives Club of Toronto. Among the fifteen other people receiving awards were Johnny Wayne and Frank Shuster for their *Wayne and Shuster Show*, Gordon Sinclair and Alan Savage for *Ontario Panorama*, Babs Hitchman for writing and producing Eaton's Santa Claus Parade programs, and Eve Henderson, women's editor of CKRC Winnipeg, for her women's programs.[21] There were only three women among the sixteen winners. Mary had previously received an honorary mention at the annual Ohio awards for the circus episode of *The Children's Scrapbook*, but this was her first radio distinction earned in Canada. Since it meant a great deal to her, she arrived at the dinner for over five hundred people as spectacularly dressed as she could be. She wore, cocked at an angle, a flat, black hat with sweeping wide brim, a white blouse with small ruffles at the neck, and a black skirt with matching cape through which her white sleeved arms poked, highlighting the broad silver bracelets on each wrist — all custom designed, of course.

Well settled into her routine, Mary wrote scripts at home in the morning, sitting at her portable typewriter set up on the kitchen table, with nearby reference books, including an encyclopedia of names, and cups of tea to keep her going. Out the window, she could look down on St. Joseph's College School. She did not prepare many meals at home, often preferring to eat at the CBC cafeteria. Since her first stories in print were published by the *Country Guide* from Winnipeg, she continued to send them a monthly story, more out of loyalty than anything else. Letters to her sisters were hurriedly typed, often in stages, and mailed along the way to the office in the afternoon. Once at the office, she clattered away on the typewriter, polishing scripts and answering the growing abundance of mail, cited in the CBC Annual Report of 1946–47 as reaching twenty-five thousand letters and requests for an illustrated brochure about her.[22] Colleague A. J. Black used to tease her that the floor outside her office vibrated from her furious typing. She quipped that one thing she couldn't seem to do well was to type with correct spelling.

After a hard day's work, she might treat herself by going shopping. Supper was often in the company of female friends, such as Grace Athersich or some of her apartment neighbours. Occasionally, she would go to movies or the theatre with friends, and sometimes she was invited to dinners or parties. With her high public profile, she continued to give more than a dozen talks annually to groups and service clubs and occasionally took part in special events, such as a broadcast to aid crippled children and one for Boy Scout–Girl Guide Week, and in 1944 she acted as a judge for a national essay contest.

Most people at the CBC were fond of her: she was warm, friendly, down to earth, and funny. Often sitting with Grace Athersich in the cafeteria, Mary enjoyed the social atmosphere, telling colleagues a few good yarns. Many felt that it was important for their careers to be seen in the cafeteria. Jack Mather contended that many a producer came to the head of the stairs in the cafeteria and looked around the room to mentally cast for his next production.[23] One had to be there for these opportunities. The social interaction offered welcome balance to the solitary time Mary spent writing.

With a fondness for candy and a lack of the walking exercise she used to get in her Devon School days, Mary began to gain weight, about which she was sensitive. However, she took great care with her appearance, often helping to design her custom clothing, hats, and jewellery. This helped to offset the weight gain, creating the impression among her colleagues that she had just stepped out of the fashion pages of a magazine. She was coy about her age, and many articles written about her underestimated her age by about ten years. That was perfectly fine by her — she had an image to preserve.

In June 1947, Max Braithwaite, Beryl's father, wrote an article about Mary for *Maclean's* magazine, noting the discrepancy between the vision conjured up by the sound of Mary's broadcast voice and the reality of her physical appearance: "Like most radio personalities, Mary Grannan doesn't look like her voice sounds. She is a plump, rather tall woman in her late thirties, who dresses almost always in black and has a weakness for oversized metal earrings and bracelets and for extravagant hats which she has designed. She has a rather sharp nose, a broad forehead, thick rather frizzy dark hair which she brushes back, and blue eyes."[24]

In his flattering article, Braithwaite, presumably quoting Mary, contributed to a myth about the *Just Mary* program when he said, "Just Mary has never repeated a story."[25] While repetitions were only occasional, stories were sometimes repeated, either because they were favourites, such as some of the Christmas stories, or perhaps because Mary's hectic schedule sometimes caused her to fall behind. Braithwaite wrote:

> Some people mistake her easy-going, unaffected manner for an inferiority complex and point out that she could be making three or four times the salary the CBC can afford to pay her if she would just branch out. But Mary is perfectly happy with the CBC. She is doing what she wants to do — tell stories to children.
>
> She knows that every Sunday thousands of children wait for the sprightly tune, "In a Clock Shop," that introduces Just Mary. And she knows that they'll be completely lost to everything except the story until it is over and Mary says, "Just Mary says good-bye, and until next Sunday — happy playtime."
>
> That knowledge means a lot to Mary Grannan.[26]

December 1947 Letter to Sister

Dear Helen,

Enclosed find check for $28 — It's a 10% increase on our checks for high cost of living and I've decided to put it in your care for income taxes. How are you making out these days getting ready. Are you excited. I can't seem to get Xmas spirit! I've ordered a fat capon which we can enjoy — I'd not try to shop there at all if I were you. You're here in time to mail Win something anyway. and I'd do it. Just forget struggling Remember the nights you and I used to go down town when the stores were open – struggling & striving to get something for everybody. I get lonesome sometime for those days. I bought a new dress today — another black. I've been going so many places that I need two to appear. The Simpson thing will be a big do — hundreds! And I have to go to a CBC party for kids on Dec 21. Couldn't say no to that when I said yes to the commercial. Course I don't get paid for Simpsons it's book promotion. I start Enchanted Pine, on Dec. 8 at 6.30 here. I'm repeating the same stories. Got to do something for Xmas night, music behind it, so it has to be good. I hope I can think of something & write it well.

Mary & Dons stayed at hotel. I was down there. Gladys came down & [Frank] picked her up after his shows. Count up how much insurance I owe you & I'll settle when you're here. Don't worry about short skirts. There's hundreds of them around. Tell me about reservations. Did you get fixed up? Get a porter in Montreal to take you to taxi and another to take you to your chair car in CNR station. Its a good idea to leave here at night. Then you won't have your day spoiled with wondering about the train waiting,

Love,
Mary[27]

In early December, Mary was harried enough that the Christmas spirit was eluding her, although she was looking forward to her sisters' visit and feeling a bit nostalgic for Christmases of old. With two new books out, sales were bustling, and the only damper on the book scene came from the libraries. While the public appeared to greatly appreciate her books, Lillian Smith and the Toronto Public Library decided they were not worthy literature for children and refused to carry them in their collection. As went the Toronto Public Library, so went most, but not all, of the libraries in the country. It was a frustration for Mary and Dud Allen, especially when various boards of education had bought the first three *Just Mary* books for schools. The consolation was that Mary was receiving royalties on these sales.

The following story, "Why O'Casey Barked at the Moon," which appeared in *New Just Mary Stories* in 1946, featured Frank and Gladys Willis, their dog O'Casey, and Frank's brother Austin:

> "Sure an' I needn't have done it," said the big Irish setter. "And it's happier I'd be if I'd been after minding me own business ... but it was Christmas Eve."
>
> It all began in the month of June when Little Joe came to the house. Little Joe was a black kitten. The blackest kitten that ever was black, and just as saucy. "Miew," he said, and reached out and struck sleeping O'Casey right on the nose. O'Casey woke, stretched his great brown body and proceeded to strike back.
>
> "No ... no ... Casey," said Frank.
>
> "No ... no," said pretty Emma.
>
> "Joe's just a little fellow," said Austin.
>
> "Just a baby," said Gladys. "You mustn't strike Joe, O'Casey."
>
> "Miew," said Little Joe, smugly, as much as to say...
>
> "See, you Irisher, I got the upper hand here ... Miew!"
>
> ... and straightway climbed to the lap of O'Casey's favourite person, Frank. He sat on the very knee that O'Casey liked to rest his chin on. This was more than O'Casey could bear. He growled and with his nose he pushed this black stranger to the floor.[28]

Tenth Anniversary Broadcast

July 1948 marked ten years since Mary had first broadcast her *Just Mary* stories over the CBC network from Saint John during the summer before she joined the corporation full-time. Since the City of Fredericton was celebrating its one-hundredth birthday at the same time, CBC Press & Information Service thought it was a splendid occasion to present a dramatization of Mary's life, to be broadcast from Fredericton during the celebrations. The Programme Department and Fredericton Mayor Ray Forbes responded enthusiastically, and so the planning swung into action.

RE: NATIVE OF MARITIMES HONORED ON CBC BROADCAST

One of Canada's outstanding writers of children's sto-ries, Mary Grannan, a native of the Maritimes, will be honored by the CBC with a special broadcast on July 30. Better known to thousands of listeners, young and old, as "Just Mary", Miss Grannan has been invited to attend the centennial celebration of her native city of Fredericton, New Brunswick. Following a twenty-five minute dramatization of Miss Grannan's life story, she will be interviewed on a coast to coast network by his Worship, Mayor Ray T. Forbes, in a broadcast from Fredericton. The broadcast will be heard between 9.30 and 10.00 pm ADT on the Trans-Canada net-work stations.

This special broadcast observes Miss Grannan's 10th anniversary with the CBC. During this period she has written and presented well over 1000 National Network programs for children, has had several chil-dren's books published, and this year will see the cre-ation of a doll named after one of her best known char-acter creations, "Maggie Muggins."

Because of the wholesomeness of her children's stories, Miss Grannan has been widely commended by parents and teachers. This year some of her "Just Mary" stories will be broadcast by educational networks in the United States.[29]

Mary wrote the script of her life story, presenting a light-hearted portrait that focused on several scenes in the Grannan home. While the broadcast originated from the facilities of CFNB in Fredericton, technical limitations and limited availability of actors meant that the program, except for the live presentation, was recorded in advance. As producer, Frank Willis was in a position to add a number of personal touches, arranging for DeB. Holly to be the announcer since he had been Mary's first announcer in Saint John, Beryl Braithwaite (Maggie) to play the role of young Mary, and Lou Snider to provide the music since he had been the musician on most of her programs. It was a kindly touch from a friend.

On the day of the broadcast, J. Stewart Neill proudly joined her and Mayor Forbes in the studio. Forbes ended his presentation by saying, "Your contribution, Mary to happiness and inspiration of Canadian children is outstanding in radio annals. You have demonstrated what a combination of devotion and ability can do for children everywhere. So I am asking you here, to sign the Golden Book of the Centennial, and to accept the key, to the city of your birth."[30]

As she accepted the key, Mary thanked the mayor, concluding with a tribute to Neill.

I have reason to be grateful to the many who have made these ten years in radio possible, but my greatest debt is to the man who started me on my radio career … Mr. J. Stewart Neill who is with us in the studio. It was quite an effort to get Mr. Neill to appear here tonight, microphones frighten him, he says. He has always brushed my "thank yous" aside. But Mr. Neill, my anniversary programme wouldn't have been complete without your being here. It was you urged me to change my profession.[31]

After responding that he thought her imagination should be shared by all the children of Canada, Neill, in his nervousness, knocked over a glass of water. The microphone picked up the sound, providing Frank Willis with an opening to later tease Mary about dropping the key to the city on a national broadcast.

For Mary, this was truly a special occasion to be honoured by both the CBC and her hometown. The recognition from Fredericton especially meant a great deal. As the city continued its celebrations, she participated in a number of events, including helping to judge a beauty contest.

The CBC was pleased with the program; Donald Manson, Assistant General Manager, sent a note of congratulations to the Supervisor of Press & Information:

> Thanks for sending me the report on the Mary Grannan programme. As a matter of fact I listened to it and thought it was very well done. It was entertaining while giving due credit to Mary Grannan for her good work over the years. At the same time I agree that it was an excellent piece of public relations work for the CBC.
>
> What I liked about it, too, was the general restraint which marked the whole show making it no less impressive.
>
> You and those responsible for the programme deserve credit and congratulations.[32]

Plain Advice from Noel

Another of Noel Langley's regular dispatches arrived in April 1949. Since Mary's letters to him have been lost, this particular letter is interesting because it reflects what she wrote to him. Judging from his comments, she must have been pleased with her publishing progress at that point and happy with Dud Allen's encouragement. Noel, however, was still lecturing her on this topic. Worthy of particular note is his statement in the second last paragraph. Mary must have asked him if he still believed she could write.

Castledore
April 15 I think
Friday, anyway

Dear Ma'am Goddam,

"Dud Allen urged me on … he says I'm good for four or five more years with them anyway."

Dud Allen is a blood-leech who has done very nicely off you, you gullible & naïve slut, because you never hired a good solicitor to handle your contracts & get a standard percentage as laid down by the Writer's Guild. He & his firm owe you as much again as they've paid you. You're damned right he says you're good for four or five more years with them any-way. Fly & get away. But dont break your leg or go sick, because you've been so sweat-shopped that you have no nest-egg; & once you're limping they'll cut you dead & never knew you. That, my fluff-minded friend, is your business acumen captured in a few short, terse phrases.

For about $150, a good N.Y. lawyer recommended by the Author's Guild or Writer's Guild or whatever they call themselves, would set you up so it was worth your while to whore for mediocre pea-&-three-shell men, instead of doing it for love. And don't think they'd hate you for it. They'd moan & try & scare you back to your old rates, & when they saw that their lit-tle racket was up; they'd adjust themselves sunnily & happily to the new terms & think a hell of a lot more of your work _and_ of you.

I'm glad you got the bigger flat: fix it the way you really want it instead of handing-out to bums. I'll dig around for a map or a picture of Fowey. Good ones are hard to come by.

I certainly still believe you can write. Depends how much you want to; not on what gift lies dormant there....

I'm turning into a crusty old misanthrope. Can't burn your end at both candles indefinitely without crusting up. We're in the house too early & it's damp. Fires going all the time.

Bestest love,
Noel[33]

Chapter Ten
Visit to the Old Countries, 1949

The Ballad of Alan Cole

In July 1949, Mary left Toronto for a seven-week overseas trip to Ireland and England. Officially, she was going there to visit the London CBC offices and the BBC, where she would do a guest broadcast. Unofficially, she was visiting friends and touring through Ireland and England for the first time. The visit to Ireland carried the emotional impact of setting foot on the land of her ancestors.

Tucked in her handbag, Mary took along a trip diary in which to record the places and people she visited and the things she did on this momentous trip. The diary was small, six and a half by four inches, with a soft, dark cover, and "My Trip" written on it in gold script. At first, Mary briefly recorded the day's events in the expected manner of such a diary. But she was, after all, a writer, and the blank space soon invited more. She wrote it for her eyes only, likely never expecting anyone else to read it. Thus, it reveals some unadorned, intimate comments.

While in Dublin, Mary planned to visit Alan Sargent Cole and Paul Smith, whom she had met previously in Toronto. Paul, a native Dubliner who had apparently worked briefly as an announcer at the CBC in 1948, appreciated Mary's friendship when he first began his job there: "Your face was the first good sight that had met my eyes since I had left Dublin. You'll never know how good you made me feel and how terribly welcome I felt that first night in the CBC. Then afterwards in your flat I loved it — you made me feel at home from the very first and your books — they saved my life."[1]

Alan was an American, and, while it is not clear what he was doing while in Toronto, he began studying for his doctorate in English at Trinity College in Dublin in 1949. Once back in Dublin, Paul had returned to his previous position working in the wardrobe department of the Gate Theatre.

Mary left Toronto on the evening train bound for Montreal on Wednesday, July 6. After taking her out to dinner, Frank and Gladys Willis stayed with her on the train in her assigned room, bedroom F, until the train's departure at eleven-thirty. "Frank inveigled door man to let them on," Mary wrote.[2] The train arrived in Montreal the next morning at eight, and by nine, Mary had her hotel room for the night. After shopping for books at the large, red-stone Morgan's department store on St. Catherine Street and then lunching at nearby Eaton's large dining room on the ninth floor, she met Mr. Anglin from the CBC and three other gentlemen for drinks followed by dinner at the Windsor Hotel. She then spent the evening socializing in Anglin's room, meeting, among others, Charles Jennings.

The next day, Friday, July 8, Mary was supposed to go to the ship the *Empress of Canada* with Anglin, but he overslept, so she went alone and proceeded through the formalities of settling on board. Her luggage consisted of a large, yellow suitcase of the steamer trunk variety into which she had placed a prayer to Saint Anthony of Padua, signed by Rev. Charles P. Brown. Mary enjoyed the eight-day ocean journey to England, her first experience on a ship, sharing her room with sisters Jess and Ann Stottar. The sea was rough at times, but she was never sick, saying she "rather liked the roll."[3] Above all, she enjoying talking to interesting people she met, including a group of Ontario teachers, while tolerating the boring ones. She dressed up for drinks, dinner, and dancing, saw a couple of movies, one of which was *Look Before You Love*, attended Mass, toured through the ship's kitchen, and listened to music.

On July 13, which she noted as being "Helen's birthday at sea,"[4] Mary gave a talk and read one of her stories. Among those listening was a thirteen-year-old girl, Ann McNally, who was a fan of Mary's. The first hint of any excitement was noted on July 14, the day before docking at Liverpool, when Mary wrote, "What will tomorrow bring?"[5]

As the ship passed the coasts of Ireland and England, Mary thrilled at the sight. After docking, Mr. Emsley from the British Railways delivered Mary's ticket to Dublin, which had been purchased for her by the CBC, and then escorted her through customs and immigration. Since the boat to Dublin left later that evening, Mary and Esther Lunney, one of the women she had met on board, spent the day touring around Liverpool, taking pleasure in the scenery, shops, and stories they heard from people. Mary noted, "Talked to two girls in restaurant, and on telling them I was going to Ireland for two weeks she said 'that is long enough to become mad.'"[6]

Evidence of the war was still visible. "Sitting in hotel window I can see where buildings were bombed. The old lady in the cloak room told me she'd been tossed into the air — that there were funny things however — when the butcher shop nearby was bombed it seemed as if every dog and cat in Liverpool ravaged the meat."[7]

Since it was her first time in England, Mary could not help but notice some of the immediate differences. "The voices all sound so 'la-de-da' around me. […] Once I was terrified when I saw a bus looming — thought it was for us, but then discovered we were driving on other side of road."[8]

After parting from Esther, who was travelling to Belfast, Mary boarded the boat to Dublin. She spent most of the night's journey walking the decks, sleeping in a deck chair for a while once it was daylight. Arriving in Dublin on Saturday morning, July 16, Mary found the sight impressive and moving.

> Morning wet, but I almost cried at the beauty — We
> sailed right into the middle of Dublin — The stone walls
> steps down into sea of stone — ships, gulls, etc. The
> crowd was so great the stewardess brought me tea and
> advised me to wait till it thinned. I saw Alan through

porthole, and went crazy because he couldn't see me. Finally I got porter and was coming down stairs inside boat, head down watching my step when he grabbed me. We got a taxi and went home. The streets are like pictures. Rows of four storey brick Georgian houses. Alan and Paul are on third floor — I mean fourth — The flat is sweet. Paul couldn't go to boat. He's wearing a complete jacket of plaster. The welcome was all I could desire — Had breakfast Sat in front of open fire — drank whiskey — Later Alan and I went out — shopped — went to a pub. so's I could see one Had dinner — then champagne — to celebrate my coming. Planned to go walking but rain torrential. Later an artist Phyllis Hayward-Teak came in. She is English — gushing, pleasant, liked my bracelets and red house coat. She left at midnight — We had tea & then to bed.[9]

Mary was in her glory as Alan and Paul, each about twenty years younger than she, warmly welcomed her to their flat at 104 Lower Baggot Street, not far from Trinity College. Alan, quiet and likeable, was tall, thin, and good-looking, with his light brown hair in a crewcut. Paul, the more talkative of the two, was medium height, blond, and slightly plump. With little formal education, Paul had worked at a variety of jobs, including hairdressing, before making his way into the wardrobe department of the Gate Theatre. He was fond of referring to Alan as "the doctor."[10]

After Mary went to church on Sunday morning, the three of them went on a walking tour of Dublin, visiting landmarks — Mary loved Dublin. In the evening, they stayed up late talking over drinks with a friend of Paul's. More walking and shopping — especially book shopping — followed over the next two days. On Tuesday afternoon, friends dropped by.

Mary wrote, "In the afternoon we had a tea party: Mrs. Vigers, Beryl Franks, Paddy McAvoy. After supper we acted foolish, dancing, telling stories etc. Very pleasant until company went. This was the night! Alan and I walked streets."[11] She added the next day: "Unhappy situation."[12]

While Mary did not explain in her diary the nature of the unhappy situation, she later told Grace Athersich and Regina Clarke, a Fredericton friend, that she had discovered during her visit that Alan and Paul were homosexual.[13] "Grace said Mary was absolutely shocked when she found out they were homosexual," Donald Roberts said.[14]

Nevertheless, Mary carried on. She and Alan kept busy on Wednesday, walking, shopping, eating at restaurants, having a drink at a pub, and attending the play *The Magistrate* at the Gate Theatre in the evening. On Thursday, they travelled to Howth on the Irish Sea to visit Mary Rose McMaster, daughter of Anew McMaster and niece of Micheál MacLiammóir, both well-known Irish actors. MacLiammóir was also co-founder of the Gate Theatre. Mary Rose lived in a seaside stucco cottage full of art treasures. After a steep walk down many steps to the shore, Mary sunned herself on the rocks while Mary Rose and Alan swam. It must have been a pleasant day full of diversion, but more trouble awaited Mary back on Lower Baggot Street. They returned to Alan and Paul's flat to find Beryl Franks.

"Beryl there and comes the 'reconciliation,'" Mary wrote. The next day, Friday, Beryl returned. "Beryl makes scene. I am evicted — Go looking for place find Russell — had lunch — came back — packed — moved in. Met Bill West who asked us to beer parlor next night. Depression and disbelief very great."[15]

What had begun as a happy visit full of all the warm welcome she could have desired had turned sour. Mary felt depressed and bewildered as she was forced to vacate Alan and Paul's flat, seeking a room at Russell's Hotel on St. Stephen's Green. Why Beryl insisted Mary should leave is unclear, but Beryl, who lived nearby on Ely Place, appeared to have an attachment to one of the men. Mary's notations were cryptic, leaving much unsaid, but she was clearly deeply hurt. As if the shock of finding out that they were homosexual was not enough, she then suffered the embarrassment of having to leave their hospitality.

Plucky and determined, Mary kept busy; she and Alan went bicycling around Enniskerry Bray on Saturday, followed by a cheerful evening at the pubs The Pearl and The Dog and Waffle with new acquaintances Bill West and his wife, whom Mary found to be "charming people full of gaiety."[16] After the pubs, the Wests invited Alan and

Mary to a party. "Would like to have gone," wrote Mary, "but Alan felt he must go home. He's a dead duck."[17]

Following mass on Sunday, Mary and Alan once again took the train to Howth, enjoying the scenery as they passed Ireland's Eye. Mary Rose joined them for a trolley ride up the nearby mountain, where the three had a picnic. Later, while Mary Rose and Alan were swimming, Mary talked "to some Sunday 'tourists.' When kids heard I came from Canada they went crazy to hear about cowboys. Did my best. Their mothers gave me a lucky farthing."[18]

On Monday, Mary spent the morning alone, followed by a quiet afternoon with Alan. They saw a movie, went shopping, and then had dinner and a drink. Since she planned to leave for London the next day, Paul wanted her to go back to the flat to say goodbye. She refused, feeling he should have come to see her. The next day, Alan took her to the boat.

"Said a sad farewell — sorry to leave him,"[19] Mary wrote.

Emotion was there, whether romantic or merely friendly. Mary's hopes, whatever they were, had been dashed, her affection misplaced. So, Mary took her leave of Alan, Paul, and Ireland.[20]

A Glimpse of Broadcasting and Life in London

Once in London, Mary had a happier visit with a coterie of familiar CBC people. Her host, Andrew Cowan of the CBC London office, met her when she arrived in the early evening, checked her quickly into Durrants Hotel, and whisked her off to the theatre and dinner, followed by a visit to the House of Lords. Swept into a bustling schedule, Mary recovered from her disappointment and sadness over the Dublin visit, making only a few remaining notations in the diary concerning Alan and Paul. On July 29, she wrote, "Two weeks tonight since I left Liverpool for Ireland so full of the warm welcome I was to get. What a short lived commodity."[21] On August 4, she added, "Got letter from Paul and Alan, ho hum."[22]

With many fascinating things to see, Mary eagerly toured London, browsing through bookstores and antique shops whenever she could.

Sightseeing included stops at Madame Tussaud's Wax Museum, Westminster Abbey, and Harrods and Liberty stores. She also went with Cowan to an English court in Soho, where they sat and watched the proceedings in which barrow boys and a prostitute were fined for minor offences.

The CBC London staff — Andrew Cowan, Mrs. Dan Barrett, Joan Kimber, and Eleanor Swallow — fed and entertained her well. Mary also made time to visit a number of Canadian actors working in England — Bernie Braden, his wife, Barbara Kelly, and Art Hill — and some friends — Joe Hurley, originally from Fredericton, then in London as liaison officer in the Canadian air command, and Tillie and Noel Langley.

Some of the stage productions Mary saw were *The Lady's Not for Burning* with John Gielgud and a young Richard Burton, *Brigadoon*, *Her Excellency* with Cicely Courtenicke, and the ballet *Sleeping Beauty*, which she particularly enjoyed. Several times, Mary and her friends went backstage to the dressing rooms of those they knew, joining the actors for food and drinks. During her stay, Cowan threw a large party in her honour, while meals and gatherings at various homes led to many late nights. Social and busy it was, with little time to be bored.

Often finding the English accents and manners stuffy, she eventually left Durrants Hotel, which she called sticky and stuffy, for the Cumberland, noting that she felt "like a human being since I got out of Durrants."[23]

Since she had work to accomplish, Mary spent time at the CBC office working on scripts. She was scheduled to take part in a BBC Commonwealth broadcast and to give a talk for women. In addition, she met some people who were producing children's shows in Britain, including a Miss Jenkins, and attended a rehearsal for *The Children's Hour*.

While the BBC had begun television production in 1936, the CBC was still in a preparatory state in 1949, sending a number of its people to London to observe. Thus, with television of prime interest, Mary went several times to Alexandra Palace, the BBC television studios, touring through the facilities and watching a number of productions. On a couple of occasions, she simply watched television for an entire afternoon or evening at someone's home — it was a wonderful opportunity for learning.

During her second day in London, a reporter from the *Daily Herald* interviewed her over the telephone. In the middle of a gossipy column called "Notebook" that appeared on Thursday, July 28, Chanticleer, after describing Angela Lansbury's indecision on where to get married, introduced Mary to readers.

Maggie Muggins

Into London yesterday came Mary Grannan, a soft-voiced Canadian woman in her early forties. She is Canada's best-known teller of stories for children. ...
Chance gave her a broadcast talk. One of Canada's broadcasting chiefs heard her. Now she puts on three children's story programmes a week, writes books, and all Canadian children know her principal character, Maggie Muggins. Last Christmas there was a Maggie Muggins doll in 13,000 Canadian stockings.[24]

A Visit with Noel

After meeting with Tillie Langley on three occasions, including a visit to her home in Kingston, Mary took an overnight train to Cornwall to see Noel, who was living in Castledore with two of his children, Jacqueline and Christopher. Noel and Tillie were beginning to have marriage difficulties. Noel and the children met Mary at the Par train station on Wednesday morning, August 10, and took her by taxi back to their home, an old stone cottage, formerly a forge, that was owned by neighbour Jack Vickers. After meeting Jack and eating breakfast, Noel and Mary walked and talked, taking the children on a bus to Fowey for lunch. Noel then hired a motor-boat, letting the children take the helm so he and Mary could continue to talk.

"It was wonderful to be with him — He's so unhappy but a tower of strength,"[25] Mary wrote.

Visiting Noel for the first time since he left Canada in 1945, Mary had originally planned to stay only one day, but that evening, while they were washing the supper dishes back at the cottage, Noel convinced her to stay another day. She was happy to have the extra time, finding the visit particularly delightful.

A tall man, at six feet, five inches, Noel was handsome, charismatic, and quick-witted. He had resumed writing once he returned to England, productively turning out books, plays, and screenplays and getting involved in some stage and film productions of his work. He was highly critical of the state of theatre production, having recently outlined his thoughts in *Theatre World*.[26] Quite opinionated, he did not mind letting his views be known. In the evenings, he liked to relax by drinking and talking at length.

"He used to drink a bottle of gin a day," said his daughter Jacqueline. "While drinking, although never appearing drunk, he would talk. Somehow, it was easier for him to talk while drinking — it opened him up. He would expound. He liked to mentor others; sometimes during this period of talking, he would say things others would find useful."[27]

Noel may have been trying to mentor Mary with his letters encouraging her to expand her writing horizons. She would have appreciated his confidence in her ability.

After lunch in Fowey the next day, Mary and Noel hiked a long stretch over the picturesque area to visit an old stone church at Lanteglos. Noel felt this special church in the vicinity of where King Arthur once lived was located in one of the areas of the earth's forces. During the long hike, they had plenty of time to talk. The large issue in Noel's life at that time was coming to grips with the difficulties in his marriage and deciding what to do. That this was a topic of conversation during that walk came to light in a letter Noel wrote to Mary later that year. On November 23, after returning from Rome where he had been working on a film job for two months, Noel wrote that he had at last begun divorce proceedings and had come to a decision regarding his role as father, ending the letter by saying, "All this started that day in Lanteglos Church — in a way, you felt it at the time. I was given an Absolution."[28]

Among the things on Mary's mind that were probably discussed was what had happened in Dublin. Noel alluded to this in a later letter: "Have you heard from your Abbey Theatre* mushroom lately, or has Booboo the Dogfaced woman put him down with hydrophobia?"[29]

After taking a wrong turn coming back, which Mary did not mind, they took a ferry back to Fowey and a bus back to Castledore. The evening concluded with supper, some lighthearted play with pets in the yard, more talk, and finally a taxi ride back to the train.

Three days later, Noel wrote Mary.

My dear Mary,

Your departure left a large gap, & it serves you bloody well right for not spending all your holiday in London, instead of tip-tapping all over Dublin.

Jack was enchanted by you. There was I just about to play Coopid & off you buzz.

We've had 2 days perfect weather & we all feel like a million dollars — but I can't can't can't face London, Mary, I just bloody well can't. All my messed up life is there, & all my dreary parlour-maid problems that can't be solved.

I've finished my shooting script, & will now tackle a novel. I was delighted & relieved to find no change in you, but of course, real people seldom change — they have only one pair of pants.

Would you get me the enclosed [magazine] for $2? I think it's a much nicer way of spending $2 than some people do.

Best love from the salvaged branch of the Langleys — Jackie says don't forget the doll!!!

As ever,
Noel[30]

---

* *Paul Smith worked at the Gate Theatre, not the Abbey.*

Journey Back Home

Back in London, four busy days ensued for Mary, including both record-ings for broadcast with the BBC. The first recording session was done the afternoon of Friday, August 12; after travelling all night on the train back from Cornwall, Mary grabbed one hour's sleep at the hotel in the morning before she plunged into the day's activities. She completed her script on Saturday, went to Alexandra Palace on Sunday for observation of television productions and tours, and recorded the second BBC broadcast on Monday. While at the BBC that day, Mary and Andrew Cowan were photographed in front of the building. In addition to work, those last few days featured dinners and socializing every evening, two more parties, theatre and ballet, some more shopping — including pur-chases of a magazine for Noel and a ballet doll for Jackie — and, oh yes, church on Sunday at Westminster Cathedral.

But all good things must come to an end, and on Tuesday, August 16, Mary packed up to leave. The entire staff of the CBC's London office — Andy, Dan, Joan, and Eleanor — came to see her off at the Euston train station. From there, she travelled to Liverpool, where she boarded her ship bound for Canada.

The voyage home to Canada was stormy in part but mostly uneventful. Mary arrived in Montreal on Tuesday, August 23, after being delayed eight hours by a forest fire outside Quebec City. Finally, at suppertime, Mary arrived in Montreal and met Dud Allen on Peel Street. Following dinner together, they went to his hotel room for a while before he took her to the evening train for Fredericton.

On Wednesday, Mary arrived back home in Fredericton, where her sister Helen met her at the train. The local newspaper promptly fea-tured an article about her in the next day's paper: "'Just Mary' Back from U.K. Visit: Featured Radio Writer in Fredericton Again after Study in Ireland."[31]

During the next three days, Mary continued to make brief notations in her trip diary. She visited Stewart Neill and his secretary, Vera True, and good friend Gertrude Davis. The final few notations seemed to be the winding down of a wheel that had been spinning very fast. "Friday —We sat around. Eddie called. Sat. Same. D. Weldon in — Gertrude — Vera."[32]

But, of course, this would be only a short rest before she geared up to go back to Toronto for the new broadcasting season. Furthermore, she was scheduled to speak at an education conference in Chatham, New Brunswick, five days after arriving home.

It had been an eventful summer.

As Christmas approached, Mary sent gifts of candy and food to the Langleys, for which Noel thanked her, saying, "You've been a very real influence for good in my harassed jabberwocky of a life."[33]

In the December issue of the CBC's staff magazine, *Radio*, Mary published a thank-you to the London office, accompanying it with the photograph of her and Cowan in front of the BBC.

A "Mary" Merry Christmas

This is a "Just Mary" story that just must be told. Its title? A "Mary" Merry Christmas to the London office.

To you, Andrew Cowan, who met me one mid-summer evening in Euston Station, with the same twinkle in the eye, with the same eager enthusiasm, that I remembered from York Street days. Did you really have a "red carpet" tucked under your arm, or did I imagine so because I had come that day from Ireland, where imagination runs riot and where goblins hide under every cobblestone? In either case, you did roll out the red carpet for me, and I trod its plushy folds for three happy weeks. For those weeks of pleasure, interest and value, I thank you and wish you a "Mary" Merry Christmas.

To you, "Dan" Cooper Barrett, of the shaggy hair and saucy nose ... you made my journey along the carpet so very easy ... you, with your blue paper and solicitous telephone. You arranged the meetings, the luncheons, the broadcasts ... You were my guide to shops and shows. You made me feel like a visiting celebrity instead of the renegade school marm that I am. A "Mary" Merry Christmas indeed.

To you, Joan Kimber, of the wide blue eyes and infectious laughter. To you I owe much for services rendered. I liked your insatiable curiosity about Canadians and things Canadian. "What is he like … what is she like … what is it like?" We all hope that you can find out for yourself someday. If we can do half as well by you as you do by us, we shall accomplish much. A "Mary" Merry Christmas to you.

To you, Eleanor Swallow, of the slow and quiet ways … you with your amusing instructions to yourself on the wall, you who took me to Paddington to send me off to discover Cornwall … you with your diverting stories of life and living … A "Mary" Merry Christmas.

To the Big Four in London … to those four who serve the Canadian Broadcasting Corporation with verve and honesty, who offer hospitality with spontaneity and charm … a Merry Christmas from us all.

— Mary Grannan[34]

Chapter Eleven
Prelude to Television, 1949–1954

Preparing for the New Broadcast Medium

"Give the gift the whole family wants! RCA Victor Television," declared the *Globe and Mail* advertisement on Friday, December 2, 1949. "You get the headline shows of all 4 U.S. Networks direct from WBEN-TV Buffalo."[1]

Canadians were buying television sets in 1949, with sales of 4,163 between September and December alone that year,[2] even though there was as yet no television broadcasting in the country. Those living close enough to the border with the United States could receive American signals, tuning in to such favourites as the *Milton Berle Show* and *Kraft TV Theater*. Canada was behind in television production.

While the United Kingdom and the United States had begun regular television broadcasting prior to the war, the CBC and the Canadian government debated and waffled for several years about television, with people in both groups arguing for and against. In the CBC, Alphonse Ouimet was the major television proponent. Considered the greatest technical authority on television in the country during the late forties, Ouimet, an engineer, had begun researching and working with television as early as 1932. In 1947, Ouimet and H.G. Walker toured the United Kingdom, France, the Netherlands, and the United States to study television facilities and production.[3] Finally, in 1948, the Liberal government made the decision to proceed with television, while the Conservative opposition decried the decision to give the CBC a monopoly. It was then that the CBC began to plan for television in earnest.

Ernie Bushnell, Fergus Mutrie, and Frank Willis were all busy studying British and American television production at about the same time that Mary visited the BBC in the summer of 1949. She had strong connections with many of the major players at the CBC, Ernie Bushnell and Frank Willis in particular, and she naturally would have been involved in office and cafeteria discussions about current issues, television certainly among them. It is not known whose initiative led to Mary's visit to the London CBC offices and the BBC, but it was certainly a boost to Mary to be able to examine what was going on in children's television in Britain prior to the start of television in Canada.

While many in radio had some doubt about the eventual place of television, Mary's curiosity allowed her to keep an open mind, and thus she viewed what British television was doing with immense interest. In September 1950, in what was undoubtedly a frequent exercise for many at the CBC, Mary prepared a memo of new program ideas that included suggestions for television as well as radio:

> New Programme Ideas
> Having heard that Mr. Bushnell wished a presentation of new programme ideas, I am listing some thoughts here, which may or may not fit into the scheduling needs.
>
> TENTATIVE PROGRAMME TITLES
> The Victoria Club. (Adult).
> An Adaptation of the "Anne" books by L.M. Montgomery. (All ages)
> Late Delivery. (A one time Christmas programme)
> One Thousand and One Nights. (Adult)

Moon Man's Diary. (Children)
Let's Have a Show. (Children)
Roadside Philosopher. (Adult)
Peter Pop-up. (Television — children)
Paper Doll Palace. (Television)
Appointment with Antoine. (Women)
The Peabody Millions. (Adult)
Cross Country Circus.[4]

In the rest of the memo, Mary sketched an outline for each of these. Whether or not any were eventually used, the outline nevertheless showed that she had a good grasp of the basic needs and imaginative possibilities. Following is her description of the "Peter Pop-up" television suggestion:

Peter Pop-up
I visualize here a large box decorated with Mother Goose characters and fastened with a huge hook. Inside this box is Peter Pop-up. (Here again must be a man with easy laughter, a man who has a very mobile face).

A child opens the box and Peter Pops up. Inside his box Peter might have many gadgets such as a tiny umbrella, a funny hat, etc. After preliminary chatter with the child, Peter might read a story. I think such a character could be developed.

If more than one camera were available, the story book characters could come alive.[5]

In September 1952, CBC Television went on the air, first in Montreal on September 6 and then in Toronto on September 8 — it was a new era. Among the many changes taking place at the CBC was a change in the staff dynamics. The close-knit family of the early radio years was evolving into a larger and more diverse group. With these changes, Mary's relative position of influence within the organization would have been diminished, although she continued to hold her popularity and recognition with the public.

Over the next few years, Mary presented other television suggestions. In April 1953 she sent proposals to Mavor Moore, who was in charge of television production, and in May 1954 she sent ideas to Harry Boyle, Program Director for Ontario, mentioning one television production in which she had been involved:

(6) THE GYPSY AND THE SONG (Television)
Previously presented.
PURPOSE:- Entertainment for 6-9 age level.
I made a kinescope under this title with Tony Stecheson in December feature. Viewing the film, I wrote a criticism to Mr. Griffiths and Miss Peggy Nairn, who produced the show. It was done hurriedly and I felt that, were the suggestions I made carried through, it could be an interesting and attractive show.[6]

Nevertheless, however hard she tried, she appeared to remain largely outside television production, at least in terms of continuing programs, through 1954. At the end of that year, it was an old radio favourite rather than any of her new ideas that aroused interest for television.

Popularity and a Couple of Honours

The *Maggie Muggins* radio stories matured as the broadcasts continued, eventually emerging into their settled format with the usual array of animal characters accompanying Maggie and Mr. McGarrity. The gentle relationship between the young, inquisitive girl and the kind, older neighbour formed the backbone of the stories, which opened and closed with playful conversations. Maggie relied on wise Mr. McGarrity to help solve the daily crises in the lives of her meadow friends, each of whom had special characteristics and foibles. After patiently listening while Maggie breathlessly explained the problem, Mr. McGarrity, often stifling laughter, would offer his sage advice. Following the always-successful outcome, Maggie would come back to Mr. McGarrity to end the story with the usual refrains and a small rhyme about the day's happenings. For example:

"He can indeed," smiled Mr. McGarrity. "Well, Maggie, all in all I'd say you'd had quite a day."

"Yes, because tra la, la la, la la, la lack, Big Bite dropped a tree on the railroad track. I don't know what will happen tomorrow."[7]

With time, the adventures became more inventive, humorous, and full of familiar things that would appeal to children: conceited and mischievous Fitzgerald Fieldmouse played his piano while singing self-flattering or teasing songs; elderly Grandmother Frog complained about her rheumatism; Petunia 'Possum spoke in a southern drawl — "Lan' sakes, Honey Chil'."[8] Maggie's usual expression of surprise was "My gracious, Aunt Matilda,"[9] while Mr. McGarrity's was "Well upon my word."[10]

In the following story, "The Ironing Board," which appeared in *Maggie Muggins and Her Friends* in 1954, Maggie and Mr. McGarrity discuss the speech habits of her animal friends:

> Maggie reached into her apron pocket and handed a small envelope to Mr. McGarrity. He reached into his overall pocket for his spectacles. He put them on, opened the letter, and read,
>
> "Honey Chil', will you please bring your lil' iron, for ironin', when you come to the meadow today.
>
> I's goin' for to iron for Honey Mouse. He done got some things he like me for to press. I is your friend, Petunia."
>
> Mr. McGarrity laughed. "Petunia has a funny way of putting things, hasn't she?" he said to his little friend.
>
> Maggie nodded her red head. "Yes, she has, but I don't mind. I like it. Big Bite Beaver talks funny too, because of the way his teeth stick out, and Fitzgerald has a squeaky voice, and Harry Rabbit lisps, and Grunter Pig snorts, and Mr. Goat says 'Maaaa' in front of almost every word he speaks. But it's their way, and I don't mind."[11]

Mary had developed a winning story formula, while her abundant imagination and wit made the stories appealing to children. In the broadcast studio, Mary, Beryl Braithwaite, James Annand, and Lou Snider enjoyed a harmonious working relationship that amplified the sweet nature of the program.

In her 1949 article about Beryl as Maggie, June Callwood declared "the Muggins child an industry," citing the program as drawing the largest audience of youngsters of any children's broadcast in the country, spurring the sale of eighty thousand copies of the two Maggie books then in print and twenty-five thousand Maggie dolls since their release the previous November.[12]

Although she appreciated the popularity, Mary had the greater pleasure in 1950 of seeing *Maggie Muggins* win an Honorable Mention from the Institute for Education by Radio at Ohio State University "in recognition of outstanding educational value and distinguished radio production."[13] The *Maggie Muggins* radio series ended in June 1953 when Beryl graduated from high school.

In 1951, Mary received her most cherished honour. The International Mark Twain Society of Saint Louis, Missouri, which conferred honorary memberships on those individuals throughout the world whom it considered worthy in the arts, made Mary an honorary member in recognition of her books. As a result of this membership, her books were placed in the Mark Twain Library collection maintained at the Library of Congress. For Mary to be included among the company of authors such as Rudyard Kipling, James M. Barrie, Thomas Hardy, Sir Arthur Conan Doyle, and Franklin D. Roosevelt was humbling, but pleasing, especially while many Canadian libraries were still refusing to carry Mary's books.

And what a growing number of books there were. Mary and her publisher were turning out a new book every year, alternating between *Maggie Muggins* and *Just Mary*. According to John Allen, Thomas Allen Limited did not edit her manuscripts but printed them as they were received.[14] Running out of variations in titles, the *Just Mary* books began to be distinguished by colours, with *Blue, Green,* and *Red Stories* appearing between 1950 and 1953. Beginning with the *Just Mary Blue Stories,* Pat Patience became Mary's illustrator, providing cheerful drawings of cherubic-looking children for almost all of the remaining books Mary published with Thomas Allen. In 1950, the John C. Winston Company introduced *Maggie Muggins Stories* to American children.

As a seasoned writer, Mary was turning out some of her best *Just Mary* stories: "Timothy Tomilson, Detective,"[15] in which a boy who wants to be a policeman solves a burglary by catching the culprit squirrel; "The Jewels of Fermanagh,"[16] in which Kitty Clover uses a magic flute to capture the thief who stole the king's jewels; "Mrs. Waddle and the Roller Skates,"[17] in which Johnny Fenner helps overweight Mrs. Waddle get to her newsstand on time by pulling her on his roller skates; "The Knight of the Hornet,"[18] in which Hippolite Hoppolite Humphrey is knighted by the king for accidentally scaring away robbers when he disturbs a hornet's nest but discovers he is happier scrubbing pots; and "Louis the Lobster," in which a group of sea creatures who are tired of being frightened by Louis concoct a plan to get rid of him. The story begins this way:

> Somehow I can't help feeling sorry for Louis. He's not very happy these days. He's in an Aquarium. You know what an Aquarium is. It's a sort of a zoo for fish. There, in tanks, you will see catfish and dogfish, seahorses and sticklebacks, carps and codfish, sunfish and snappers, tuna and trout, suckers and salmon, minnows and mullets, flukes and flatfish, halibut and halfbeaks, sardines and swordfish, marlin and mackerel, and lobsters too, of course, because Louis is there.
>
> Louis was the largest lobster that ever walked the seafloor. He was proud of his great size. He was proud of his great strength, and he was proud of his shining armour.
>
> All the smaller creatures of the sea feared Louis. He liked it that way.[19]

Mary continued the tradition of occasionally honouring a young fan or acquaintance by including his or her name as the principal character of a story. Some of these stories were meant to please an adult friend, such as the one for her publisher, Dud (Forbes Duncan) Allen.

In his tale, Duncan Mouse was so upset at not getting his toy piano from Santa Claus that young Martha Star (daughter of a friend), who "found truth in the eyes of Duncan Mouse," sent a message to Santa, asking him to come again and bring Duncan his piano.[20]

Sometimes the honour of being named in a story had a surprising effect, as in the case of a young British girl called Pat Webb. This story began with a letter another Webb girl, Penny Webb of Vancouver, had written to Mary about her disappointment of missing the circus because she had the measles. Fully understanding the sadness of a child unable to attend the circus, Mary wrote a story for Penny called "Penny Webb and the Spider," which was broadcast on *Just Mary* on Sunday, May 15, 1949.[21] In the story, Penny Webb misses her class's nature outing because she is sick with the measles but instead goes to the spider fair thanks to a magic spell by Grandmother Spider.

A few months later, Mary left on her trip to Ireland and England. During her talk in August on the BBC program *The Women's Hour*, Mary spoke about where she got her story ideas, telling as an example about the recent story for Penny Webb of Vancouver in response to the girl's letter. Hearing the broadcast near Southampton, England, was a British woman by the name of Ivy Webb, whose daughter, Pat, suffered from epilepsy triggered by the anguish of living through bombing during the war. After taking an accidental overdose of medication, she was languishing in a hospital, having given up the will to live. Moved by the broadcast, Mrs. Webb wrote to Mary about her daughter and soon received a reply. During her next visit to Pat, Mrs. Webb spoke about the Canadian storyteller and her story of the magic spider web but substituted the name *Pat* for *Penny*. Surprised to see young Pat responding, her mother persisted with the tale, eliciting further positive reaction. Mrs. Webb wrote again to Mary, asking for a copy of the story. Changing the story name to Pat, Mary promptly sent the story along with some *Just Mary* and *Maggie Muggins* books. With help from repeated readings of a story featuring her own name, Pat gradually began to regain her joy in living. The family and doctors credited the story with playing a significant part in her recovery.

When Pat wrote Mary in early 1952 to say she had recovered, the *CBC Times* related the entire story in an article called "A Grandmother

Spider and Her Magic Web."[22] The *Prairie Messenger* in Saskatchewan subsequently picked it up — "Grandmother and Her Spider Web: Mary Grannan Credited with Saving Girl's Reason."[23] While this was one of the most remarkable and touching responses to her work, Mary preferred to minimize her role by saying "a letter from a little girl in Vancouver helped another little girl in the south of England."[24]

In late December 1954 or early 1955, Mary received an envelope from Britain sent "On Her Britannic Majesty's Service," and stamped "Salvaged Mail Aircraft Crash Prestwick 25-12-54." Inside was a partly burned airmail letter from Mrs. Ivy Webb. The Webb family was alive and well, but their Christmas letter had a harrowing trip to its destination. The news it carried, however, was happy and welcome:

> Dear Miss Grannan,
>
> It is Christmas time & we would like you to know, that we have never forgotten the great kindness you showed to our daughter, Pat. We all wish you a very Merry Xmas and a prosperous New Year.
>
> Pat, you will be pleased to hear, has made steady progress, & was discharged completely from the hospital after eight years of treatment, last month. She now works as a clerk in an office & does shorthand & typing. Your books are her dearest treasure & we often speak of you & all that you did for her.[25]

Jubilee Road

In addition to her principal shows and seasonal specials, Mary was writing some programs to fill her summer time slots: *Karen Discovers America* in 1952, *The Cotton Sprouts* in 1953, and *Mr. McGarrity's Garden* in 1954–55, specifically intended to provide summer work for James Annand. In the fall of 1953, she further began to write a new regular season radio series called *Jubilee Road*, the story of three children who lived on that street — Johnny Little, his sister Patty, and their friend, Salty Pickle. Geared for slightly older children than *Maggie Muggins* or *Just Mary*, the fifteen-minute drama series followed the characters' adventures as they frequently got into trouble.

Produced by James Kent, with music provided by Lou Snider and later Lloyd Edwards, the show featured in the lead roles three adults in their twenties and thirties who specialized in authentically portraying children's voices on the air. Billie Mae Richards, who was perhaps best known for her role as the Kid in W.O. Mitchell's *Jake and the Kid*, portrayed Johnny, the lead character and narrator. Her companions and culprits in action were Maxine Miller as Patty and Bobby Jackson as Salty Pickle. These experienced actors who had begun their acting careers at early ages did a variety of other radio work, including an extensive number of school broadcasts. They were part of a large, well-trained pool of actors who were kept constantly busy — except they were part of that unique group that depicted children.

"Everybody that did [radio], did it a lot. We were called radio babies,"[26] said Maxine, who also acted in the radio programs *The Tyler Touch* and *Alice of Orchestralia*, as well as in the television series *Howdy Doody* as Princess Haida.

"[*Jubilee Road*] was one of hundreds of shows that we did," said Billie Mae, while explaining that she and Maxine worked extensively together through the years. "Oh, yeah, we did all the children — I was the boy and she was the girl. ... I was always a child — only did boys' voices."[27]

As with the selection of actors for *Maggie Muggins*, Mary was actively involved. Maxine remembers:

> Oh, yes, she pretty well had the say ... because it was
> her show. And her *Just Mary*, of course, was herself. But
> *Jubilee Road* — she wrote it and she wanted to make sure
> who the people were. ... I always thought she was larg-
> er than life. She always was made-up and always dressed.
> ... I was always mesmerized by her make-up. She was
> larger than life with her make-up; it was quite bright —
> the cheeks and the lipstick, and the eye lashes. ... And
> I remember that she wore a lot of black and a big, black
> hat. I remember that. But other than that, she was there

and she was pretty well in the booth most of the time with the director. … It was kind of nice because if there was anything she didn't want or if they wanted to change it, she could re-write it or do anything like that. That's the nice thing of having a writer on the show. They can always change things.[28]

Seldom seeing the scripts before the day of broadcast, the actors arrived a couple of hours in advance, picked up their scripts, read and marked them, and then proceeded with at least three rehearsals before going on the air. As capable actors, they knew how to read scripts quickly. And the scripts were humorous.

"We had a lot of fun doing it,"[29] said Maxine.

In order to produce the required essence of childhood in their voices, they allowed themselves to behave physically in front of the microphones as children would under those circumstances. Maxine explained:

On radio, it's only your voice, and you have to portray what's there but … I was always told by Esse [Ljungh], "It's your voice, but you have to create the feeling and what it sounds like, what it feels like, but it has to be in your voice." Whoever watched us doing [shows] as kids would see our hands going and doing all the … crazy things. Anybody watching would be in hysteria because we're "doing the kids," you know. It doesn't matter whether we're older, we're still "doing the kids." Or even if you're doing a funny little old lady, you're still doing something with your hands at the same time. …You get into the part, but it comes from here and here. But it doesn't come from looking like the part.[30]

On the same subject, Bille Mae said:

Radio is a very specialized medium. It's not the same as television at all. … Radio — it doesn't matter what you look like. It's what your voice is. It's what you can do with your voice. And if you've been on television, of course, it's how you look. So, I am not going to be able to do little boys, am I? ... But there is an upside, and that is, after we got going and we got through all the pitfalls of live television ... the upside of radio is that from that you go into cartoons because that *is* radio. That's all it is — it's radio. 'Cause it's only your voice, and you just have to look at the storyboard, see what kind of characters, and then decide on what kind of a voice you think would suit.[31]

How did listeners respond to *Jubilee Road*? "It used to be if the show went on for another year, you were alright," said Maxine. "Or if it went on past the thirteen weeks, and we were picked up again, we figured we were wonderful. ... We did get a little bit [of fan mail]. Every once in a while, somebody would bring it in the studio. There might be two or three letters for Billie, one or two for me. And I always answered them."[32]

While the *Jubilee Road* stories derived part of their humour from the antics of the child characters, a good portion came from the device of having the lead character, Johnny, narrate the stories as he told events from his eight-year-old point of view. In his opening narration, Johnny would bring listeners up to date on any necessary facts they might have missed from previous episodes. In the following broadcast from October 14, 1953, Johnny introduces the day's story:

ANNCR: This is the story of Jubilee Road and the people who live there. I don't even pretend to tell that story. I hand that chore over to Johnny Little. Johnny lives on Jubilee Road.

JOHNNY: It's my street, and as I told you before, it twists and turns through our town like a grass snake ... [full] of wiggles you know. It's a nice street and an exciting street. I hope you won't think I'm bragging if I say that Patty and Salty Pickle (he lives across the street) and I help to keep it that way. Patty's my sister, in case you don't know. She's a year younger than I am. She's just as good as a boy, honest she is, because she never tattle-tales, and she's always ready for anything. And if we get into trouble which I'm sorry to say we sometimes do, (although it's never our fault, because we never intend to get into trouble), Patty never complains. We're pretty good kids, all in all, and we try to be thoughtful and kind, but do you know that kindness will sometimes get you into a mess, too? Now take last Saturday. We had only the best of intentions. It was a nice day. October has some nice days as you know ... we sing a song in school called "October's Bright Blue Weather" ... well, it was bright blue that day and we were feeling in the pink. And when you feel in the pink, you should always do something about it. No use of sitting around. We were up early, Patty and I, and so was Salty. Mum and Dad had gone away for the week-end and sort of left Kathy in charge. Kathy's my other sister ... she's sixteen ... guess you know that by now. She wasn't too fussy about having us on her hands because it sort of meant that she had to stick around the house more than usual, so she was glad when the phone rang at breakfast time.[33]

In the story that followed, the children went to visit Salty's grandfather's farm, bringing home a crate of hens that had fallen from a passing truck. Naturally, a bit of chaos ensued as the hens got out of the garage and into the house when Kathy opened the door to see what the noise was all about. Each week's story built on the previous one, ending with Johnny's closing statement, "There's Salty. I have to be going … see you next week." The series continued for three years, ending in June 1956.

Discovering the West

While the Maritime provinces had long been prime supporters of their native daughter Mary Grannan, many of their radio stations, including Fredericton's CFNB, stopped carrying *Just Mary* in the fall of 1952. Alerted to the fact, the head of children's programs, John Dunlop, initiated a query into the matter through George Young in Halifax station relations. Drawn into the effort to help was Ann Grannan, Mary's sister, who wrote to Ted Briggs in Halifax:

> Dear Commander Briggs,
>
> I am Mary Grannan's sister Ann, and at her suggestion I am writing you to ask if you could do anything to get the "Just Mary" program back on the air here in the Maritimes. Mary said if any one could get the program back it would be you.
>
> I am a teacher here in Moncton and day after day children in my school are asking when Just Mary is coming back — children and teachers from other schools are phoning and stopping me on the street asking about it — and then my own disappointment at not being able to hear my favorite program!
>
> Mary really has many many fans here and at home in Fredericton who are all disappointed about not being able to hear her. Last summer when she was home children were calling at our house day after day to see and talk to her — and when we came visiting to a cottage at Shediac Bridge they came from all around the shore asking for stories and inviting her to children's parties.

> We use her stories in school for written and oral composition — even the primary children retell them.
>
> I won't go on at length but <u>hope</u> you will be able to get her back on the air.
>
> Mary said to mention to you that if the Weatherman <u>had</u> to be at 2.15 perhaps you might pick up the show and put it on at another time.
>
> Thank you <u>ever</u> so much for reading this long letter and hoping you will do your best to help us.[34]

However, the efforts were unsuccessful, with probably no one more disappointed than Mary herself. Briggs replied to Ann that having decided to drop one of Mary's programs in order to carry *Folk Songs for the Young Folk*, they chose to keep *Maggie Muggins* instead of *Just Mary*.

Such occasional disappointments soon passed, as Mary was too busy with work to dwell on them. By the fifties, with Mary's popularity solidly entrenched, her appearances, speaking engagements, and book signings were numerous enough that these activities took up a significant amount of time and energy. For example, in November 1952, Mary spoke to the Prince Charles Home and School Association in London, Ontario, and the Summerlea Home and School Association in Lachine, Quebec, and attended a powwow in the museum at Caughnawaga (now known as Kahnawake). There she met Chief Poking Fire, who listened to her programs with his grandson. Then in Brockville, Ontario, she visited the Commonwealth School, where she told stories to the kindergarten class, spoke at the Rotary Club's annual "ladies' night," and signed copies of her books at Copland's store because it was Young Canada Book Week. She loved it all.

As much as she enjoyed her work, she took time in the summer for rest and recreation. In the summer of 1954, Frank and Gladys Willis took Mary with them on a car trip to the Canadian and American West. Both Frank and Mary were interested in the Old West and the famous characters that had lived there. After enjoying the Calgary Stampede and the friendly Albertan people, they continued to South Dakota, where they visited Deadwood in the Black Hills, seeing such famous sites as the Mount Moriah Cemetery, where Wild Bill Hickok and Calamity Jane were buried. While there, Mary collected a number of books on the Old West, later using some of the ideas in her writings.

"I remember Mary telling me that the car broke down out on the desert," Donald Roberts said, "and they thought surely they were going to die. They had to take off their petticoats, as she called them, and make things to put over their heads ... They didn't have anything to drink ... Fortunately, anyway, they got the car going."[35]

"[Frank and Gladys] would take Mary on a lot of these things because they felt Mary was lonesome," Austin Willis said. "Indeed, she was, although she had lots of chums at the station. You know, their [lives were] pretty much the same day in and day out."[36]

Chapter Twelve
Maggie Comes to Television,
1954-1958

Television Beckons at Last

Dr. Fred Rainsberry's arrival at the CBC as head of children's television heralded a new era for Mary Grannan. Frustrated by the continuing lack of interest in her television suggestions, she mused to her sisters in early November 1954 that she would love to write for television, but perhaps she was not forceful enough or maybe she should submit a script under another name.[1] Then, on November 25, she met with Rainsberry at his suggestion; he told her that he wanted her to learn television technique and scriptwriting because he liked her work. Asking her to attend some of the children's television shows they were doing, he requested three written program suggestions after Christmas. She, in turn, gave him her latest *Maggie Muggins* book. Mary wrote to her sisters about the meeting: "I don't feel much like the effort, but it's a struggle to keep up with the times and keep people aware of me, that I'll make the effort. This business is one in which you can't lag, and TV has sort of knocked us on our fannies, a little bit."[2]

Within a few days of that meeting, Rainsberry had turned his attention to *Maggie*.

[November 30, 1954]

Dear Girls,

[...] Rainsberry of TV called again ... this morning ... wants me to meet a bunch of them on Friday ...
They're interested in Maggie Muggins, and GOD how
I'd love to get that on TV ... We are to talk techniques
and I hope I'll be able to understand ... Rainsberry, a
former professor at U of Michigan* seems to find merit
in my work ... the others you see, who are old CBC
staff, Radio, have ignored all suggestions ... A new
man comes along ... I hope I don't get too involved
this time of year ... with no shopping done ... and I
mean none and no ideas ... and all ... I'm up to
February 7 with Jubilee Road, but only till the Sunday
after next with Just Mary ... I'm going to use some
oldies at Christmas time ... I'm not saying anything to
Athersich or Willis about this deal ... I talk too much
about some things ... I'd like to be able to have somebody to say something to that wasn't jealous. I miss
Henri [Edey] for that ... I could talk things over with
her. I wish I weren't so conscious of my figure [...] Bye
for now. Love Mary.[3]

Fred Rainsberry had accepted the position of supervising producer
of children's television at CBLT, the CBC's Toronto station, on March
29, 1954, at the invitation of Chief Producer Mavor Moore and
Program Director Stuart Griffiths. With a background in education
and having recently completed his Ph.D. in English and philosophy
from Michigan State University, Rainsberry arrived with plenty of
knowledge about educating children but little about television.
Nevertheless, he was eager to establish programs and policies that
would protect children from the negative aspects of television by man-
dating wholesome and educational material. The Canadian general
public and the television industry itself were debating the potential

---

* *Fred Rainsberry taught at Michigan State University, not the University of Michigan.*

evils posed by the new medium, speculating the possible effects it would have on children. With CBC television in its second year of operation, the executives thought it was time to build the children's department by putting some guidelines and policies in place. Fred Rainsberry was hired to accomplish this.

Fred's wife, Margaret Rainsberry, said her husband had expected to remain teaching at Michigan State University, where he was employed in the Department of Effective Living, an outreach department. However, the native of Sarnia, Ontario, seized the opportunity to branch off in a new direction at home in Canada when he received the CBC's offer.

"Fred was very relaxed," Margaret said, "but he went a mile a minute; he was energetic ... and very intelligent."[4]

Rainsberry's connections in the United States led him to return from time to time to seek talent he could use. Among those he later brought back to Canada were Bob Homme (*The Friendly Giant*), Fred Rogers (*Misterogers*), and Ernie Coombs (*Mr. Dressup*).

Prior to Rainsberry's arrival, Joanne Hughes (later Soloviov) and Peggy Nairn (later Liptrott) had been the first producer-directors for children's television. When CBC Television was organizing in 1952, they were two of the four women hired as script assistants, Peggy in April and Joanne in August. By 1953, they had become producer-directors. Peggy said:

> Everyone was learning [his job] then. We had a month to prepare for the shows, and we just pitched in and did it. ... It was a matter of sink or swim. The cameras were huge, with lenses two, three, five and eight inches; five and eight were close-up. We had to decide ahead of time what camera shots [we] wanted; we needed a list of camera shots ahead of time. You had to 'rack over' the lenses — squeeze the lever to rack over to the next lens. In the control room, there was a bank of monitors. As soon as the camera was ready, we moved to the close-up.[5]

The first children's television programs on the CBC included *Pepinot & Capucine* and *Children's Corner* from Montreal, and from Toronto *Uncle Chichimus*, *How About That* with Percy Saltzman, *Hobby Workshop* with Tom Martin, *Pet Corner* with Rick Campbell, *Planet Tolex*, an outer space story series with puppets by Leo and Dora Velleman, and *Ed's Place* with folk singer Ed McCurdy and actor Joe Austin. There were also serialized productions, such as *20,000 Leagues Under the Sea*, *The Mysterious Island*, *Roger Sudden*, and *Space Command.*[6]

In 1954, the Canadian *Howdy Doody Show* began its successful run with a host of talented writers, producers, actors, and puppeteers. It was at this time that attention turned to the television potential of the pop- ular radio program *Maggie Muggins*. From that first meeting Mary had with Rainsberry and others on Friday, December 3, 1954, the staff of the children's department worked to develop the television production of *Maggie Muggins*, and the first broadcast was aired just two months later, on February 4, 1955.

Maggie in a New Dimension

Maggie Muggins's first television producer, recently married Joanne Hughes Soloviov, was away in Europe on an extended vacation as the show was in its early planning stages. She returned to discover that the staff had programmed all the characters to be played by puppets, includ- ing the main characters, Maggie Muggins and Mr. McGarrity. Telling the staff this would never work, she cast Maggie and Mr. McGarrity to be played by actors. Since Maggie's animal friends were presumed to be imaginary, the idea of having puppets portray them seemed appropriate. On the other hand, Maggie and Mr. McGarrity were meant to be real people, so having actors play these roles allowed for a clearer division between the real and the imaginary.

"I got John Drainie as the first Mr. McGarrity," Joanne said. Referring to the program as "her baby," she was particularly proud of cast- ing the eminent Canadian actor as the first Mr. McGarrity and young Beth Morris as the first Maggie. "*Maggie Muggins* was always a success,"[7] she said.

Because of a shortage of available studio and camera time, the low-priority children's program was broadcast in a small studio with its rehearsals elsewhere. Joanne greatly admired Mary and respected her scriptwriting abilities.

"Mary was terrific," Joanne said. "She wore big hats and huge earrings. The most amazing thing was that we never had to have a script rewritten. We would just get the script and do it. It had wonderful humour. They were great shows. … She was known as a character. The Jarvis Street building had a cafeteria in the basement where everyone congregated. Mary was frequently there, always chatting. She was charming."[8]

Beth Morris, who had been acting since the age of three, including in numerous CBC productions, was eleven years old when she assumed the role of Maggie. She recalled that her audition for the part was probably more like an interview than an audition, since the producers knew her. She met Mary only a couple of times, once after getting the part and then at rehearsals.

"Mary Grannan was a big person with a big personality and flamboyant clothing," Beth said. "She was amazing for a little girl. She really stuck out as a unique character. … Mary was very glad that I was going to be Maggie Muggins. She talked warmly to me and clearly loved her stories. I felt invited in by her."[9]

During the first season, *Maggie Muggins* was broadcast live on Thursdays from the basement of the Jarvis Street building in the same studio where *Howdy Doody* was broadcast, while the rehearsals were held on Tuesdays on Broadview. There were two sets — the shed where Maggie met Mr. McGarrity, and the mouse house or other places where Maggie met her animal friends. In between these two sets were Lou Snider at his celesta and novachord and the actors in front of microphones doing the voices for the puppets.

The puppeteers, husband and wife John and Linda Keogh, stood on a raised platform behind the mouse house set. In the beginning, Linda also provided the voice for Grandmother Frog. The well-designed marionette puppets with eyes that could close and wink were often dressed up according to the particular script.

"John Keogh managed Fitzgerald and Linda managed Grandmother Frog," said Beth. "John would sometimes make Fitzgerald snuggle up to

227

me or kick me or something. ... I felt that the puppets were almost real. I never saw them unanimated."[10] Once they were out of their boxes, the puppets were in motion. The sets full of miniature things also appealed to the young actress.

In a scene with John Drainie as Mr. McGarrity during one of the live broadcasts of the first season, Beth was holding a large book as a prop.

"I got carried away with acting and slammed the book shut," Beth said. "The dust flew up, causing us both to cough. It was live, so John Drainie began ad libbing to make it seem that this was all part of the show."[11]

During the preparations for the new series, Mary wrote to her sisters with news of the progress. Her letter offers some insight into her thoughts during the period just before the first broadcast:

> [January 1955]
> Dear Girls
>
> Monday, and I've been to a rehearsal for Maggie Muggins. The little girl is cute, but she's on the way to grow out of it soon ... She must be ten ... She's pretty, and has hair long enough for pigtails. Using John Drainie for Mr. McG. It breaks my heart to leave Jim Annand out, but they say he can't study ... he got nervous at anything out of the ordinary in radio ... and so when he'd be surrounded by cameras etc. I'm sure he'd forget everything and fluff badly. I guess you can't be sentimental in this business ... and my own day will come. I worked the whole weekend ... writing Maggie scripts ... Joanne Hughes called me that maybe it would start Feb. 4 ... then she called me that John Drainie had to go to NYC [New York City] for ten days, and they'd want to have two scripts done ... Well I sure enough worked ... Have to get at the book too ... Funny I always get into the urgent jobs. Guess there's not much chance of its going commercial, because it is to go between 5 and 5.30 which time they reserve for CBC sustainers. However, it might revive interest in the dolls

… The physical end is most of the work, because I'm
going to draw from the scripts at hand … If it is shown
down there, maybe you can see it somewhere … I hope
so. Watch the schedule after Feb 1 […]

Love Mary[12]

Shortly after *Maggie Muggins* began to be televised, Joanne Hughes
Soloviov, in her capacity as the show's producer, prepared a highly
complimentary report analyzing the scripts and submitted it to Fred
Rainsberry. He agreed, adding his own comments as he passed both
reports to the supervisor of programs. Favourable comments on Mary's
work also came in from John Dunlop, head of children's programs.
Someone, likely Mary, prepared a typed copy of their remarks:

From Dunlop to Supervisor of Programmes

Mr. Rainsberry and Joanne Hughes have sent you separate reports on Mary Grannan's work in television,
which has been outstanding not only on the MAG-
GIE MUGGINS series, but she has been most helpful
in reviewing films and passing onto us, some very
sound comments on programming for children.

Miss Grannan is at the top of her group and because
of the extra work of television, should be put in a higher
category so this work is properly recognized. W J Dunlop

FROM RAINSBERRY

I am submitting for your reference, the attached report
on the work of Miss Grannan as a writer for the television show of MAGGIE MUGGINS. I concur with
Miss Hughes' estimate of Miss Grannan's work. We
have been able to produce a most charming children's
show with Miss Grannan's script. Her amazing capacity to adapt her style for television production deserves
great praise. I hope that we may be able to use her services in the future as script writer for television.

Supervisor Children's Pgs TV

JOANNE HUGHES REPORT

MARY GRANNAN SCRIPT WRITING

I find MAGGIE MUGGINS scripts very satisfactory for the following reasons.

1) Very good ability to create an infinite number of situations within a very limited framework. Mary's fund of plot lines seems inexhaustible. Plots are usually slight, but very real and very adequate to a 15-minute show. I think the pattern of repetition is very good for young children.

2) Fine appreciation of the individual line. The actors have little trouble in dealing with dialogue. Great variety of word play and puns add spark to otherwise wordy passages.

3) I think the speed with which Mary has made the adjustment to TV is amazing. She is infinitely practical and seems to think in terms of pictures. Usually a very difficult transition for radio-trained writers.

4) Mary's co-operation has been first class. I have taken exception to only one character and upon that occasion she rewrote exactly as I suggested and with no apparent objection. She is not "sensitive" ... if I suggest we cut this or that or change a line or two, I do not get an argument unless there is a reason for one.

5) I have never been held up for lack of scripts. We are about ten weeks ahead and ordering them is at my discretion. All this makes the job much easier.

6) While the scripts are essentially entertainment, there is usually a little "lesson" worked in unobtrusively. Example ... last week, a small instruction on safety. Occasionally a word explanation, or a spelling lesson.

7) Scripts have a consistent standard of quality. We don't have three good and one bad.

March 16, 1955 Joanne Hughes[13]

After the first season, Joanne Hughes Soloviov stepped back from the role of producer to that of program coordinator because of health problems, and Peggy Nairn Liptrott became the next producer of *Maggie Muggins*. Peggy said:

> I loved working with Mary Grannan. … Her scripts were so creative — a child and her imagination, with an adult there for help. The premise was that children's imagination should never be curtailed. Mr. McGarrity lets Maggie come around to the solution, lets the child develop her own cognitive skills. … John and Linda Keogh were the puppeteers, the only sensible puppeteers I have ever met. They were so much fun, but once the puppets were put away, they were gone. … We had good actors as Mr. McGarrity.[14]

After John Drainie left the show, Mavor Moore stepped in to fill the role, followed by Frank Peddie.

"Mary Grannan was very professional," Peggy continued. "She wore gorgeous hats and earrings; she was a big woman and played up on that with the big hats and so on. She had a wonderful naive quality and never lost that. She worked with sophisticated people and yet never forgot her roots."[15]

Joanne and Peggy outlined the steps in producing a show, which began when the script was received. The producer would review the script with the writer, or perhaps call a meeting only if there were questions.

"[Mary's scripts] were so good that we didn't have to meet much,"[16] Peggy said. "Her scripts did not need re-writing," Joanne said. "There were cuts for length only."[17]

The producer would then plot out the work to be done — the set, the puppets, etc. "The Keoghs were so creative that they came up with good ideas," Peggy said. "It was so exciting to start with a germ of an idea — the script — and then everyone would add to it. It became so creative."[18]

At the production meeting, usually held ten days before the broadcast, the producer would meet with the script assistant, the technical director, and sometimes the sound person, the properties people, and the set designer as well. The standard sets for *Maggie* were Mr. McGarrity's garden and the treehouse.

"We would get the tail end of the set designers,"[19] Joanne said.

For the props on the set, the producer had to differentiate between those for the people and those for the puppets.

"One time," Peggy said, "we ordered puppet-sized furniture and the stage hand brought in doll furniture that was too big."[20] It was so close to production time when this was discovered that the stage hand was sent off in a hurry, but he did manage to bring back something appropriate in time.

From the second season on, the rehearsal was held in the studio on the day of production. There was a walk-through, a dress rehearsal with the cameras and all scenery, and then the show was done "live to kinescope." The location of the studio was changed a lot because children's features were not top priority and could not generate revenue.

Mary was not always present on the set but came whenever she could, sitting in the gallery to watch the rehearsal and production without interfering.

"Once an author has produced a script," Peggy said, "it is difficult to have it taken away. It's difficult not to be there."[21]

Peggy also produced a Christmas special for Mary in December 1955, *A Gift for the Princess*, with actor Frank Peddie and young actress Deanne Taylor in the role of the princess. To express her thanks, Mary gave Peggy a *Webster Biographical Dictionary* as a gift, inscribing it, "To Peggy for her assiduous and creative efforts in producing my 'A Gift for the Princess' December 1955."[22]

Deanne Taylor's role in this production brought her talents to Mary's attention. As Beth Morris outgrew the role of Maggie, Deanne was selected to step in to replace her.

In the following letter written during the first television season of *Maggie Muggins*, Mary provided more detail about what was going on behind the scenes:

[Winter 1955]

Dear Girls ... Sunday at five. [...] I didn't see Maggie Muggins on Friday ... went to get my poor permanent fixed [...] When I went over to TV that evening to watch next week's kinescope, I heard that five o'clock came and the film hadn't been found ... They finally got it on and played HALF of it ... then it was cut off for next show. That makes me mad ... they're so slipshod ... not at all like Radio ... Imagine watching a show and then BANG ... it's off ... another on. It's unforgivable to me, but I don't know who's responsible ... In radio it is the producer's job to check and see everything is in order for a recorded show. I read in paper John Drainie is thinking of going to NYC to live. If so ... what about our McGarrity. If he is, he knew when he took on the series, but people in this business are not honorable ... unless forced by contract. [...] I was also mad ... I heard some of them talking ... somebody asked how long series was going to run ... one said 13 weeks? Another said oh no, I happen to know 23 which will bring it to first of July ... Joanne Hughes says "It may run all summer" This, as if the scripts came out of bureau drawer. I'm going to tell Rainsberry it would be nice if the AUTHOR knew how long it was going to run.

Had a note from Toddy and a clipping from another paper. I must write to her ... still haven't answered Mary Jane or Noel ... can't seem to get letters written... I did write to the newspaper at home, Hel ... said you'd sent me the copy ... told them that my hometown paper meant a bigger thrill than any other place I found my name ... that all I was in Radio or TV was due to Stewart Neill, whose foresight and understanding had made it all possible. I hope someone there tells him. [...]

Toddy seems to like Maggie Muggins ... They made a new mouse house which is very cute. Amazing but I'm writing right to TIME [i.e., script is correct length] ... I seem to have a lot of natural instincts, don't I. Nobody taught me to write ... and nobody taught us to draw. [...]

I'm going to Henri's on Sunday and do I ever despise it [...] Henri decides the time you go and the time you leave ... and it's a bore all the way to me. Wish we were putting the last book on the shelves ... God give us health to see it all through and to settle down for some happiness together.

Love, Mary

MONDAY It's 7AM ... and raining. I just thought I'd finish this off before I start to write. I'm going to a rehearsal this morning, and TV rehearsals are away out east. Joanne Hughes is not doing it today ... she's being replaced by a fellow. He called me last night, so I won't get a drive out. I am sticking to going to the first rehearsal ... keeping my finger in. I had the puppeteers over for tea Friday night ... made sandwiches in the morning. So it wasn't too bad [...]

Wrote a note to Toddy. Had a letter from Capital Press [Fredericton]. They say "It was such a nice tribute to Mr. Stewart Neill, that we are taking the liberty of running it as 'a letter to the editor.' We trust you <u>will</u> not object." Hope Stewart will be pleased. The crow puppet is wonderful. They dyed feathers black. It's covered all over [illustration of crow] Got a top hat — eyes move. I didn't get any scripting done today & I feel I'm getting behind when I don't write.

Love, Mary[23]

234

Cupboard Love and Paper Romance

Finally, Mary had made the successful leap to television, while contin-uing her radio perennial, *Just Mary*. More positive developments arrived in 1956 when she published her first full-length children's nov-els, *Kim and Katy: Their Summer Holiday* and *Kim and Katy: Circus Days*, based on her radio scripts *The Cotton Sprouts*. As well, she began to do occasional scripts for school telecasts, such as the April 1956 one called *How Does Your Garden Grow?* However, she was not pleased when Richard Lambert, head of school broadcasting, made unwelcome changes to her scripts:

> In the school broadcast, the actor was saying plant bean one inch … I whispered to Monty Fotheringham … the one for whom I did script. He's got that wrong … I had FOUR INCHES … he said … I know but Mr Lambert didn't agree with that … I said but I took it out of a book on Vegetable gardening … Well Mr Lambert did-n't agree. I said Mr Lambert COULD be wrong, you know … he said "Oh do you think so?" I asked one of the men from farm broadcast … he measures about four inches with hand … I said how about an inch … Oh, first rain, a heavy seed like a bean would be washed right out. … Can you beat it … Mr. Lambert didn't agree! He didn't agree earlier that leaves were storehouse of food for the seed, either … although I called up and read it out of a science reader.[24]

Because of her years of experience, she was sometimes critical and impatient with what she saw as sloppy work, venting her frustra-tions in letters.

> I wonder if you heard the show yesterday and HOW it sounded. I didn't hear it … and this is the reason. It was a half hour show. It was timed perfectly for that time, and when our time came up the NBC opera

235

announcer was still spouting. It's courtesy show or something and you have to wait till it's over … We didn't know how much he was going to run over … he went FIVE minutes all but about three secs. Imagine the consternation … If I hadn't been there, it couldn't have been fixed … but quick like a flash and with really superlative thinking for an emergency … I began to hack … I cut scenes out of the last half … took the pages into the studio and with the poor actors still on the air … lined the cut pages up on organ where they came to look for them … then hunt through their scripts … cut … rush back to mike … It sure was something. Fred [not Rainsberry] had come over for the show and he saw one of the greatest crises ever. Young Dan who was producing it said if I hadn't been there, he just couldn't have gotten through … I knew the script so well, and thank goodness I got it cut so that it sounded OK … IF we'd had forewarning what was going to happen I could have cut the gimmick off the front but we didn't know when Milton Gross was going to shut his damn mouth.[25]

Small annoyances aside, all appeared to be going well in her work with the breakthrough into television. Nevertheless, her regular letters home to her sisters were infused with a sense of loneliness: "Saturday afternoon … wet and lonesome … I seem to be wasting time … but I don't know what I want to do, except maybe speak to somebody I guess I'm getting impatient for your coming … and the minute you step OFF the train, I'll be begrudging the passing of the days."[26]

Other than occasional movies, theatre outings, dinners, and parties, Mary's social life largely consisted of meals and evenings of television shared with her apartment neighbours and girlfriends — "all cupboard love,"[27] Mary called it. She and the girls liked watching the shows and even the wrestling, watching it "till last full nelson was full nelsoned."[28]

Sometimes others' happiness left her feeling lonelier:

> Grace [Athersich] is going to Maxine Miller's wedding
> today …. she went to Europe with Grace. […] Peggy
> Brown … an actress here … and a lovely girl … col-
> lege grad … smart dresser, went to Europe in May last
> year … met an Englishman on the boat … He came
> here to see her … now she's engaged and is going to be
> married in November … give up acting and live in
> England. He's a motor sales manager or something.
> The only romance I have is on paper.[29]

While paper romance could refer to anything from reading romance novels to her own fairy tale writings, it might also have referred to the continuing fond letters from Noel Langley. In missives full of his own brand of humour with his strange salutations, such as, "Dear Countess Rockbottom,"[30] or "Dear Mary Mother of Boston Cod,"[31] he poured out his complaints about life, while still nagging her for the earlier loss of royalties. He moved to the United States around 1955, looking for work in the film industry, but still issued an open invitation for her to visit. But their relationship, in spite of the fondness, was friendship only.

During the late fifties, there was a particular marriage announcement that upset Mary. In 1957, twenty-year-old Beryl Braithwaite (the first Maggie), after returning the previous fall from her acting studies in Britain, took a three-day role on an episode of the television series *The Last of the Mohicans* that was being filmed in Ontario. Within two weeks of meeting the show's star on the set, Beryl married John Hart, twenty years her senior. The newspaper photograph of the pair on their wedding day featured the caption, "Maggie Muggins Weds Lone Ranger,"[32] as that was one of the acting roles Hart had played. In public, Mary often playfully quoted that catchy phrase, but in private, she disapproved of the large age difference between them.

"When I met John, I went to tell Mary, and she was just appalled; she was so upset," Beryl said. "After John and I were married, we were only in Toronto about another six weeks. We met Mary and a friend coming out of the Odeon Theatre. … I went rushing up to her to introduce her to John, and she simply looked right through him. She would not acknowledge that he was there. ... But I sent her Christmas cards every year and she never answered."[33] Beryl and John Hart, however, have the last word on the wisdom of their choice, for they have had a long, happy marriage together.

Although her workload was heavy, Mary did make some time in the fifties for her hobby of painting, turning out a few works to decorate her apartment walls. After practising portrait painting with a variety of famous faces, including that of Princess Elizabeth, she painted a portrait of actress Alice Hill, drawing the likeness from a photograph. "At least Alice and all her friends recognized whom it was supposed to be — without prompting, either,"[34] she was quoted as saying in the *CBC Times*. Mary submitted it to Simpson's Homemakers' Show, where it was accepted for display in the Amateurs' Art Gallery in January 1952.

Aware that retirement was only a few years away, she was reluctant to spend too much money fixing up her Toronto apartment, while she and her sisters were doing what they could to repair and upgrade their shared Fredericton home. Mary expressed the frequent wish that the sisters should stay healthy so they could enjoy happiness together during retirement. Occasionally her letters contained happy reminiscences of earlier days and sometimes a less happy memory of their blustery mother. "I'd be able to get my pension now, if I'd stayed with [teaching] ... twenty years teaching ... fifteen here ... how life has flown away from me ... seems like last year that I was dragging home at 3 PM expecting a blast the minute I opened the door and nine times out of ten, getting it ... and for what, I don't know .... just for being, I guess."[35]

Mary was a mixture of daring and timidity — plucky enough to try writing for television, but too frightened to travel by airplane. She warded off disasters through "blessed candles and a crucifix over my door."[36] Although she was a sophisticated public personality, she was still at heart a small-town girl.

With so much time spent alone writing, Mary's visits to the studios for work and to observe the *Maggie* productions must have had an important social function in her life.

Deanne Taylor Becomes the Next Maggie

When the auditions were underway to select the next young actress for the role of Maggie, Mary was in attendance as usual but happened to catch herself on camera at one of the readings. She told her sisters of her reaction, which was likely something no one else at the audition could possibly have imagined that Mary was thinking, especially the young girls who looked up to her with such admiration.

> [Friday, September 28, 1956]
> Dear Girls
> [...] This week has been a series of reading with kids ... we're ending up with the one who was the princess at Xmas ... she's a nice little thing ... rather studied in personality but we sure read a lot of them. Tuesday I was on camera with two of them reading. GOD I looked awful ... came home real depressed ... Had my best hat on ... my Montreal hat ... but looked like this ... [sketch] Of course as an alibi ... I had no makeup on ... but it was the shape of me. Looked like Muriel. Oh well ... guess if I KEEP well, as my grandfather says ... it don't matter a damn how you look if you feel well. I'd asked Grace over to see the reception on new aerial ... Peggy asked me to go read so I took Grace. She got a bang out of it I think. [...]
> Love Mary[37]

When Deanne Taylor stepped into the role of Maggie Muggins at the age of ten, she felt that she had entered a wonderful world. Experiencing a brief spell of nerves when she was selected for the final cut of those vying for the role, she burst into tears in Beth Morris's living room when her parents took her to meet the previous Maggie. But Deanne's anxiety quickly passed and she sailed through the final audition to become the new Maggie.

"It was just the most fun any kid could have to go play act with very intelligent, witty, kind, clever grown-ups, who were kind of child-like themselves," Deanne said. Given the script a week in advance, Deanne always arrived on the set with her lines fully committed to memory.

> I used to get my new script for the following week, and I could learn it knowing there would be no huge changes. That's how good [Mary's] scripts were to begin with. We could rehearse and produce [the show] in a day, and then that was shrunk to half a day, from one o'clock until six. There'd be a read-through, a walk-through, a dress rehearsal, and a taping of a fifteen-minute show. In between each of those there would be notes, and revisions to the plan usually, but not to the script. ... The first read-through would be rather genial and friendly, getting to see each other again after the week. I wanted to be on best behaviour and know all my lines. ... And then we would be up and active. I'd hear Mary's voice perhaps speaking a suggestion over the P.A. And, of course, I could make suggestions at that point if it would be useful. If I could help a puppet get on stage or get dressed, or pick up a prop, or be helpful as one member of an ensemble, then I would start to be able to contribute.
>
> Between the dress rehearsal and the show, I'd go have a snack and ... then lie down. The cast would have a coffee or whatever they were drinking at three-thirty and four in the afternoon. ... I would go to the Greek restaurant at the old Jarvis brownstone downstairs, and the grown-ups would go across the street to that quite well-known club where all the CBC gang went.

For a wide-eyed, eager young child, the exhilaration of closely observing and working with these fascinating adults was intense and left a lasting impression. "All those women told me to stay away from show business, and get my university education because there was no glamour and no glory and no money whatsoever — there were no mink coats and Cadillacs for little Canadian child stars, or even grown-up

Mary in her CBC office on Jarvis Street, circa early 1950s.

John Drainie as Mr. McGarrity and Beth Morris as Maggie Muggins with Fitzgerald Fieldmouse and Grandmother Frog puppets, in the first year of the *Maggie Muggins* television show, 1955.

Beth Morris as Maggie Muggins with the second Maggie Muggins doll by Reliable Toy, 1955.

Deanne Taylor as Maggie Muggins with Fitzgerald Fieldmouse and Grandmother Frog puppets, circa 1956.

Deanne Taylor as Maggie Muggins and Frank Peddie as Mr. McGarrity, circa 1956.

"JUST MARY"

AUTOGRAPH PARTY 1957

MARY GRANNAN

Mary Grannan, "Just Mary," Autograph Party, 1957.
Sketch by J. Frank Willis.

Mary Grannan in her apartment on Breadalbane Street, 1958.

Mary Grannan in front of her apartment building on Breadalbane Street, Toronto, 1958.

From left: F.D. (Dud) Allen (President of Thomas Allen Limited), Mary Grannan, Deanne Taylor, and Robert B. Pennington, Jr. (President of Pennington Press), at the Chicago launch of the *Maggie Muggins* books by Pennington Press, March 1959.

Mary Long as Maggie Muggins holding a toy bear in a scene from the show with puppets Fitzgerald Fieldmouse, Benny Bear, and Reuben Rabbit.

Doug Master as Mr. McGarrity, Mary Long as Maggie Muggins, and Winnifred Dennis as Miss Merryweather, the toy shop owner, circa 1961.

Mary Long as Maggie Muggins with Fitzgerald Fieldmouse, circa 1959.

Mary Grannan's retirement party, February 26, 1960. From left: Lois Pope, George Taggart, J. Frank Willis, Mary Grannan, Sydney Brown, Henri Edey, Grace Athersich, DeB. Holly, and A.J. Black.

From left: Ruth Springford, Alice Hill, Linda and John Keogh, and Mary Grannan exchange teasing glances at Mary's retirement party, February 26, 1960.

Mary with a puppet from the *Just Mary* television show episode "The Chinese Bracelet," 1960.

Mary at the end of her career, 1962.

Mary at her typewriter on the kitchen table, Breadalbane Street, 1962.

Photo by John Reeves

Mary, Toronto, 1962.

From left: Helen, Mary, and Ann at their Fredericton home circa late 1950s. Mary wrote on photo, "Back yard, Three of us."

flashback

Mary Grannan with Paul Soles on the CBC television show *Flashback*, April 1963.

Portrait of Alice Hill by Mary Grannan, 1952.

Beautifully Designed
and always in the best of taste,

We've lately heard rumours
That you're stealing bloomers
To wear as a scarf
That gives us a larf
We suggest in this letter
That an ascot is better.

A card Mary designed for Donald Roberts, circa 1960s.

stars. On the other hand, while they were saying this, I noticed that they were laughing and joking and having a ball; it didn't escape me."

The author of the show made a singularly deep impression on young Deanne:

[Mary Grannan] was a real sparkler. I remember a glow, a fire in the eyes, a light in the eyes, and wonderful smile, and the kind of face you wanted to have turned on you with approval. And this is a child speaking. Whom do you look up to? Whose approval and benef- icence do you want to conjure? And I was so proud. I remember being incredibly proud that she liked me, and approved of what I was doing with *her* work. Because that's what an actor craves. … you are carrying someone else's words and work and soul and guts and heart. So, the author's approval means everything to you — more than the director's. It means everything to you that the author is fond of you and smiles when she looks at you. And she was absolutely great to me.

I think of the dressing room times more than the work times because in the work times, we were all in our separate areas. … So, the times I remember Mary are really in the dressing room with the girls [Margo Christie, Ruth Springford, Alice Hill]. … We had these four women regularly, the costume wardrobe woman, the female directors, [and] my mom. And it was a gas, the most fun you can have as a child, to be a child that adults are not trying to get rid of, in a room full of really wonderful, witty, mature women — all artists, all with stories and anecdotes of the show busi- ness, and gossip and dish on this person and that per- son, and lots of rolling eyebrows and lots of covering it up for me, making sure that their language was not being completely penetrated by me. … But Mary was the glowing centre of all of that. …You'd think [that between the] actresses and an author, the author

would be one of the more reserved, but she was a performing writer.

[Mary] was extravagant, and her voice was good,
her way of delivering up a line. She could tell jokes, she
could crack wise, she could tell anecdotes. Her laugh
was great — that beam. I would say that actually she
was the most radiant one of all those gals. … Mary …
[was] the most chic, really — the slave bracelets, the
fabulous four-inch earrings, the tall turbans of many
shapes, many, many decorations, coupled with these
wonderful suits, waisted suits with darts and sewing,
with breasts in them, and waists in them, and hips in
them — a woman's suit, very business like and feminine
at the same time. Great legs, as I recall, and high heels
… Painted nails, painted lipstick, eye makeup, I bet.
She was the picture of stylish grooming all the time.

As well as being fond of Mary and the others associated with the
show, Deanne demonstrated a deep affection for the *Maggie Muggins*
stories and their characters.

People might say, "Oh, it's just L.M. Montgomery
again, another red-haired, freckled, pigtailed
orphan." But the Maggie Muggins stories are completely unique — the meadow stories, the Aesop's
Fables, the talking animals, the Greek roots of it all,
the metamorphoses, the moral crisis, the resolutions,
the use of the adult to be a sounding board for the
child. And the form — the three visits to McGarrity
and the two visits to the meadow is a form, something [Mary] invented, and then could fill with the
writing. She didn't have to reinvent it every week. …
The meadow disasters were [usually the result of]
Fitzgerald's arrogance or shortcut style. He's the
quick, clever one who thinks maybe he could cheat,
maybe he could steal, maybe he could nick a carrot

from the farmer, or fool somebody somehow. Reuben was more of a fearful sinner. Reuben lied because he wasn't brave enough to tell the truth, or stole by accident because he wasn't clever enough to figure out it belonged to someone else, or was then afraid to return it or own up. They all had their own ways of messing up. … And somewhere in there, before the disaster occurred — the sin, the evil — they would be off for some innocent sport, like a play with a theme, or a game, an adventure. Those meadow activities were each really well defined. Sometimes I had costumes, dances, songs to carry the theme of the day — a circus, or dance, or some historical character. … The scripts were incredibly well structured to hand out riches, like ideas about hobbies and crafts and skills from Mr. McGarrity, ideas for play from whatever Fitzgerald and Grandmother Frog and the animals were cooking up for the day's delights. The little moral upshot was just the result of all of that. It's wonderful stuff.[38]

During the first two years that Deanne acted on the *Maggie* show, she was accompanied by her mother, Violet Taylor (later Armstrong). Finding herself among a group of actors familiar to her from years of listening to CBC Radio, Vi was pleased with their warm reception, frequently joining them during the break between dress rehearsal and broadcast. On the set, Vi remained quietly in the background in the small area off-camera where the actors performed the voices of the puppets and music director Lou Snider played the theme, various songs, and sound effects. She remembered Mary coming to the studio to watch the production from the control room.

Mary Grannan was a large presence. You knew when she had entered the room. She was a large, tall woman with large jewellery and hats and well dressed. She had a theatrical presence with dramatic gestures. …

243

The veteran actors who were the voices of the puppets enjoyed a kind of earthy humour, which Mary shared ... but Mary was very sensitive to and protective of her message. She believed children should be allowed to be children and that fantasy was important — no adult innuendo was allowed to creep into the dialogue and her message.[39]

Mary related her thoughts about Deanne in the role of Maggie in a letter to Helen and Ann on October 28, 1956:

I'm glad you like the new child in Maggie ... she's working hard and loves it. The rabbit was in a kiney [kinescope] we made for filing in case anyone took sick. She told me that she knew she SHOULD like Fitz best but she loved the rabbit better. She had a crying scene in the show and she cried ... Bob Christie wiped her eyes. She did a terrific scene.[40]

"The True Princess"

The following television script for "The True Princess" episode from May 1958 demonstrates the evolution of the *Maggie Muggins* stories. Also evident are the production instructions required for television, which were different from radio script requirements. Mary adapted to the changes quickly.

MAGGIE MUGGINS	KINE: MAY 16/58
SCRIPT GRANNAN	T/CAST: MAY 22/58
MUSIC SNIDER	NET: CBLT
PRODUCTION [RENA] ELMER	TIME: 5.00–5.15

MUSIC UNDER
OPEN ON TOOL SHED. MR. MCGARRITY IS CUTTING THE PAPER STRAPPING ON A MEDIUM

SIZED BOX ... A CARTON TYPE. INSIDE THERE IS A PENCIL SHARPENER WHICH HE WILL SCREW TO EDGE OF COUNTER IN HIS SECOND SCENE.

MCGAR: (LOOKS UP) ... Maggie Muggins is fun and she has freckles on her nose and it's turned up and she has two pigtails the color of brand new carrots and she has a friend named Mr. McGarrity. That's me. I garden here in my garden and on days when Maggie can't think of a thing to do, I always think of something ... I'll never forget the day that ... Oh here comes Maggie Muggins now.

MAGGIE: (ENTER ... SHE IS CARRYING TWO DOLL'S MATTRESSES AND AN "EIDERDOWN" ... THESE WILL BE MADE TO FIT THE DOLL BED IN MEADOW SET ... SEVERAL MAT-TRESSES ARE NEEDED TO PILE UP THE BED FOR THE STORY OF "THE TRUE PRINCESS")

MAGGIE: [Tra] la la la la la la lee Here comes Maggie Muggins me ... and I'm coming la lipperty larrety, to say hello to Mr. McGarrity ...

MCGAR: Hello yourself, Maggie Muggins .... You can't guess what I have in here ... (POINT TO BOX)

MAGGIE: (LAUGH) Tra la la la la la lee I think it's something nice for me ...

245

MCGAR: (TAKE OUT SHARPENER) Sorry to disappoint you ... But it's something nice for me ...

MAGGIE: Oh ... it's a pencil sharpener ... That is something nice for you.

MCGAR: Yes, but right now I'm more interested in why you're carrying all that bedding. That's off your doll's bed, isn't it.

MAGGIE: Yes sir ... Fitzgerald Fieldmouse has written another play ... "The True Princess" ... do you know it Sir ...

MCGAR: Yes ... yes ... I know it well. It's the story where the [queen] wants her son to wed a true [princess] and they test her royalty by [putting] twenty mattresses and twenty eiderdowns on the bed and between the bottom mattresses they put one little green pea.

MAGGIE: Yes, Mr. McGarrity, are the peas ripe in your garden?

MCGAR: Well now I'm doubtful ... but you might find one little green pea in a pod for your play ... You're welcome to take a look ...

MAGGIE: Thank you Sir ... I'd better be going. I have to put these on the bed and then go to Fitzgerald's house.

MCGAR: Goodbye ... I hope you have a successful play ...

MAGGIE: (EXIT) Thank you sir …

As the play got underway, with Grandmother Frog as the queen, Fitzgerald Fieldmouse as the prince, and Reuben Rabbit as the princess, everything came to a halt when the bedroom chamber scene was found in disarray, mattresses strewn around, and Princess Reuben Rabbit missing. With Mr. McGarrity's help, Maggie realized that her mistake was placing a baby carrot under the mattresses when she couldn't find a ripe pea pod. Reuben, being a rabbit, had sniffed out the carrot, knocked over the mattresses to get at it, and then gone to nearby Farmer Feather's carrot patch to eat more. Maggie and friends rescued Reuben from the farmer after promising that Reuben would stay out of his field. Maggie returned to Mr. McGarrity to wrap up the story.

MCGAR: (SITS ON PATIO … LOOKS UP … CALL) Take your time Maggie … take your time … Whoops … Fell eh? That's what you get for not looking where you're going.

MAGGIE: (ENTER BRUSHING APRON … APRON) Yes sir, but I'm all right, because Farmer Feather gave Reuben back to me.

MCGAR: I thought he would, and all in all Maggie, you've had quite a day.

MAGGIE: Yes, because tra la la la la leather, Reuben got caught by Farmer Feather … I don't know what will happen tomorrow…

EXIT[41]

Chapter Thirteen
Many Books but No Cartoons,
1956-1960

Rainsberry's Proposal

Impressed with her scriptwriting abilities, Fred Rainsberry approached Mary with a proposal in the spring of 1956. She, however, was uncertain what to do.

> [April 1956]
> Dear Girls […] [Rainsberry] really put a proposition up to me, and I am supposed to keep it confidential, and I wish I had someone to talk it over with. This gist of it is, that he'd like me to go to TV as script editor to rewrite scripts that come in with good ideas, but poor showmanship … to be sort of an educational guide to script writers. etc. I asked him if afternoons would be enough of my time … It wouldn't. He said that if I considered it, he'd talk the matter over with Jack Dunlop and then Mutrie who heads TV and so on … I said if it would mean resigning from radio, I wouldn't, as I had my pension to consider … that I would not at this stage, take over contract work … He

said I'd still be staff … I said that I'd not give up Just
Mary … I said it was my outlet creatively … but really it's my royalties … I somehow don't think, I may be
wrong of course, that they'll stop Just Mary now, before
I'm through here. He asked me if giving up Jubilee
Road would mean much to me … It really wouldn't,
but I don't know what to do. It's sure something to
have him recognize in me, that ability to be able to put
my finger on what's wrong with a script … that he sees
I KNOW enough to do it … I'd love to be able to do
this job … He'd want me moved over to the TV building … God, I'm a scaredy-cat about things … I never
know what to do. I don't know if I'd like to edit other
scripts … I prefer to write my own … He said that it
was such a joy for a producer to get a practical script
like mine … that would lift off the paper and work. If
I had SOMEBODY to talk to … If Henri were here, I
could trust her, and she's level headed. I don't believe
I'd have the freedom I'd have now … it would be more
binding. Anyway. right now, I'm sort of confused about
it. I think I'll send a buck to Fr. Brown … If he'd said
afternoons would be enough time, I'd have taken a
crack at it, but as it is, I'll have to think and probably
will dream tonight of scripts and scripts and scripts I
was thinking the other day, that LITTLE WOMEN
would make a good TV show, and bought a soft covered edition. You know it's as prudish as it can be, but
of course that could be cut from it. He liked the idea
… said he liked Emily of New Moon … I forget it, but
I think I'll get a copy and read it. He remembers having it read aloud to him in elementary school days. I
completely forget Emily.[1]

Three years later, Rainsberry finally accomplished his plan for
Mary, transferring her in April 1959 to the National Children's
Department under his supervision in a special position created for her,

"Program Organizer H-I." He was highly complimentary in his report requesting the reclassification:

> I have been associated with Miss Grannan in the pro-
> duction of the television show MAGGIE MUGGINS
> and two or three other children's "spectaculars" which
> she has written for me. As you are no doubt aware,
> Miss Grannan has recognized skill as a writer of televi-
> sion scripts. She has co-operated successfully with the
> television producers and has made very significant
> contributions to our schedule. MAGGIE MUGGINS
> is one of the best children's programs for the age group
> 4 to 8 available anywhere in North America.
>
> In addition to the artistic endeavor and excellent
> co-operation given to the television service, Miss
> Grannan has repeatedly been able to meet emergen-
> cies in the radio schedule. The reputation which she
> has built up as a writer of children's broadcasts is a dis-
> tinct asset to our enterprise.[2]

While continuing her regular programs, *Just Mary* on radio and *Maggie Muggins* on television, as well as seasonal specials, Mary's new duties involved participating in program development in radio and television, evaluating scripts, interviewing personnel and talent for children's programs, and evaluating films. In the job description for her new position, Mary cited writing a total of ninety-nine shows the previous year. Certainly, she regularly accomplished a substantial amount of work, receiving genuine recognition from Rainsberry.

The Children's Department

By acknowledging her skills and bringing her into a higher position, Fred Rainsberry greatly influenced the last part of Mary's career in the children's department. Under his guidance, policy and programming began to evolve, shaped by his background in education and philosophy. Moreover, he had a congenial approach to the people with whom he worked.

"[Rainsberry] was just a very solid person," said John Twomey, who worked for years under Rainsberry as assistant national supervisor of Schools and Youth Programming, "and he knew that to get the best out of creative people, you support them. You bring them in and you communicate."[3]

The gentle, intelligent nature of Rainsberry's character was also described by Joyce Le Maitre Bradshaw, who arrived in Toronto from Guernsey in 1957 at the age of nineteen and quickly found employment as Rainsberry's secretary:

> Dr Rainsberry ... was a real darling. It was a privilege and a thrill for me to work as his secretary. ... I am sure Fred gave me the job because he originally came from Sarnia, Ontario. Sarnia being the old name for Guernsey and many Guernsey folk settled in Sarnia so it was his little in "joke" that we both came from the same place! He was your typical absent minded professor and had I been older and wiser I probably could have helped him more. He would always remember to check that I was living "properly and having decent meals" and seeing that I was apportioning my money to good effect![4]

When Joyce arrived in the department in 1957, CBC Television and the children's department were five years old. While still having much to learn about television, Rainsberry was intent on developing policies to produce children's programming that was worthwhile, beneficial, and would do no harm.

Joyce continued:

> Fred Rainsberry was a caring, sincere, well educated man whose experience prior to coming to Children's television was as an educationalist and he brought these skills with him, knowing little about television

and the technical side of the business. He was often the butt of good natured jokes about this fact when the department viewed and dissected our own programmes because he could not understand camera angles, etc. It was an important quality at a critical time [one can see] with hindsight and hence one can see that having Mary Grannan within his sights on the same floor of the building presented just a small step to including her and her writings in programming. The content of everything that went out from that department was well researched, decent and considered. … Of all sections producing programming within CBC at that time, Children's had the most viewing hours to fill as we had a two hour slot each day (4-6 p.m.) plus a 2 or 3 hour slot on Saturday morning (Junior Magazine).[5]

Part of Rainsberry's work involved speaking to various organizations concerned with children's television. As well, he organized many conferences with American television stations on the topic of the effect of television on children. Joyce wrote:

There was such a lot of concern about the effects that TV might have on children and no experience to go on, and I can remember it as being the guiding aspect in all programming. Research into any effects on behaviour from watching TV were sought and investigated and ideas like how and why can children accept cowboys and Indians at the movies but could be upset by Snow White and the wicked witch on television were the order of the day. …

During the first year I worked for him when he was Supervising Producer I guess the development of the department, staffing and programming ideas were the most important to Fred but it soon became clear, once he moved up a notch to take on responsibility for TV first in Ontario and then across Canada, that the effects

TV was having on children was a major concern to all
— both the programme makers and the viewing public.[6]

By 1965, Rainsberry had developed the philosophy and policy into a written document called *Children and TV: The Moral Concern*. However, his concerns for children's television extended further to include his view that those involved in the department should be truly interested in being there and that children were an important audience.

"A lot of interesting people come and say, 'Well, I really want to [do something else, but] they tell me this is a good place to start,'" John Twomey said. "But Rainsberry said, 'We wanted people committed to this thing. They're not going to move through.' In fact, one of my colleagues said at a meeting, he said, 'Fred, I'll give you a couple of good years, but I want my credit on the air at six o'clock. That's prime time, that's people. These are just kids.' And Fred kept saying, 'Yeah, but these kids are so important.'"[7]

Joyce also recalled the excitement of the early years in the department. When Rainsberry's duties expanded to include school broadcasting and children's radio, she took on more work.

> By this time Stan Cox and I could run the programme scheduling and other aspects of keeping the office ticking and it really was an exciting time. ... CBC had numerous locations and addresses around the city and the great aim then was to one day get into one building. The [crises] we have had when the wrong film was found to be in the can and I have actually dashed off in a CBC car from Jarvis to a street down at the Lakefront where the film library was whilst the programme was running to collect the right one — it was very much flying by the seat of your pants in those days. On another occasion smoke couldn't be created for a scene because in rehearsal it was a quick dash to the ladies loo to get water to pour on dry ice — the loo was occupied and locked at the time of the actual broadcast![8]

Near Joyce's office in the Jarvis Street building was the office of Mary Grannan, whom Joyce found to be "a very kind sweet person with a warm personality — well endowed with wispy hair."[9] Mary was curious about Guernsey.

> She showed a great deal of interest in that I lived in Guernsey, in the Channel Islands and I frequently wandered down the hall to have little chats. By December 1957 my girlfriend and I had made many friends and were invited by one male friend's mother to spend Christmas. No sooner had we accepted this invitation than Mary Grannan asked me what my friend and I were doing for Christmas as we would be welcome to spend Christmas Day with her. Unfortunately my girlfriend wasn't keen on the idea, not having met Mary, and felt it was not etiquette to cancel our first acceptance so I have now spent many years celebrating Christmas Day with the lady who became my mother-in-law when I could, just once, have spent it with Mary Grannan![10]

The Rustler and the Reindeer

On Christmas Day, 1957, the CBC presented a special for children based on a Christmas story that Mary had published in *Maclean's* magazine on December 15, 1954, "The Rustler and the Reindeer." Although she had had other stories successfully turned into television productions, such as *The Jewels of Fermanagh* in 1956, the production in 1957 did not please her, as she later described in a letter to Georgina Murray Keddell. The passage highlights Mary's disenchantment with the changing culture of the CBC as television emerged and developed:

> When TV came, a different breed arrived. I got on fine with those who produced my shows. They let me

sit in the control room — no other author was allowed. But as time went on the new people got "new dimensions." For example — I dramatized a Christmas story I had written for "Macleans" called "The rustler & the reindeer." The script was assigned to a producer in June — we went over it together. Everything worked & he loved it. But that summer he left and another fellow got it. He put another writer on to make changes. When I saw it, I said "Take my name off it." Dr. Rainsberry who was then head of children's TV came over to my apt. to talk to me about it. The little boy in the story was out to get a Xmas tree, came to a red gate he'd never seen before, a little rabbit beckoned him — he climbed gate, then the rabbit could talk — said Chris Stocking, foreman of Santa's ranch was in a bad way. Someone had rustled the reindeer — it was the polar bear who had perpetrated the evil. He wanted to drive Santa. He had hidden the reindeer behind snow banks. What I wrote in for the scene was to have 8 sets of horns on springs so they could move up & down. The audience could see antlers & know reindeer were there behind snow. The new writer hired eight dancing girls, bare bodies except bra & G-strings (sparkling) with antlers on their heads. I said "It's a show for children. They will see real reindeer behind the snow." Then Rainsberry said, "But Mary — you don't understand. This is a new dimension." I said, "Naked girls do not look like reindeer to children" But they put it on with the new dimension, & they put my <u>name</u> on it, and I sat Christmas day, with Ann & Helen & <u>cried</u> as I watched it. I'd even sent to University of Oklahoma for a "Book of Western Words." The colorful expressions were cut from "Chris Stockings" speeches. "The Telegram" panned it, saying I was not up to standard or something. After Xmas I said to Rainsberry, "What did you think of the show?" He said "It was a $20,000 mistake" And later Cliff Braggins, the fellow who rewrote my script, came to me and said, "Did you see the Xmas abortion? I told the producer I didn't write for children like you did — but he wanted to turn the story into a musical and it was money for me, so I did it." That's just one example — Boy! the money they wasted.[11]

The Rustler and the Reindeer, presented as "a Christmas fantasy based on a story by Mary E. Grannan,"[12] was produced by John Kennedy, featuring Barbara Hamilton as Aunt Minnie and Deanne Taylor as the elf. The dancing reindeer appeared in the form of four men and four women, who were not naked but dressed in black body tights with little skirts or shorts and antlers on their heads. Certainly by later standards, the production appeared to be poor overall, lacking sufficient rehearsal. Above all, it did not meet Mary's standards. Perhaps it was just as well that Joyce Le Maitre Bradshaw and her friend did not join Mary and her sisters that Christmas Day, for they would have witnessed the tears.

Michael Spivak Changes the Set

Considering all the positive comments Rainsberry made about *Maggie Muggins*, one might assume he never had any doubt about it through the years. However, there were apparently times when he considered making changes.

"Rainsberry wants me to devise a new idea," Mary wrote her sisters in May 1957. "He makes me tired. I still don't know if Maggie is going on or not He thinks there should be a change. Dunlop thinks when there's a good show it should stay put. I agree."[13]

However, the show was saved from replacement after Rainsberry succeeded in getting some satisfactory production changes made.

In the 1958–59 season, Michael Spivak followed Rena Elmer as producer of *Maggie Muggins*. After beginning work at the CBC as a stagehand, he was hired by Fred Rainsberry to be a research assistant in the children's department and became a producer the next year while still in his early twenties. *Maggie Muggins*, then starring Deanne Taylor and Frank Peddie, was his first production assignment.

"Rainsberry asked me to spruce the show up — it was a bit tired,"[14] Spivak said. With the energy and brashness of youth, he prepared to confront the writer and dictate changes, buoyed by the task of bringing fresh appeal to an old show.

"So, I had sixteen or seventeen changes and I phoned the writer. The name Mary Grannan didn't mean anything to me at the time. She answered the phone herself, and it was when I heard her voice — *that voice* — that I realized she was 'Just Mary' whose stories and voice I had heard on the radio as a child."[15]

Surprised to discover not a nameless writer but a storyteller he had heard and enjoyed for years, Spivak suddenly faced the unenviable chore of explaining changes to someone he admired. After a brief pause, Spivak plunged ahead undaunted with his suggestions. His main suggestion involved redesigning the set of Fitzgerald Fieldmouse's house. In the original set design, Maggie approached the mouse house set from the front, which required her to have to turn to face the camera. To Spivak, this created a sense of phoniness, as Maggie divided her time between facing the puppets and facing the camera. In the new design, Maggie approached the mouse house from the back of the set, so that she was always facing the camera, thus able to focus solely on the puppets and the story. This change also allowed for greater interaction between Maggie and the puppets.

Mary was somewhat reluctant, thinking the children might be confused by the changes. Convinced he had good reasons, Spivak suggested she could write an explanation for the change into the first script.

"She probably went off and talked to Rainsberry," he said. "To her credit, after the change of set was implemented, she said she approved."[16]

Whether or not Michael Spivak and Mary Grannan realized it, they were actually firmly in agreement on a basic principle. Mary called it honesty or sincerity in a story, while Spivak called it a dislike of phoniness or artificiality. It amounted to the same thing. So, it was not surprising that Mary liked the new mouse house set.

During that year on the show, Spivak also recalled the day that actor Frank Peddie did not show up for work. "I called him. Frank had just found out he had cancer. He said, 'I'll never work again, laddie,' in a soft Scottish burr. Robert Christie took over as Mr. McGarrity."

"*Maggie Muggins* was highly regarded," Spivak said, "but you have to remember that it was the 1950s. It was post-war, post Hitler, cold war time. It would work then and not now. Shows are always set in their cultural time. *Maggie* was a sweet show, but it wouldn't work today."[17]

Pinnacle in Publishing

Beyond the continuing Canadian editions of Mary's books, Dud Allen had been actively seeking markets elsewhere, bringing about an especially pleasing development in 1958 with her first British edition by Frederick Warne & Co., publishers of Beatrix Potter's books. Calling it simply *Just Mary Stories*, Warne selected a compilation from across Mary's published books, editing them for British children and supplying new illustrations by Jennetta Vise. The next year Warne published a second edited book, *More Just Mary Stories*.

The year 1959 marked the zenith of Mary's publishing years, for in addition to the second Warne book and a new Canadian one, *Maggie Muggins and the Fieldmouse*, Dud Allen had negotiated six new books for the American market with a sale to the recently established Pennington Press of Chicago, a division of Merrick Lithograph Company of Cleveland, Ohio.

Pennington designed a larger format book with a smaller number of stories, only three or four in each book rather than Allen's usual dozen. New illustrations were provided by Bernard Zalusky or Lonnie Stern. Along with Mary's books, Pennington also released a non-fiction science series, *Show Me the World* by Julian May, and several titles from another of Thomas Allen's children's library, *Dale of the Mounted* by Joe Holliday.

To launch the books, Pennington arranged for two publicity tours — Chicago in March and New York City in May. Along for the weekend promotional trips were Mary, Dud Allen, Deanne Taylor, and her mother, Violet. Arriving in Chicago on March 28, Mary was astonished to see a large billboard advertising her new books. When the women arrived at their hotel on Michigan Boulevard overlooking Grant Park and Lake Michigan, they found flowers waiting for "Maggie Muggins" with a note from Dud, "I don't know what I'll do tomorrow? Gramps Allen."[18]

An air of excitement surrounded the publicity tour, as Pennington had prepared a full promotional plan with coloured billboards and posters outside bus stops in Chicago, Cleveland, San Francisco, Los Angeles, and Boston. Dressed as Maggie, Deanne introduced the books at a book launch dinner while Mary, Dud, and Vi looked on. Appearances and press interviews followed over the few days of their visit, but the three women took time to see the movie *Auntie Mame* and the musical *The Music Man*, starring Forrest Tucker, at the Shubert Theatre. Of course, there had to be time for shopping. Both fond of hats, Mary and Vi went hat shopping at some of the large department stores. Seated in front of the mirrored vanity tables, they tried on various creations brought to them by the salesladies. It was luxurious shopping done in style — comfortably seated before a large mirror, accepting one hat after another, turning their heads this way and that to admire and assess if the bonnet was worthy of purchase.

During the visit to New York City, May 7 to 9, Deanne made a guest appearance on an ABC-TV children's television show, *Time for Fun*, modelled a line of girls' dresses for *New York Journal American*, and gave two press interviews, while Mary had a press interview published in the *New York World Telegram & Sun*. Once again, the women attended a live theatre production, this time seeing *West Side Story*, starring Carol Lawrence and Larry Kert.

"Mary left early," Vi said. "She said she couldn't take any more of the noise, but she wanted Deanne to stay and enjoy the show."[19] The trips to Chicago and New York allowed Vi to get to know Mary better. Underneath the grand and glamorous woman, Vi found someone who was serious about her writing and broadcasts, but in whom still lurked some of the small-town girl with her conservative leanings.

While the promotional book tours to Chicago and New York City were memorable, the book sales were not. Pennington optimistically had printed forty thousand copies of each of Mary's books, but the *Maggie Muggins* books never caught the public's attention in the United States as they had in Canada, where the popular broadcasts drove sales. The company eventually went out of the book business.

In a later letter to Deanne, Mary recalled the Chicago trip:

> I remembered how on Easter Sunday two years ago we hied away for our Chicago trip. The whole thing was too big. Mr. Pennington spent so much that he sort of folded in books. I was not happy with the Maggie books because by making it flat, they lowered the age level of it. No child over seven or eight would accept it, in my mind. It looked like a book for five and six and yet five and six couldn't read it. But I made some money and with no effort.[20]

Although there were plenty of publications by 1959 about which Mary could be happy, she was disappointed when Dud chose not to proceed with a fourth *Kim and Katy* book, for which she had prepared a full manuscript. After experiencing disappointing sales for the first three, Dud cancelled the series.

Thor Arngrim's Proposal

The success of *Maggie Muggins* gave Thor Arngrim an idea in 1959. Both he and his wife, Norma Macmillan, had worked on the show doing voices for puppets. After beginning theatre careers in their native city of Vancouver, the husband and wife actors had migrated toward radio drama, moving to Toronto in 1954 in search of greater opportunities that included television as well as radio.

"Norma and I played a game of guessing who would get roles," Arngrim said. "We were fortunate to be in the loop. We worked as much for Esse Ljungh as for Andrew Allan. Norma did the *Search for Tomorrow* series for Esse."[21] In addition to adult dramas, the acting couple played roles on children's programs, never making any distinction between the two in the seriousness with which they approached the job. It was in the CBC studios in 1954 that they first met Mary Grannan.

"Mary Grannan had a large presence," Arngrim said. "She was the-atrical, animated, had spirit and energy. She was excited about her work and it was contagious. When she walked onto the set, she brought an atmosphere with her."[22]

When production began in 1955 for the television version of *Maggie Muggins*, Macmillan was selected to provide the voice of Fitzgerald Fieldmouse, while Arngrim played the voice of the occasional puppet character Leo the Lion.

"Mary Grannan's stories had a great sense of humour, but she had to do a lot of pushing to make things happen," Arngrim said.[23]

In the latter part of 1956, they moved to New York City, although Macmillan commuted between New York and Toronto for most of the next year to continue with various roles. While Arngrim turned to the-atre work on Broadway and at the Gristmill Playhouse in New Jersey, Macmillan's work blossomed in animation. She became best known as the voice of cartoon characters such as Caspar the Friendly Ghost, Gumby, Under Dog, and Davy in *Davy and Goliath*. With her addi-tional work providing voices in animated commercials, her voice filled the television airways on Saturday mornings. She was one of four women in New York City who dominated voice-over work and voice dubbing for children's voices in television.

Thus, familiar with what was happening in animation work in New York, Arngrim became interested in the possibility of turning *Maggie Muggins* into an animated program. After speaking to UPA about the possibility, he found an interested partner in Gene Deitsch, who worked for many big animation productions. Then Arngrim drew up a proposal and draft contract to present to Mary. Around March 1959, he met with Mary and some executives at the CBC, outlining a pro-posal to produce and deliver to the CBC thirty-nine cartoon film episodes over a three-year period. He said:

> I tried to make a deal with the CBC, but the CBC did-n't want Americans to do this. They blocked it. There was no way to interest the National Film Board,

because this was not their type of show. The contract never got off the ground. I always felt bad about that. Several CBC people who were involved were very earth bound. They couldn't see the future. The show would have been documented forever on film. It would not have taken away from the current live actor and puppet show. The CBC was always difficult — it was a bureaucracy and semi-governmental. They had no frame of reference when it came to entertainment. Entertainment was a big aspect for Mary, but she was very discreet about comments about the CBC. She was too positive a person.

In Mary Grannan, the CBC had a star personality who could write. She delivered. She was very sophisticated about the cartoon proposal. She knew exactly what they were talking about. The CBC just discouraged her from entering into it.

Everything about Mary's personality was attractive — everything. She was in charge without rocking the boat. The way she conducted herself at the meeting with me and her attorney was utterly charming. She was nonjudgmental and asked pertinent, intelligent questions. She was a curious, inquisitive person. The CBC executives were negative, but she remained calm and listened.[24]

It was a lost opportunity. A cartoon version of *Maggie Muggins* might have generated a greater interest for the *Maggie Muggins* books that were launched that year in the larger American market. However, part of the difficulty with the proposal may have been in the language of the contract. Although Arngrim was mainly interested in making the cartoons, the contract asked for all rights connected with *Maggie Muggins*, including radio, television, books, and dolls. Mary may have had serious reservations about the proposal for this reason, although no alternative proposal was offered. In the end, Mary's loyalty and trust in the CBC remained paramount.

"In a way," said Arngrim, "the CBC was her studio system. She was protected; it was home, comfortable, and security for her."[25]

The Last Maggie

As planning for the fall 1959 television season got underway, the producer of *Maggie Muggins* decided it was time once again to replace the young actress playing the lead role. After playing Maggie for three years, Deanne Taylor was outgrowing the part. Mary and producer Dick Knowles held auditions and selected eight-year-old Mary Long to play Maggie as the production entered its sixth season.

The year that Mary Long joined the show marked a full twenty years since Mary Grannan had joined the staff. As a member of the CBC Twenty Year Club, Grannan was a senior member within the organization, at least in terms of recognition and deference, if not by rank and position. She was as strong-willed and determined as ever — even more so. Unbeknownst to most around her, she was less than six months away from her sixtieth birthday, the mandatory retirement age for women at the CBC.

Mary Grannan, who had grown fond of the outgoing Maggie, dedicated *Maggie Muggins and the Fieldmouse* (1959) to her: "To DEANNE TAYLOR who has played 'Maggie Muggins' on Television to my delight."[26] It was a difficult position into which young Mary Long stepped.

Petite and beautiful, with light brown hair rather than Maggie-red and no freckles, Mary Long came from an Italian family that had immigrated to Canada. Her real name was Barbalunga, meaning "long beard," but Long became her stage name. Her audition left a lasting impression upon her. Long described the experience:

> I was about eight years old, and my agent at the time was a cousin, Matie Molinaro, who then ran the Canadian Speakers' and Writers' Service; [she] called up one time and said that Deanne Taylor who had been playing Maggie Muggins had outgrown the role. She was twelve now, and they were on the

search for a new Maggie. And I was a sweet, effer-vescent, sort of bubbling over with enthusiasm, little Italian girl, who didn't speak English very well, as a matter of fact. So, Matie arranged for me to go and audition for the part of Maggie.

They took me down to the CBC, and there was Dick Knowles, the first producer, and Mary Grannan herself, who happened to have … one of her famous, large hats. Now, to me, she was … an enormous pres-ence. And something that I hadn't seen before, she was wearing white gloves, as I recall, and a great hat and a sort of prim suit, but was extremely foreboding [*sic*]. She was quite frightening to me, and she had me read from the script, but in that sort of school marm'y way. She would correct me, and I thought, "Oh gosh, if I'm not careful, I'll get the strap."

And then I subsequently found out — I guess it was a while. I was on pins and needles for the longest time, of course. They called and said that I had won the role. I couldn't believe it. Well, it was the very first time I had done anything at all. But I subsequently found out that I was not Mary Grannan's first choice because I was of Italian heritage and I think she really wanted a little red-headed girl with freckles. So, I think I was starting off the whole process with a strike against me. So, I remember going into studio, and, of course, they had to paint my freckles on, so I don't know how that came across. I think in the end she was quite thrilled with the energy that I brought to it, but I do remember her being quite, quite formidable.…

She was a robust woman. I mean she wasn't slight in any way. She was one of those Victorian bosomed women, whose bosom seemed to come right to her waist. [She had] quite a strong voice. I don't know if she smoked. Yes, she did because she had a cigarette holder. I remember that quite distinctly. And she really reeked of Hollywood that didn't exist. She was all that I think Dorothy Parker must have been. She really seemed to have an aura....

She certainly seemed larger than life, a character totally unique and unto herself. I didn't get much of a soft side from her, I must say. I think she was quite sure about what she wanted. And yet, there she was writing all this gentle stuff for children whom she didn't possess. So, I guess she must have had a very amazing imagination. But I didn't get to know her, me personally ... very well.

I did [the show] for three years, from the time I was eight until the time I was eleven.... It was live the first year, live to air [i.e., live to kinescope]. They taped it the year after that. So, on Tuesdays, I would have to miss school entirely, and I would go to the studio. I would have worked on the script over the weekend, and then on Tuesday, I was expected to come in, do just a slight rehearsal, which would be from about ten in the morning until 3:15 and then we went live to air. And from 3:15 until 3:30, there was that fifteen minutes of time that by necessity needed to be perfect, absolutely perfect, because there was no turning back. You couldn't stop. And now that I [have seen] some of the tapes, the kinescopes of the very early stuff ... there were a couple there where the inevitable happened, the puppet strings got tangled or something, and you could see this poor little child's mind racing as to how to fix the strings but continue with the dialogue at the same time. And it looks pretty hokey at this point in time with all the high tech stuff now ... But, as I say, I remember it with fond and harrowing moments at the same time.[27]

A few times each year, the young actress made public appearances dressed as Maggie Muggins. She would ride on a float in the Santa

Claus parade or ride the Zamboni at a hockey game, often meeting celebrities like hockey hero Frank Mahovlich. "So, it was a bit of a heady experience,"[28] Long said.

During the time that Mary Long was Maggie Muggins, Doug Master played Mr. McGarrity. For the puppet voices, Margo Christie was Grandmother Frog, Alice Hill was Reuben Rabbit, Ruth Springford was Benny Bear, and Pauline Rennie was Fitzgerald Fieldmouse. John and Linda Keogh continued as the puppeteers. Sometimes during this period, there was an additional actor on camera: Winnifred Dennis played Miss Merryweather, the toy shop owner, and Syd Brown appeared in occasional roles.

"And those were my constant companions. These were the people that I spent three years with and whom I remember as surrogate parents in a lot of ways. It was a wonderful time."[29]

A frequent visitor to the set was Miss Grannan herself, whom Long remembered being in the background on the floor of the set, not in the control room with the producer.

I was always wanting to be absolutely right for everyone, you know, and especially for Mary. And I do remember being quite nervous when she was on the set because she demanded some perfection. Of course, here was a character that sprung from her imagination and it was embodied by something less than perfect. So, I tried very hard to please her and I think in the end, she really cottoned to me, but she was formidable.

Well, I was stuck between her and sharing a dressing room with Juliette. ... You know there were big guns all around me. I remember Juliette saying to me, "Oh, you're terribly *fat*." I thought in retrospect it wasn't very kind of her to say. She didn't particularly like sharing her dressing room. This was in the old building at Studio Seven on Mutual Street and she was in Studio One and we were in Studio Two. So, we shared this one dressing room, the two of us, although she had a little compartment to herself. Anyway, I'm making it sound [as if] it was very much of an ordeal, but it wasn't. It was just very, very stress-ful on an eight-year-old.[30]

Besides being the only child on a set full of adults, Long felt there was an additional stress on her that derived from her ethnic background.

[Coming from] an immigrant family, I had the pressure of "These are the really good people and you've got to be extraordinarily good." So, there was [this idea that] I wasn't quite as good as everyone else. So, I had to really work harder to be accepted. ...

I imagine that [Mary Grannan] must have had great control because I don't remember her being up in the control room. She would be down on the floor of the set, which of course was terribly distracting. I'm not sure if they understood how difficult it was for a child ... There was lots of distraction from back here. And they'd make signs at you while you were working. That's very hard for a child to take in all at once. But they were all around you when you were working; even the voices in those days were not off in a secluded place. ... I would enter [the mouse house set] from the back and Grandmother Frog, and Pauline and Alice and [others] would have music stands set up so they would be within my eyesight. So, I'd be talking to the puppet here believing that this was the presence, but hearing voices, of course, from here. The biggest chastisement to me was "stop looking at the monitor." But I think it was just that I would be distracted because, of course, I knew that the puppet was supposed to be animated and yet something would happen out here. ... The voice and the picture or any kind of order or instruction would be coming from out here. So, I had to sort of scramble it in my brain immediately. Oh, it was hard. It was really hard. ... I remember my mother saying to me very strongly, "This is a job. You're very lucky to have this. You're a very lucky girl." I was a very lucky girl, I remember that. But I seemed to have to work very hard to be such a lucky girl. ...

The second year, I was actually able to come home and watch [the show] myself because, of course, we would tape it on Saturdays and I would be able to watch it on Tuesdays, although that proved to be a bit disconcerting, because I was like a hockey player who watches too many of his tapes. I kept seeing mistakes and know things I wanted to improve which made things difficult. So, I think I stopped watching.

[When we did the show live the first year], what we would do is rehearse and then we'd do what was called a "dry run." And in the dry run, that was when every-thing was supposed to go wrong. Of course, hardly ever in the dry run did anything go wrong. Everything *always* went wrong when you went to air. The gate wouldn't open or you would trip or you'd turn your ankle or the camera wouldn't switch from Mr. McGarrity over to where you were supposed to be, so you'd be blabbing away over here and the camera hadn't switched yet. Then you'd have to watch until the red light started, and start all over again. ... But then, when we went to tape, you were encouraged to go straight on through, but if you got into terrible trouble, you knew it was tape and you could stop. But often, you didn't. Often you just went on and then you taped it twice. ...

Because it was taped, they could edit, which they were unable to do previous to that. But *you* of course were encouraged to do it perfectly twice. ... I seem to be coming back to this perfection thing, and I think part of it had to do with Mary's presence. I think that Mary had an *overwhelming* power to want things to be right and perfect. And she was always impeccably turned out herself. So, she was something to work for and toward. I do remember that. I don't know if she had that impression on many people, but she did have an overwhelming feeling that you had a lot to live up to. ...

I was a pretty fast learner, so I actually had the scripts word perfect, certainly in the first year, very early. But if you see the kinescopes or the tapes of the third year, you can see that I'm getting very comfortable with the character and I start to take some liberties with the script. And I'm sure Mary didn't like that. But it'll happen to any actor, of course. Because they'll start to ad lib, and I remember watching the tapes and seeing sort of the perfect one at the very beginning and then by the end, I was throwing in "you know's" and "ha, ha, ha" sort of stuff. ...

I was a chubby child, I thought. I probably wasn't, but I thought I was. And I had to wear these damn crinolines ... with little ballet slippers. It really ruined my life because I wouldn't wear galoshes in the winter time. My mother tells these terrible stories that because I was wearing ballet slippers and anklets all the time [for the show], I thought that that's how I should dress all the time. So, I never wore galoshes in the winter, and I was carried from the house to the car. I was terribly spoiled in those days. But they went out of their way to make me just beautiful, beautiful costumes, all with gorgeous ... gingham, puffed sleeves, and just everything that you could imagine. And my Mom took great care with those braids. She would comb and comb and comb and comb and comb ... She would do it especially for the day when I had to be at the studio ... She combed my hair just before the show and pulled it as tightly as she could. ...

[On the set] I was concerned with doing a good job and learning my lines. And so [Mary Grannan] and I didn't come into too much contact, other than she would be around and she would be a force to sort of stay away from. ... She did spend more of her time with the adults. I think I was a fly on the wall in a lot of cases. I remember them going over to the Variety Club, which in those days was across the street. They didn't know quite what to do with me, because I always had to be dragged along. I was the only one who was under age, right? They would park me upstairs and I'd eat banana splits while they were downstairs having their drinks. You know, in those days, everyone had cocktails, smart cocktails, especially after the shows. You see, when we did the show live, it would have been a Tuesday afternoon, so about five o'clock we'd all be finished, so they'd all trounce over to the Variety Club across the street, including my mother, and they'd go and have their smart drinks and I'd be left alone upstairs eating banana splits. But I'd sort of sit around on the stairwell and listen to them talk. And she was booming. I mean her voice was booming, so you could always hear her. The topics were varied, including her family, and stuff like that. ...

I have bittersweet memories of all that time because, despite the fact that it was the happiest time of my life in some ways, it was also a time that took me away from a real sort of ordinary childhood. I spent a lot of time in studio, a lot of time around adults, so I felt a great deal of responsibility very young. ...

There wasn't a moment after I had done that program that I ever thought about what it was that I might do as an adult. I just thought that well, now I'm on the road. And sometimes when that happens when you're very young, it can be disturbing because you don't really leave yourself open for too many other options. Your mind is set on that and I was very strong willed about that kind of thing. And it taught me great discipline in terms of being able to be directed. I think I endeavored to be a perfect little girl.[31]

Chapter Fourteen
Last Years at CBC, 1960-1962

Official Retirement

In late October 1959, six months after Fred Rainsberry transferred Mary into the new position, a notice from the salaries administration officer arrived in the department, advising that Mary would reach normal retirement on February 29, 1960. At that time, the mandatory retirement age for women at the CBC was sixty years, rather than sixty-five as it was for men. To Rainsberry, her impending retirement may have come as a surprise, for he had noted in a letter prior to the transfer that she had four more years. Nevertheless, while Rainsberry set about organizing a retirement party and Grace Athersich rounded up contributions for a gift, Mary arranged to continue work as a freelancer.

At five o'clock on Friday, February 26, 1960, colleagues and friends gathered in the boardroom of the Jarvis Street executive building for Mary's party. She was dressed impressively for the significant occasion in a navy blue silk dress, adorned by a carnation corsage and topped off with a flower-decked white gauzy turban. Keith Morrow, Director of English Networks and the Toronto Area, spoke to the gathering and presented her with the gift selected by Grace, an *Encyclopaedia Britannica* complete with bookcase and green covers to match Mary's decor. After giving her a scroll with the contributors' names, Frank Willis read messages from H.G. Walker, General Manager of English Network Broadcasting; Andrew Cowan, Director of Northern and Armed Forces Services; and Bud Knapp, who had acted on many of her shows. The affection was genuine, as colleagues enjoyed her friendliness, humour, and professionalism on the job. Cowan's telegram read, "Returned from Frobisher Bay for today's party but the drifts between here [Ottawa] and Toronto are too much for a man pushing 50 even though his heart could melt a path to Mary."[1]

Morrow's later note reflected the warm tributes: "The testimonial of your colleagues, both past and present, confirmed your long record of loyalty and service to the CBC through these many years. You have become identified nationally as one of the founders of good broadcasting for children during your long career."[2]

Gladstone Murray, unable to attend the party, sent his wishes the next week: "Your contribution to the radio service of Canada has been of the highest order. You have the unique capacity of combining imagination with practical ability."[3]

After the speeches and presentations, cake and tea were served while many photographs were taken — casual groups with Mary holding tightly to Frank's arm on one side and Syd Brown's on the other, individual poses with various people, and one with several cast members from *Maggie Muggins* in which the teasing glances they exchanged captured the essence of their friendships and working relationships.

While she was pleased to be the centre of attention and affection, Mary was anything but happy about retiring from CBC staff. In spite of little and big frustrations along the way, she had loved being part of the organization. Her thoughts on the occasion were best expressed in the subsequent letter she wrote to Bud Knapp:

> Dear Bud
>
> This is to thank you for the letter you sent to "my party". Frank read it and of course in that Bluenose voice of his, it sounded like a theatrical gem. But the delivery was not what moved me. It was the contents. I was moved to tears at the nice things you said about

me. That letter will be treasured by me, always. My twenty plus years with the CBC were good ones. No one censored my work, I was given the freedom to go and come when I pleased, and under those circumstances, the corporation got many extra hours. But we 'old timers' never thought of overtime. Who cared as long as we turned out something the public liked. Many people helped me along the way. I've many to thank. I mentioned some at the party. I'm sure there were many that I overlooked, under the strain of sentimental spot I was in. To Mr. Weir, I owe a great deal. He helped me clear up the royalty mess I was in. Remember? Dr. Frigon who had the authority to resolve my predicament, did so. Wick was a good friend, in my outside broadcast efforts. He went to factories and zoo and ever so many places to show me how to get stories for The Scrapbook. Mr. Bushnell was so good to me. He even remembered I was a lone woman those first Christmases I was here, and had me to his house to dinner. Hugh Morrison did so much in those first weeks of getting started. So did George Taggart. George came to the party. He looks almost the same … same wide personality grin. I was very happy to see him, and flattered that in such weather conditions that he would come. Jim Annand, my beloved McGarrity, of early days, came from Clarkson. Syd Brown, rather dewey eyed with recalling the happy 'old days' was also present. And Neill Morrison … Hugh was there too. Henri Ball Edey, my dear friend since 1939, and Lois Pope. And then the "new ones". Almost the entire Children's Department came. I've been fortunate in having Fred Rainsberry as a supervisor during my "last" years. As you know, he invited me to write for Television. It has been one of the most pleasant chores I've had. He's always had time for me. Last spring, when he was in a real tailspin of work, I wanted to ask him what my future looked like, as far as getting work for his department was concerned. His days were booked solid but he suggested that we meet at Eaton's. Lunch time, and talk, and I came away feeling secure that he would keep me working as long as I wanted to and could turn in satisfactory material. It was Stan Cox' idea to try Just Mary on TV. He has taken a great personal interest in preparing this show. As Jackie Gleason used to say "It's a good group", at least as far as I'm concerned it is.

I suppose you were told of the wonderful gift I received. Nothing, not even a mink stole, could please me more. Keith Morrow presented it, after your letter was read. He said to Frank, "I'm glad to see someone else besides Ross McLean is writing your material." Thank you again, Bud, and may you have good health, too, to carry on for the corporation, I left so reluctantly, last Friday.[4]

Freelancing

Officially retired as well as inducted into the CBC Pioneers' Club, Mary cleared out her fourth-floor Jarvis Street office and moved her papers, belongings, and photographs into her Breadalbane Street apartment from where she would base her freelance work. Losing her CBC office was a psychological and social blow, for it had permitted more contact with colleagues and a balance to the solitary writing time. While freelancing would permit her to continue her work, it carried the constant insecurity that her shows could be cancelled suddenly without any guarantee of replacement.

One bright piece of news was that *Just Mary* became a television program on April 7, 1960, for which Mary adapted some of her best radio scripts, including "The Princely Pig." Actors and elaborate puppets by John and Linda Keogh performed the stories, while Mary narrated off camera. The series, however, was only broadcast one year. For the remainder of her work, Mary continued to write for the ever-popular *Maggie Muggins*, observing on the set as often as possible. On radio, she maintained her long-running *Just Mary*, although during her last two years of the program, she presented revised versions of a number of her earlier scripts, such as "A Home for Dinnerpail," "The Cowboy and the Pony," and "The Green Hill Mystery."

"Glad to hear you're still doing business at the old stand & hadn't eloped with Austin Willis,"[5] Noel Langley wrote in September 1960. Yes, she was still doing business at the old stand, but it was different. Feeling the loss of no longer being on staff, she faced the looming reality that an end to her broadcasting days was not far away and would likely come unexpectedly. Nevertheless, she had received assurances from Fred Rainsberry that he would always have a place for her as long as she could satisfactorily produce the work.

The finest testimony of the nature of Mary's freelancing period was reflected in her letters to her sisters. As humorous and gossipy as ever, the letters nevertheless hinted at an increasing feeling of loneliness as she recounted the various meals she arranged "for the sake of someone to speak to,"[6] wished at other times for "someone to take me someplace"[7] on a beautiful day, and told of falling asleep by herself in front of the television set during the evening. Yet, in contrast, she occasionally appeared irritated at unwanted social engagements that took her away from valuable scriptwriting time. "I told her [Henri Edey] I was NOT anti-social, but that I was earning my living and lunch didn't figure in it."[8]

While she remained a valued friend to those closest to her, such as Frank Willis and Grace Athersich, and continued to command widespread respect throughout the CBC for her broadcasting work, she gave the impression to some of a hardened personality. Mavor Moore, who was chief producer of CBC Television and also did a stint playing Mr. McGarrity on the television *Maggie*, described Mary as a "tough old bird in her later years, not quite the warm persona she portrayed or of early years. She became a real tyrant in later years, although one understands why. ... She had to develop brass knuckles."[9] Presumably, the reason behind the toughness was self-preservation in a ruthless business, although it is worth noting that this same toughness garnered admiration from others, such as Violet Taylor Armstrong.

There had always been a difference between the soft, gentle public image Mary projected as a children's storyteller and the forceful, determined, real personality behind the image. She may have allowed more of the tougher side to show in later years, possibly becoming more irritable as she aged. Her wide-eyed eagerness and energy of the early years had become a firm determination to protect what she had, coming to the rescue when necessary. However, she also displayed in the letters home an underlying insecurity.

In the following letter to Deanne Taylor on Easter Sunday, April 2, 1961, Mary recounted an incident in which she rose to defend her character Fitzgerald Fieldmouse. The tone of the letter is lighter than the one she used in her letters to her sisters and permits some reflections on her writing to surface:

> Dear Deanne
>
> I was so delighted to get your letter that I'm answering it almost right away ... this is not a habit of mine ... writing is a busman's holiday for me ... I write to my sisters ... that's about all. Thank you for the medal I greatly appreciated your thinking of me while in Rome ... and your broadminded outlook in bringing me the Catholic symbol pleased me even more I took your letter to MAGGIE yesterday. Mrs. Christie read it aloud to the others ... it was almost as if they were hearing from you too. We talked about you, and how we missed you. [...] I had to come to Fitzgerald's rescue this week. Michael Spivak is back and is doing Junior Roundup. He was doing a show about the Keoghs, and asked me if Fitz could be interviewed ... I said Yes ... but the night before the show, Pauline Rennie got the script ... she called me up and read it ... Fitzgerald was asked where he was born ... well I'll give you a rough idea of contents
>
> Fitz   ... was born in a sewer in Regina
> Westgate.   I thought you were a fieldmouse

<u>Fitz</u>	Oh no … raised in a sewer … I ran away from home. I went to New York … worked with Runyon Rat … then got into the mousehole theatre where I played King Lear …
<u>West</u>	How did you get into TV
FITZ	The original mouse in Maggie Muggins left, so Mary Grannan came to NY looking for a new mouse … naturally she came to see me … She offered more cheese, so I came to TV …
WEST	Do you like it …
FITZ	I get tired of playing underwater scenes and climbing mountains and have Gra Frog try to take spotlight from me … but it's a living … and you know how hard it is to get into CBC unless you know someone …
WEST	Is Fitzgerald Fieldmouse your real name …
FITZ	Oh no … my real name is Mickey Mouse …

Well you can see how poor little Fitz who although mischievous, always asked forgiveness … admitted he was sorry … paid back either in deed or gift was being defamed in front of the children … another thing, I'd never mention running away from home … or knock the CBC … so I called Mr Cox and had the script killed … they did a bit with him, and in it he lied twice. They used another mouse for the other script … called him Baldwin Beatmouse … and he talked "Daddy oh" and expressions like that. Children are young so short a time, as you yourself now know … that I like them to have the prettiest things they can see and hear when small. […]

279

I thought today too, of our Easter Parade experience … how cold we were Ugh … today it's only 31
with snow flurries … last night, they painted the sidewalks of Yonge Street from Gerard to King, Pink …
white curbs and planted garlands of flowers … but it's
such a mean day, I wonder how many will parade. […]
Give my fondest regards to your mother, father and
Burt All the Maggie Muggins "animals" send their
love … I do too.
Mary[10]

The Spotlight Extinguished

The year 1962 sat on the cusp of a cultural shift in Canada. The staid
fifties were giving way to the freer expression of the sixties, edged
along on their journey by the baby boomers' maturation into adoles-
cence. Canadian television was also maturing, as CBC Television
marked its tenth anniversary. While staff reflected on accomplishments of past years, they also planned for the future, looking ahead
for changes in programming. As television redefined the role of radio,
the CBC prepared to collapse Trans-Canada and Dominion into a
single radio network. Among the various changes taking place, young
children's programs were migrating from radio into the morning television slot.

On the administrative side of things in the CBC children's department, Bruce Attridge had taken over as supervisor from Fred
Rainsberry, who had moved into a higher position as head of schools
and youth programming. Attridge had been intent on teaching at
Michigan State University until his friend and colleague Rainsberry
coaxed him into coming to the CBC. Attridge, looking for change and
ways to put his own stamp on the shape of programming for children,
believed Mary Grannan's programs were outdated. In April 1962, he
cancelled *Maggie Muggins* on television and *Just Mary* on radio. Mary's
broadcasting career with the CBC was over — the long spotlight in
which she had gloried suddenly went out.

To Attridge this was perhaps a sign of progress, but to Mary it was a devastating personal blow. Since her shows were still popular with the public, she felt she had several years of creativity remaining. Yet, there was little she could do but accept the outcome. "There were no sacred cows," she told newspaper columnist Sid Adilman. "I was a free-lancer and I was let go."[11]

Rainsberry, as overall head of the department, would have supported Attridge's decision, but Frank Willis and others close to Mary were upset by the cancellations. With the terrible news coming after a frustrating winter of working in the midst of noise and dirt as the nearby school was demolished, Mary decided that she should move home to Fredericton to live with her sisters. The three unmarried women would be living together in their Brunswick Street house once again. After obtaining a quote from a moving company, she wrote to Ann and Helen over the course of three days, discussing the details of coming home, interrupted by news of talking to people about the situation.

> Dear Girls. I guess by now you have my letter … I'm so sorry to chuck the mess at you … but it would be foolish for me to hang around here with no work … Attridge didn't even offer me a chance to write CHEAPER shows … it's the department who like the Razzle dazzled type, I guess. […] Stan Cox called me last night … Stan drives to work with the assistant to one of the head programme people […] Stan said don't jump into going to NB … something will happen … said the man he drove with said I was supposed to be offered a chance to do another radio show … I said that if Attridge didn't want me … I wouldn't work on a programme pressured by someone from the top … it wouldn't be a happy situation. He said you'll be broadcasting until the day you're in your coffin […] I just called Dud … thought he should know … he said that's quite a shocker … I said well will you want another book … and he said

... Yes I think so ... and I said I'd soon be through with scripts and could start it ... He said what about other stations ... Hamilton ... etc. ... but Hamilton is local and they can't afford shows unless they have sponsors ... and besides I've not been thinking of new shows ... I suppose I will when I get around to it [...] LATER Pauline [Rennie] (Fitz) called up, full of ideas ... a NY agent is going to visit her sister in two weeks and they want me to meet him ... etc. Like Stan, she thinks it's crazy for me to think of going home ... But the Grannan guts never amounted to much ... the reason being a gal named Kate. [...] Interrupted here by Paddy Sampson, the producer who did Just Mary TV series ... He wants to meet me tomorrow to talk. I said Paddy, I can't see the use ... but I'll meet you. I said it's not the programmes ... it's I, that the children's dept doesn't want. He said "Wait ... not the children's department. Don't say that You know what WE all think of you ... sometimes a person falls on his back and gets up and sits on a plush seat." I said I heard they were bringing Fred Rogers from Pittsburg to do shows ... he said YES he'd heard that today. I said well Paddy ... I've a strange feeling about what happened to me ... a strange feeling about the setup there. And he said "God, don't we all." [...][12]

In the brief couple of months between the cancellations and the end of the regular broadcasting season in June, Mary's friends and colleagues were unable to convince her to stay in Toronto. While she prepared her final shows, she started packing to leave.

Time magazine dispatched writer Fergus Cronin and photographer John Reeves to produce a farewell article. As Cronin arrived to interview Mary in her apartment, she was busy packing up her large book collection. He noted her sadness, writing in a later article that in his opinion, "her spirit was broken by a conviction that she was no longer wanted."[13] She told him she planned to continue writing, hoping to broadcast children's stories on radio in Fredericton and television in Saint John.

When photographer John Reeves arrived at Mary's apartment for his photography shoot, he encountered a woman used to being photographed. She not only posed and smiled obligingly but also suggested several shots. Mary was an old professional at that point. While she was at the end of her career, he was at the beginning of his.

Time published the article, called "End of the Tale," in its July 6 Canadian edition, accompanied by Reeves's portrait of Mary beaming a broad smile from underneath a large hat while resting her elbow on a stack of her published books. Cronin caught the essence and significance of what Mary's departure from the CBC meant to Canada with his opening line: "Outside of the Dominion Observatory Official Time Signal and J. Frank Willis, the CBC's most durable performer has been a lively onetime Fredericton schoolteacher named Mary Grannan."[14] Canadian listeners had been hearing Mary's voice on radio since 1939, just three years after the CBC came into existence. Hers had been a long run on the air.

On CBC Radio, Mary's long-time pal and confidant, Frank Willis, arranged to interview her on his program, *In Reply*, broadcast on June 17. His interview was a fond farewell, the tone one of pride in her accomplishments and support for her viewpoints. He gave her an opportunity to review the highlights of her career, state her philosophy of storytelling for children, and mention various names of people she had met along the way. After reviewing her various radio and television programs, Frank commented on her great success with her published books. Yes, she replied, the books had come about in response to people's many requests for scripts, and she had been very happy about the way they had been received. Indeed, that was a mild way of understating the phenomenal sales she had experienced, approximately 400,000 copies at that point. Yet, she admitted, "They may not be great literature, but the children find themselves in [them], because [from] my teaching experience, I learned what children liked and how they talked, how they coined words."[15] That statement seemed to sum up her defence to any critics.

"It's been a great pleasure," Frank said to Mary as he closed the program, "and I'm sure our listeners join me in wishing you the *very* best in your move to Fredericton, a long, continuing, and productive career in writing. It certainly won't be the same here in Toronto without you."[16]

Chapter Fifteen
Journey Homeward, 1962-1975

Home Again

As the train left Union Station in early July 1962, taking Mary away from her beloved Toronto back home to Fredericton, she was undoubtedly in a different mood than she had been during the usual summer trips she had taken for twenty-three years. With a one-way ticket home, she had no plan to return for the start of the new broadcasting season in September. The trip that year was not the longed-for summer retreat to recharge her batteries, think of new script ideas, and visit her sisters. It was a sad trip homeward. Although she had frequently expressed the wish that she and her sisters would settle down for some happiness together during retirement, she found the end of her creative, productive years at the CBC difficult to accept.

The journey through Ontario, Quebec, the New England states, and into New Brunswick ended at Fredericton Junction, since train service directly into Fredericton was no longer offered. Helen would have arranged for a friend to pick Mary up and bring her to the house. When the moving truck arrived with her belongings a couple of weeks later, the delivery man refused to unload her possessions until he had received payment in full. Mary scurried around the house rounding up the final cents to complete the fee. To accommodate Mary's extensive book collection, Helen had shelves installed along one wall of the living room. With these soon filled, the book collection and Mary's other things spilled over into all rooms of the house. Ann had moved home in 1957 after retiring from teaching in Moncton, so settling Mary and all her worldly goods into the house certainly must have brought a spell of adjustment for all three women. To provide some additional living space, Mary had a room built on the back of the house where the shed had been. She jokingly continued to call it the shed.

As September rolled around, the rumblings of discontent over the cancellation of Mary's shows made their way into the press. Trent Frayne wrote in the *Canadian Weekly* a piece critical of the decision, quoting from his interview of Bruce Attridge.[1] Frank Willis wrote Mary a letter of support on September 29.

> Dear Mee-Ree:
>
> My reference to the files, this date, shows that the last peep out of you was on July 16th. From time to time I get a bulletin from my amanuensis (sometimes mistakenly called inamorata) which serves to keep me in touch at second-hand. This is not altogether satisfactory since, as you can imagine better than anyone, Grace's quotes and interpretations are not always as accurate as a tape recorder. In fact, the heavy overlay of her own opinions and prejudices so clouds any issue as to make her reportage just about worthless. She is, nevertheless, a loyal friend and much must be forgiven on that account.
>
> Speaking of loyal friends, and lest you should for a moment imagine that you have not a full complement, the old pals, co-workers and admirers, are only now bestirring themselves and getting up a full head of steam in protest against the shabby and insupportable way in which you were obliged to take your

leave of the local scene. You will have seen Trent Frayne's piece in the Canadian Weekly in which he admirably pulled that pompous Attridge's leg. I'm sure that is only the beginning of a continuing protest, couched in innocence and mild enquiry this time, but likely to get much more vehement and penetrating as time goes on. Coincidentally, there have been a number of articles in the local print in the past few weeks advocating a return to the certain verities in literature and television for the very young. It was significant, and timely, that Eatons sent out a brochure last week advertising the perfect nucleus of a child's library in a special package deal. It was very significant that, despite the fact that the selection had been made by "an international board of child psychologists" who emphasized the need for fantasy and make-believe, the recommended reading was all at variance with the avant-garde thinking of our brilliant young men and included, as you would expect, all the best of the Brother's Grimm, Hans Christian Andersen, Rob't Louis Stevenson et al. along with the standard modern classics. The Attridges of this world are not going to succeed in their efforts to make Razzle-Dazzle the epitome of juvenile literature-on-the-air. As a matter of fact I would not be at all surprised to see that department utterly discredited and cleared out if the present trend continues. Be sure that I have not accumulated a large dossier on the most modern and best accredited thinking on the subject of children's reading and viewing for nothing. I have every intention of hitting them in the eye with it when it will hurt the most.[2]

The following January, Frank reported in another letter that Fred Rogers had completed thirteen weeks of his series with no more planned. "Perhaps, after a few more disasters, the realization that

Maggie was one of the greatest properties they ever had will begin to dawn. I hope it will not be too late then for them to do something about it."[3] As encouraging as these supportive words must have been, nothing changed in the decision over Mary's shows.

In the fall of 1962, Thomas Allen published Mary's last book, *Maggie Muggins and Benny Bear*. While she still had many scripts from which she could have produced more books, she did not do any writing after returning home. Indeed, if ever she had longed for more time to write or to try other types of writing, she should have found that opportunity during retirement. In later letters to Fergus Cronin, Helen wrote about Mary's return to Fredericton: "When she came home after 23 years in Toronto it was a great change for her. For one thing, she left the big city for the little one & [left] the job & the life that she loved. As you yourself said she was completely disheartened — I ached for her."[4]

With her move into the family home, Mary had lost the privacy of her own apartment where she had an established writing routine and more control over her daily schedule. Since Helen continued teaching children at the hospital polio clinic until 1967, Mary insisted on doing many of the household chores. In addition, Ann was ill with diabetes, growing increasingly more difficult to manage until the doctor insisted that she should move to a nursing home in 1969. Helen told Cronin that the new living arrangements affected Mary's freedom to write, as she was reluctant to disturb her sisters by thumping away on her typewriter early in the morning, which had always been her best writing time.

> She didn't feel that she should start typing early, early & look for books she might need & so the habits of years were broken. Then there were casual callers coming to see dear Ann & cups of tea to be made etc etc. [Can't] you see how difficult it would be to put ones thoughts on paper? ... Between you & me though I do think that she would still [have been] writing if she hadn't felt that she was no longer wanted. It was a great pity but she was that kind of person & could be so easily rebuffed.[5]

Helen confirmed to Cronin that Mary had always aspired to write for adults but blamed her busy schedule of producing children's scripts for keeping her from doing it.[6] While she could have pursued such writing after she left Toronto, she did not succeed in accomplishing it. At first, Mary did plan a few writing ideas, such as a play called "High Heels."[7] To his credit, Dud Allen remained supportive, encouraging her in January 1964 to further her proposal for a book for older children based on her radio program *Karen Discovers America*. He suggested that she arrange the material by province with a map at the beginning of each chapter, writing the book under another name, perhaps Mary Evelyn. In November 1968, Dud responded to a letter from Mary, saying he would like to see any ideas she had, "so pretend you are in the kitchen at 89 Breadalbane, and get on your thinking cap."[8] But the usual deadlines that had helped spur her work were absent.

The only other recorded effort to produce a book after retirement involved Michael Wardell, a former Brigadier in the British Army, who owned the Fredericton *Daily Gleaner* from 1951 until 1968. After Wardell expressed an interest in her writing, Mary gave him a manuscript she had ready. But Wardell not only failed to publish the book but also did not return the manuscript before he moved back to England. Unfortunately, Mary had not kept a copy.

"I tried many times to get her to look for it or find out what happened to it," said Helen. "But she said, 'Oh, well.' She thought nobody cared now, so she let it slide."[9]

In the interview with Fergus Cronin before she left Toronto, Mary indicated she might try broadcasting on the local radio and television stations. Jack Fenety, station manager of CFNB, the station that gave Mary her radio start, said this certainly would have been a possibility for her.

"She could have come to the station once a week or once a month or whatever," Fenety said. "She appeared there once, I think. That's all. … I think she was greatly disappointed when she came home, and I think the big city life had changed her. To come back here to little old Fredericton to be with [her sisters] — she never got orientated in Fredericton after she left. As I say, the best way I could describe her would probably be a semi-recluse."[10]

However, Mary accepted some of the invitations she received from local groups, making appearances to support the local Kindness Club and giving a speech at the Community Concert Association dinner, for example. At one such event, on October 24, 1966, she spoke at the Fredericton and Area Council of Women, where she was introduced by her friend Muriel Burtt Walker, then the mayor's wife. She made at least two appearances at Teachers' College on the campus of the University of New Brunswick, speaking to students. Had she the energy and desire, though, she could have filled her schedule with more than a few occasional appearances.

Mary took a few trips to Montreal and Toronto between 1962 and 1965, including one in April 1963 to appear as a guest on the CBC Television show *Flashback*, with host Paul Soles. For the most part, though, she dropped out of public sight, unless a magazine or newspaper writer inquired what happened to her: "What's happened to Just Mary"[11] (1963); "Say, Just What Did Happen to Just Mary?"[12] (1966); "The (Lost?) World of Maggie Muggins"[13] (1967); "Missing Persons: Whatever became of Mary Grannan?"[14] (1969). She had been a constant for so many years that her absence was noted.

Even though the broadcasts were off the air and there were no new books, children continued to write to Mary up to 1974. In May 1970, she received a package of letters of appreciation for *Maggie Muggins and Her Friends* from the Grade 2 class at Sunalta School in Calgary with a request for an autographed picture for their Favourite Authors' Gallery. The children particularly enjoyed the stories when Grandmother Frog complained about her rheumatism, when Fitzgerald Fieldmouse painted his toenails or became a cowboy mouse, and one thought Mr. McGarrity must have been a brain to solve all the problems. The continuing affection of children would have brought Mary great satisfaction, but it was not enough to cause her to write again. Some of those closest to Mary were not surprised that she did not write after leaving Toronto.

"[Frank] said, 'She'll never do anything in Fredericton, once she's out of the rat race, the limelight, the cocoa in Toronto,'"[15] Austin Willis said.

Mary frequently said she brought children safely back home at the end of her fantasies. Her life story appeared to play out according to that same plan. She went away to Toronto on a fantasy that lasted twenty-three years, doing more than she had ever dreamed of accomplishing. Then, when it was all over, she came safely back home — safely, perhaps, but not happily.

Friends Old and New

Missing her friends in Toronto, Mary attempted to keep in contact by writing letters. Many wrote back, while a few visited her, such as Frank and Gladys Willis. One memorable visit of old friends occurred on September 5, 1964. One hundred years after the Charlottetown Conference, eight actors portraying Fathers of Confederation arrived by boat in Fredericton as they recreated the historic journey. Dressed in top hats, beards, and costumes were Robert Christie as Sir John A. Macdonald, Bertrand Gagnon as Georges Etienne Cartier, Andrew Allan as George Brown, James Barron as Thomas D'Arcy McGee, Austin Willis as Alexander Galt, Larry Mann as Sir Leonard Tilley, Peter Donat as Dr. Charles Tupper, and John Vernon as Col. John Hamilton Gray.

Following an elaborate welcome at the wharf by Mayor William T. Walker, military bands, and local Native chiefs, the actors and a number of costumed local ladies travelled by horse-drawn carriages to the legislative building to deliver their speeches. After an evening of riding around the city, a dinner, and a reception, a group of the actors who knew Mary — Austin Willis, Robert Christie, Andrew Allan, John Vernon, and Larry Mann — descended on 325 Brunswick Street to visit their old friend, soon filling the small living room with a lively scene. While such a party had been a regular occurrence in Toronto, it would have been a welcome and extraordinary evening for Mary and her sisters in their small home in Fredericton. Recalling that the room was quite crowded, Austin said he spent most of the evening talking to Helen.[16] Mary, apparently worried about his intentions, walked over and asked him to leave her sister alone. It would have given the women plenty to talk about for days.

Besides these occasional outings, Mary stayed at home, creating a private, comfortable world for herself within the bounds of the old family house. The sisters read books, frequently reading aloud to each other, watched television, wrote letters, and entertained friends. Since the women shared an artistic bent as well as years of grade school artwork, they often busied themselves with paper and felt crafts, making greeting cards for friends, decorations for holidays, and whatever other notions came into their heads.

"They kept themselves busy with projects," said Muriel-Ann McKenna, Muriel and Bill Walker's daughter, "one of which ... was a study of Queen Victoria which ended *abruptly* when they researched about Mr. Brown. They were most offended and stopped their study."[17]

One of the most welcome new friends that the sisters made during their retirement years was Donald Roberts, a younger neighbour who arrived in their lives shortly after Mary first returned home. After meeting Don in McElman's Bookstore, where he was store manager, Ann invited him to come to the house to meet Mary, whose stories he had enjoyed since he was a boy. Soon he was stopping by their house frequently to deliver magazines and newspapers on his way home at the end of the day, and before long he was staying for dinner several times a week. A warm relationship quickly arose, as the women enjoyed his companionship. In many ways, he may have represented the son or nephew they never had.

"We got to be really just like relatives, very close relatives" Don said. "In fact, they used to tell me that. They said, 'You know, we forget that you're not our relative.'"[18]

On one of her trips to Toronto, Mary wrote a note of appreciation to Don, saying, "As Helen says, 'You're one of the nicest things that ever came into our lives.' I hope we never disillusion you in any way."[19]

Captivated by her personality and stories of her broadcasting days, Don clung to every word. "Mary would sit there after we'd have dinner, and ... she could tell story after story. She was a smoker — and a different one, sort of like you'd expect Marlene Dietrich to [be]." After lighting the cigarette with a flourish, she would smoke only three or four puffs, putting out the long butt by tapping all around the edge of the ashtray and then immediately pulling out another cigarette. "Her mannerisms were not of Fredericton, or of a small town. She was an actress, but she didn't know it. She was very natural with it."[20]

As well as being helpful to the sisters, Don encouraged Mary to accept a number of the invitations and opportunities that arose. He arranged twice for her to appear at McElman's to sign books, including after the Christmas parade on December 5, 1964, when Mary signed and sold nine hundred copies; another time, he organized an autographing session at the Fredericton Exhibition. As a result, she called him her great promoter. It was he who pasted into scrapbooks the mass of unsorted memorabilia and clippings that Mary and Helen had collected through the years. Whenever he met an interesting visitor to the city, such as Donald Wiegand, the New York representative of the Community Concert Services, he would invite the person to visit the Grannans. Don was so attentive to the sisters' needs and such good company that they missed him when he went away on business trips. Often on his trips, he would have a small shopping list of items to bring back for the women, including Mary's favourite Daniel Green slippers in various shades to match her smocks. Mary found particular joy in mailing letters to him just before he left on a trip so that the letter would be at the hotel waiting for his arrival.

Laughter and good-natured fun appeared to be the dominant characteristics of the relationship, as Don became the frequent recipient of imaginative paper crafts and handmade cards with humorous rhymes designed by Mary. At times, the elaborate paper creations stunned Don — a paper model of theatres displaying names of famous plays on their marquees, a stagecoach, or a treasure hunt that would send him searching all over their house until the prize was uncovered. When there did not seem to be enough to do, to lift their spirits Mary would decide that someone should have a second birthday party so they could celebrate. It was all light-hearted fun meant to amuse and to pass the time, almost as if the sisters were once again back in their childhoods playing make-believe.

Mary designed one silly card after Don had given them a good laugh one winter evening. He had put his coat and red scarf in the closet as usual, but when he went to leave, he was not paying close attention.

> So, this night we were sitting there talking, and suddenly I said, "Oh, my gosh, I didn't know it was that late. I've got to go home. I've got to work tomorrow."

293

So, I reached in [the closet] and got my coat on, and
then I reached in and I pulled out the scarf — I *thought*
— and put it on, and then I looked over on the chester-
field and they were in convulsions. They were laughing.
And I said, "Well, what's so funny?" And they couldn't
tell me because they couldn't talk. Finally, Helen says,
"You've got a pair of our pants on."[21]

The next day, Don received a card:

We've lately heard rumours
That you're stealing bloomers
To wear as a scarf
That gives us a larf
We suggest in this letter
That an ascot is better.[22]

On October 26, 1969, Frank Willis died suddenly of a heart attack
at his home in Toronto. Although Mary was among many across the
nation who were saddened by the loss, she would have felt it particularly keenly since they had been such close friends. In his Christmas
card the previous December, Frank had written of many friends moving away from Toronto, saying, "Having now completed all my 35 years
of bondage to the CBC I may be moving on soon meself. At least we
will have some time now in the summer months for cruising around so
hope to see you this coming year."[23] During Frank's last visit to
Fredericton in the summer of 1969, Mary and Helen asked him to read
to them because they loved hearing his voice.

Mary continued to exchange letters with Noel Langley, who
remarried in 1959. However, his letters grew more infrequent, with a
final Christmas card in 1967. Mary often wondered aloud to Don and
Helen if he might have died. He became ill in his later years, but did
not die until 1980. While Mary did not see him again after the visit to
England in 1949, she had enjoyed his letters, keeping them all.

Although the number of Mary's Fredericton friends had dwindled
during her long absence, she resumed her friendship with two of her

best long-time pals — Muriel Burtt Walker and Gertrude Davis, both of whom remained considerably more active in the community as seniors than Mary. Muriel was busy for a number of years with activities as the mayor's wife and was involved as well in numerous church and social groups. Gertrude, also active in a variety of local associations, continued as church organist and choir director for several years after retiring from teaching and broadcasting at CFNB. In contrast, Mary's community activities consisted of occasional guest appearances, even though she might have been fairly active in the community prior to leaving the city years earlier.

Muriel regularly joined Mary and her sisters for Friday evening meals, usually fish cakes, at the Grannan home, but the highlight of their shared activities was the annual summer vacation, whose sole objective was having fun together. Muriel-Ann McKenna recalled those holidays.

My Mom used to go on trips with Mary and her sisters. … These were the stories that you heard them yakking about the most. They were like children. They would go away — my Mom would drive, of course, because the three of them were housebound by choice almost, except for Helen. They'd go off to Portland or Bangor or somewhere like that for three or four days, and they'd giggle like fools — just giggle like fools. They talked about times when they pulled down the curtains in a hotel because they were trying to close the blinds, and all the curtains came off. My Mom had this [kettle] for heating water that used to blow all the fuses and they kept taking it with them. So, that was a central thing to them, were these trips that they used to take, and they just absolutely counted on those. … They went to have this foolishness together. And they got into trouble doing it. … But they loved it. It was girl stuff. They didn't go to go to theatre — no, no, nothing at all like that. It wouldn't have mattered where they went. It was just off to stay in a hotel and laugh and giggle and carry on.[24]

After Muriel-Ann gave birth to her son in 1970, she used to bring the baby for a visit with Mary and Helen, who were fond of seeing Muriel's first grandchild. Muriel-Ann remembered how much they laughed during these visits, especially when she left them in charge of the baby one afternoon while she attended a baby shower. "I couldn't have been at this baby shower more than two hours when they phoned me to come and get him. They were so excited — they had a wonderful time, but they just had enough. They had to change him, and they got laughing over that ... because they didn't know how."[25]

In spite of all the times they shared laughter, however, Muriel was bothered by Mary's lingering sadness over the loss of her career as well as her sadness over Ann's illness, finding it difficult to watch such a good friend become inactive, spend too much time simply sitting, and not look after herself properly. After Muriel's husband, Bill, died suddenly in 1970, she reduced her visits to 325 Brunswick Street. Muriel-Ann explained:

> I think after my Dad died and because Dad had died suddenly, [my mother] didn't like thinking about mortality. ... The following summer — that would have been in seventy-one — we went on a trip with *another* friend of my mother's, and gosh, were their noses out of joint. They were very hurt. ... They were devastated that she didn't visit as often. But she just couldn't watch Mary. ... She loved Mary; she loved her dearly, but ... it just was a time when she needed somebody to giggle with, that [wasn't] so blue.[26]

Muriel's son, Bill, had similar recollections. "My mother did not want to be affected by Mary's attitude and stopped going over to visit suddenly. The Grannans didn't understand why. Helen would say, 'We never knew what happened. She just dropped us.'"[27]

The friendship between Mary and Muriel had been a long, close one, with Mary one of the members of the bridal party at Muriel and Bill's wedding in the early thirties. "I don't think my Mom had another friend like Mary," Muriel-Ann said. "I don't recall her hanging around with any one person the way she did with Mary and the girls."[28] Sadly, in 1972, within a year of the change in their friendship, Muriel suddenly took ill and died. It was an unfortunate ending to their friendship. At a time when Mary needed friends perhaps as never before, Muriel did not understand the great emotional difficulty of ending a creative career.

Final Years

On the Victoria Day weekend in May 1971, Mary began a long letter to Georgina Murray Keddell, reflecting on many memories through the years:

> I'm sure you had a lovely party at Gladys's. She is a wonderful hostess. And the house is lovely. It's sad that Frank did not live longer to enjoy it. He loved it. Their back lawn in the spring is beautiful with the flowering trees. I was amused at your aunt being another victim to Austin's charm. The Willis boys just can't help it — Frank was the same as far as the charm goes. But he had a good wife who stuck by, no matter how hard the going. It made a difference in his basic character. I remember once, years ago, saying to Austin, "I like you _very_ much, but I don't admire you at all." He couldn't understand that. [...] He'll be 55 in September. Frank would have been 62 on May 15.
>
> He and Gladys were here for four days in August 1969. Did we ever enjoy them. Ann's being in a home is a depressing thing for us. And Frank brought us laughter on his last visit. He took us out to see Ann (It's 29 miles from here.) and most of the nurses recognized him and was there a buzz and a thrill around the place. Ann has advanced diabetes, hardening of the arteries, and two years ago she fell & broke her hip.

Up to that time, Helen & I were looking after her, and it was hard. We had to bathe her, give her insulin, watch her diet etc. She'd take fits of crying — she was tottery on her feet & sometimes — <u>most</u> times, she'd not make it to the bathroom on time. When she broke the hip, her doctor told us she needed intensive care of which we were not capable. We had an awful time finding a suitable nursing home. This one is in a village — there's a small hospital there, a doctor, and the nicest people. They are so kind, and give her such good care. We've managed, through the kindness of friends, to get to see her every week. [...]

I was interested that Gladys said our house "was something." Once after being here, she wrote & said it was "a doll's house." It is arranged as artistically as we know how. We have hundreds & hundreds of books & they always add — we have some lovely pottery — good prints — good china for eatin' off. The rooms are green with exception of kitchen which is yellow & white. We figure having the greens, the transition from one room to another is good — not broken. We always (so far) have had nice flowers. Ann used to do that — she loved working in the earth — her face would glow as she transplanted. God help us all — we never know. It's an awful heartbreak. Helen has taken over the flowers. We have a good man who digs and Helen tells him where to put what. I take on the big chore of picking and arranging. I just can't garden — I'm sort of stiff and sore. [...]

Now to the CBC. I had some very happy years there. No one ever checked on my comings & goings. I wrote at home so they got lots of extra hours out of me. And I had so many good friends in all the departments. [...]

I was sorry to leave Toronto. The "Maggie Muggins" cast gave me a lovely party at Alice Hill's. Grace Webster shared. They asked a great many of my friends. The CBC on my retirement gave me an Encyclopedia Britannica. Grace Athersich was responsible for that. Grace is a real go-getter. They had been giving barometers at the retirement parties. I said once, I wouldn't want one of those. Grace knew I wanted an Encyclopedia & she started the ball rolling. More than a hundred contributed and on the first volume their names appear. It was a wonderful gift, and a wonderful retiring party held in the "Kremlin." It took me a couple of weeks to write personal "thank yous." I stayed 2 years after retiring, freelancing. Then they got a new supervisor, who killed my shows and brought a friend of his "Mr. Rogers" up from Pittsburg.[29]

Mary set the letter aside until August, when she heard that the Murrays' place in Lillooet was on fire. She picked up the letter again, adding another page, but once again abandoned it, never actually mailing it.

Later that year, on Christmas Eve, 1971, Ann died at the nursing home in Harvey. Within three or four months, Mary had a bad fall, injuring her back seriously enough that she was hospitalized for a while. Upon her release, she recuperated at home in a hospital bed on the ground floor, attended by her ever-faithful Helen. Physiotherapist Jack Ross, Helen's colleague and friend from the hospital, came to the house to do what he could to alleviate the pain in Mary's back.[30] She walked with the help of a cane after that, but fell again in 1974, breaking her arm. In spite of it all, she remained mentally alert, retaining her sense of humour. She occupied her time with many of the same activities as before — reading, watching television, writing letters, doing paper crafts, and talking with friends who dropped by. While she was bedridden, she sometimes put a note on the back of her hand-crafted cards with a small drawing of a bed, "The Very Sick Card Company, Very Sick."

During these later years while Mary was mostly at home, Don used to visit on Sunday mornings while Helen went to church. During the private talks that Mary and Don had on these Sunday mornings, she reflected on her life, confiding in him many things that even her sisters never knew. Mary told Don that she wished she had travelled more and felt she had not been religious enough. She did not regret passing up marriage and children, for she had loved her broadcasting career, which had brought her great joy and fulfillment.

On January 3, 1975, Mary died unexpectedly of heart failure. Having just finished breakfast, she was sitting on the side of her bed when she fell backwards. Helen soon found her and telephoned the family doctor who lived across the street. After examining Mary, the doctor telephoned Don to come over.

"When I got in," Don said, "the doctor had left. Helen was out back screaming. Of course, the shock."[31]

Tributes for Mary flowed in the newspapers, radio, and television. Many people wrote Helen to express their love and appreciation of the woman they had known and worked beside. At the CBC in particular, staff who had known Mary felt a deep sadness. June Graham, Toronto Radio Promotion Representative, wrote a tribute in the staff magazine, *Closed Circuit*:

> In the sadness over the news of Mary Grannan's death at 73,* the main thing I recall is that no one enjoyed a good giggle more than she, or could invoke one with more style. She was one of the funniest people I ever met. When she launched into an anecdote about some of the strange or amusing people she'd encountered, she'd have you clutching your sides in seconds. It was partly her sense of timing, her mobile face, the warm innocence that cosmopolitan life never erased, the seriousness with which she could drop a devilish chortler, and her unawareness of how vastly amusing she really was. Mark Twain would have adored her, and we were all happy when she was made an honorary member of the International Mark Twain Society in 1951, joining the ranks of Eugene O'Neill, John Masefield, Lionel

---

* Mary was 74, not 73, when she died.

Barrymore, and Albert Einstein. Just Mary with the likes of those! She chuckled — and purred.

Part of her loveableness stemmed from the fact that there were two Marys. That tall, well-built, sophisticated-looking woman in couturier gowns, enormous hats and oversize jewellery, who enjoyed a bit of ribaldry, good food, and a drink or two, was a rather shy insecure little girl underneath, who loved and needed people, and, after decades of city life, was still a bit superstitious, religious, and upright, who got goose bumps when the Big Top hit town or she discovered a new book about the Wild West. ...

Mary was one of the handful of imaginative, hardworking, humorous, knowledgeable, charismatic characters who poured themselves into the CBC unstintingly, and made the golden days of radio and early television so hard to live up to today. On January 3rd, Just Mary became just memories. But they're warm, happy ones. She was fun.[32]

When radio and television were young, Mary Grannan was part of the popular culture that was airborne across our country, drawing us together. For more than two decades, we heard her voice, listened to her stories, and she was part of us. To those of us who particularly enjoyed her stories in our youth, she was an inspiration.

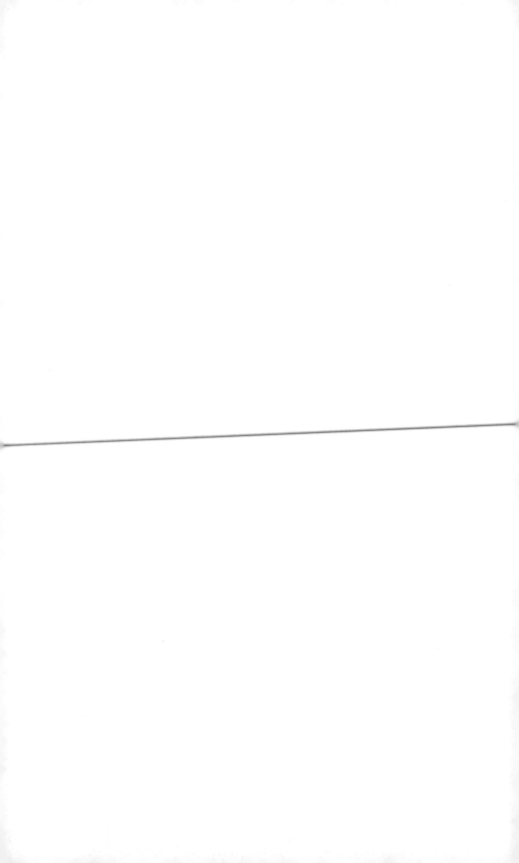

Epilogue
The Last Public Performance, 1967

It took a telephone call followed by a personal visit to 325 Brunswick Street, but finally Hayden Leaman succeeded in convincing a reluctant Mary Grannan to come and read some of her stories to his second-year class at Teachers' College. Leaman described the class, entitled "Creative English," as including all those things not normally done in English classes but would be interesting to try.

"I was asked to do something to try to improve the sterility of what goes on in classes," he said. "I wanted to show the student-teachers how to bring things alive by reading to their students, so that they themselves would learn to read."[1]

Often drawing on talented individuals available in the community, Leaman found that Mary was a uniquely interesting resource since she had started out as a New Brunswick teacher before launching her broadcasting career. Retired and living in Fredericton again, she would be an inspiration to the aspiring teachers.

On Thursday afternoon, March 9, 1967, Leaman drove her to the University of New Brunswick campus where Teachers' College was located and ushered her to the classroom on the ground floor. He noticed she was physically aging and having some difficulty moving around, but she was attired magnificently in a dress and matching coat, turban hat, dangling earrings, and broad silver bracelets — "a Parisian costume with a touch of gypsy,"[2] Leaman said. He introduced her to approximately thirty skeptical nineteen-year-olds who responded with absolute silence. Sitting in the class as well that day was Eileen Wallace, who taught children's literature at the college. Mary, on her first teaching assignment in 1918, had boarded at Eileen's mother's house a few years before Eileen was born.

After the introduction, Mary sat down at the front of the room, settling into a comfortable position. As she began reading, the years appeared to drop away, her animated voice and lively face dramatically engaged in the storytelling. Her talent and charisma revealed that the full impact of her legendary tales lay as much in her capable delivery as in the construction of the stories. Part of the magic was Mary Grannan herself. When the hour ended, the class burst into applause, giving her a standing ovation. The skeptics had become believers. Mary was obviously delighted, but as Leaman took her home, he realized that she was also exhausted from the physical and emotional demands of the reading.

The class that day had most likely witnessed Mary Grannan's last public performance.

Notes

Abbreviations

CBCMG   CBC Mary Grannan Personal File

CBCRF   CBC Reference Library

CON   Centre for Broadcasting Studies, Concordia University

DR   Donald Roberts Collection

LAC1   Library and Archives Canada, RG41, A-V-2, v. 867, file PG4-Just Mary Pt.1, 1938-1947

LAC2   Library and Archives Canada, RG41, A-IV-2-C, v. 276, file 11-42-9-4

LAC3   Library and Archives Canada, RG41, A-IV-2-C, v. 393, file 21-10, "Complaints and Appreciations — Sale of 'Just Mary' books, 1941-1945"

PANB1   Provincial Archives of New Brunswick, Mary Grannan fonds, MC1052

PANB2   Provincial Archives of New Brunswick, Fletcher Peacock fonds, RS116 D18d

Foreword

1. "John Interviewing Mary Grannan (Maggie Muggins Author) in Her Home In Fredericton, N.B., Spring 1972," ts., John Moss, 18. I am

indebted to Dr. John Moss, FRSC, Department of English, University of Ottawa, for giving me this unpublished typescript for deposit in the University of New Brunswick Archives, Harriet Irving Library.
2. Ibid., 21.

Chapter One: The Departure, 1939

1. Mary Grannan, interview by J. Frank Willis, *In Reply*, CBC Radio, 17 June 1962, transcription recording, DR.
2. Donald Roberts, interview by the author, 10 February 2001.
3. Helen Grannan, interview by the author, tape recording & transcript, 30 October 1993, 1.
4. Ronald S. Ritchie, letter to the author, 19 November 2001.
5. Canadian Pacific Railway public timetable, 25 June 1939, Table 12A, 10. There were two overnight CP trains to Montreal with no evidence available to indicate which train MG took. Most likely she took the earlier train, as the later one would have placed her in Toronto after ten o'clock on the night before she had to report for work. For purposes of description, it is assumed she took the earlier train.
6. Eleanor Stillwell, interview by the author, 30 September 2001.
7. Environment Canada, *Climate Data Online*, Daily Data Report for June 1939, Fredericton CDA New Brunswick.
8. *The Daily Gleaner*, 30 June 1939, 1.
9. Ibid., 14 June 1939, 4.
10. Gladstone Murray, letter to Mary Grannan, 5 January 1939. DR.
11. Mary Grannan, letter to Gladstone Murray, 15 June 1939. CBCMG.
12. Details of train journey, Ronald S. Ritchie, letter to the author, 19 November 2001.

Chapter Two: Birth of a Storyteller, 1900–1914

1. Mary Grannan, certificate of baptism, St. Dunstan's Church, 31 May 1954. DR.
2. Bill McNeil and Morris Wolfe, *Signing On* (Toronto: Doubleday, 1982), 11.
3. F.H. Leacy, ed., *Historical Statistics of Canada*, 2nd ed. (Ottawa: Statistics Canada, 1983), Series A2-14 Population, census dates 1851–1976.

4. *Daily Gleaner*, February 11, 1900.
5. Desmond Morton, *A Short History of Canada*, 5th ed. (Toronto: McClelland & Stewart, 2001), 144-158.
6. W. Austin Squires, *History of Fredericton: The Last 200 Years* (Fredericton: City of Fredericton, 1980).
7. Ibid.
8. William Peter Grannan, birth, marriage, and death records; Catherine Teresa (variant Theresa) Haney, marriage and death records. PANB.
9. Helen Grannan, interview by the author, tape recording & transcript, 30 October 1993, 10.
10. Ann Grannan, late birth registration, PANB; Francis Murphy, letter to Ann Grannan, 24 April 1948. DR.
11. *McAlpine's New Brunswick Directory for 1903* (St. John: McAlpine Publishing Co. Ltd., 1903), PANB.
12. Helen Grannan, "My Sister Mary," *Atlantic Advocate*, May 1957, 58.
13. *Hutchison's New Brunswick Directory for 1865-1866* (Saint John: 1965), PANB, MF F-1412, 244.
14. *Fredericton Census of 1871*, 88. PANB.
15. Helen Grannan, interview by David McCormack, tape recording, 28 March 1992. DR.
16. Rohal, "Just Mary," *Teen Talk*, summer 1945, 6.
17. *4th Census of Canada* (1901), PANB, F15365, Fredericton Carleton Ward, no. 4, 17.
18. Squires, *History of Fredericton*, 89-90.
19. James O'Neill, interview by the author, 5 June 2000.
20. Squires, *History of Fredericton*, 48.
21. Ibid., 49.
22. Helen Grannan, interview by the author, tape recording & transcript, 30 October 1993, 10.
23. Ibid., 11.
24. Donald Roberts, interview by the author, 10 February 2001.
25. Mary Grannan, *Just Mary Anniversary Programme*, CBC Radio, 30 July 1948, 6-7. CON.
26. Rohal, "Just Mary," *Teen Talk*, summer 1945, 6.
27. Helen Grannan, interview by the author, tape recording & transcript, 30 October 1993, 1.

28. Teacher's Reports, Fredericton (1906-1914). PANB.
29. Helen Grannan, letter to Fergus Cronin, 14 August 1985, 4.
30. Ibid., 4-5.
31. Helen Grannan, "My Sister Mary," *Atlantic Advocate*, May 1957, 58.
32. Ibid.
33. Mary Grannan, *Just Mary Anniversary Programme*, CBC Radio, 30 July 1948, 11. CON.
34. Squires, *History of Fredericton*, 140-141; Ted and Anita Jones, *Fredericton and Its People, 1825-1945* (Halifax: Nimbus, 2002),145.
35. Helen Grannan, letter to Fergus Cronin, 2 June 1982, 4-5.
36. James O'Neill, letter to the author, 9 June 2001.
37. Mary Grannan, *Just Mary Anniversary Programme*, CBC Radio, 30 July 1948, 9. CON.
38. James O'Neill, interview by the author, 5 June 2000.
39. Description of the Mighty Haag Circus based on "The Haag Circus Draws Big Crowd This Afternoon," *The Daily Gleaner*, June 18, 1914, 10; Charlie Duble, "A Tour with the Mighty Haag Circus - season 1911," *Hobby-Bandwagon*, November-December, 1948, 3-4; Charles E. Duble, "The Mighty Haag Circus, 1912", *The Bandwagon*, 2, no. 3 (May-June, 1958): 6.
40. Duble, "A Tour with the Mighty Haag Circus", 3.

Chapter Three: The Schoolmarm, 1914–1934

1. Canadian Pacific Railway public timetable, 25 June 1939, Table 12A, 10.
2. Ibid., Table 10, 9.
3. Ronald S. Ritchie, letter and memoranda to the author, 19 November 2001.
4. Ibid.; Canadian Pacific Railway public timetable, 25 June 1939.
5. Teacher's Reports, 1915-1918, Fredericton City. PANB.
6. Ibid.
7. Rohal, "Just Mary," *Teen Talk*, summer 1945, 6; Kay McMullen, "Just Mary, Herself," *Catholic Youth*, June 1944, 9.
8. Helen Grannan, letter to Fergus Cronin, 5 November 1981, 3-4.
9. Mary Ann Robertson, deed to Patrick Haney, no. 29987, Registry Office Province of New Brunswick, 3 May 1879.

10. Helen Grannan, interview by David McCormack, tape recording, 28 March 1992. DR.
11. Helen Grannan, interview by the author, tape recording & transcript, 30 October 1993.
12. Mary Haney, will no. 66344, Registry Office Province of New Brunswick, 14 April 1916, registered 17 June 1916. (Variant spelling, Margaret Flannigan.)
13. Mary Grannan, Provincial Normal School record. PANB.
14. Mary Grannan, Trustees' Return for Maplewood, December 1918. PANB.
15. Helen Grannan, letter to Fergus Cronin, 20 July 1986, 3-4.
16. Ann Grannan, Teacher's Reports, Minto, 1918-1919; Mary Grannan, Teacher's Reports, 1919. PANB.
17. Rohal, "Just Mary," *Teen Talk*, summer 1945, 7.
18. Marjorie Taylor-Morell, *Of Mines and Men* (St. Stephen, N.B.: Print'N Press, 1981), 50.
19. *Daily Gleaner*, 25 April 1919, 10.
20. Helen Grannan, letter to Fergus Cronin, 20 July 1986, 4.
21. Ibid.
22. Fred Mawer, letter to Mary Grannan, 23 October 1919. PANB1.
23. Ted Jones, "Bittersweet Memories of Devon Superior School," *Daily Gleaner*, 26 March 2005, B2.
24. Pat Barry, interview by the author, 27 June 2001; Lila Titus MacPherson, interview by the author, 25 September 2001.
25. Mary Grannan, Teacher's Returns, 1920-1939. PANB.
26. Pat Barry, interview by the author, 27 June 2001.
27. Interviews of former students by the author: Mavis Williams Dunn, 11 June 2001; Pat Barry, 27 June 2001; Mary Galen Cassidy, 27 June 2001; Donna Bolster Rickard, 26 September 2001; Eleanor Monteith Stillwell, 30 September 2001; Mary Hayes, 1 October 2001; Mary Kessom Grandy, 2 October 2001.
28. Susan Manzer, "Fredericton Writer Had Vast Audience," *The Atlantic Advocate*, February 1973, 47.
29. Mary Hayes, interview by the author, 1 October 2001.
30. Pat Barry, interview by the author, 27 June 2001.
31. Mae Savage Nicholson, interview by the author, 28 January 2004.

32. Mae Savage Nicholson, letter to the author, 8 August 2001, 2.
33. Mary Kessom Grandy, interview by the author, 2 October 2001.
34. Mary Grannan, "Students MSS Book," 1928-1933, [116]-[127]. U.N.B. Archives & Special Collections, Harriet Irving Library.
35. Rohal, "Just Mary," *Teen Talk*, summer 1945, 6.
36. *The Daily Gleaner*, 17 September 1929, 3.
37. Mary Grannan, drawings, clippings from *The Daily Gleaner*, June 1930. DR.
38. Mary Kessom Grandy, interview by the author, 2 October 2001.
39. Pat Barry, interview by the author, 27 June 2001.
40. Mary Grannan, "Students MSS Book," 1928-1933, [1-3]. U.N.B. Archives & Special Collections, Harriet Irving Library.
41. Ibid., [102].
42. Donald Roberts, interview by the author, tape recording & transcript, 28 October 1993, 10-11.
43. Muriel-Ann McKenna, interview by the author, tape recording & transcript, 18 May 1999, 13.
44. Gertrude Davis, interview by the author, tape recording & transcript, 9 June 2000, 2.
45. Eleanor Monteith Stillwell, interview by the author, 30 September 2001.
46. Gertrude Davis, interview by the author, tape recording & transcript, 9 June 2000, 2.
47. William Walker (Jr.), Gwen Kitchen Herbin, Nancy Herbin Beltrandi, interview by the author, 2 October 2001.
48. Ibid.
49. Photograph. DR.
50. Mary Grannan, "Students MSS Book," 1928-1933, [111]-[113]. U.N.B. Archives & Special Collections, Harriet Irving Library.
51. Helen Grannan, letter to Fergus Cronin, 20 July 1986, 4.

Chapter Four: The New Circus, 1935–1939

1. Knowlton Nash, *The Microphone Wars: A History of Triumph and Betrayal at the CBC* (Toronto: McClelland & Stewart, 1994), 15-49.
2. Donn Downey, "Malcolm Neill: New Brunswick broadcaster was radio pioneer," *Globe and Mail*, 3 April 2000, R6.

3. Jack Fenety, "CFNB Anniversary: They Raised their Family in the Studio," *Canadian Broadcaster*, 23 January 1958, 16, 18-19.

4. Jack Fenety, interview by the author, tape recording & transcript, 8 February 2001, 5.

5. Fenety, "CFNB Anniversary," 16; Squires, *History of Fredericton*, 70.

6. "Canadian Education Week," *Educational Review* 49, no. 6 (February 1935): 5.

7. Gertrude Davis, interview by the author, tape recording & transcript, 9 June 2000, 2.

8. [Gertrude Davis], letter to P.S. Watson, 23 September 1936. PANB1.

9. Rohal, "Just Mary," *Teen Talk*, summer 1945, 7.

10. Mary Grannan, letter to Gladstone Murray, 12 January 1939, [1]. CBCMG.

11. Ernest B. VanDine, "'Aggravating Agatha' of CFNB Concludes Successful Season," *Daily Mail*, 21 July 1936.

12. Mary Grannan, "My Favourite Laugh," *Liberty*, 27 September 1947.

13. Gertrude Davis, interview by the author, tape recording & transcript, 9 June 2000.

14. Mary Grannan, *Aggravating Agatha*. DR.

15. William P. Grannan, Certificate of Registration of Death, Department of Health, New Brunswick, PANB.

16. "The Late W.P. Grannan," *Daily Gleaner*, 5 March 1935, 12.

17. Ted Jones, "Bittersweet Memories of Devon Superior School," *Daily Gleaner*, 26 March 2005, B2.

18. Teachers' Reports, Devon School, 1921-1935, PANB.

19. Marsh Jeanneret, *God and Mammon: Universities as Publishers* (Toronto: Macmillan of Canada, 1989), 18.

20. Wilfred Wees, letter to Mary Grannan, 5 July 1937. PANB1.

21. Mary Grannan, *Just Mary Anniversary Programme*, CBC Radio, 30 July 1948, 18. CON.

22. Wilfred Wees, letter to Mary Grannan, 12 July 1937. PANB1.

23. Wilfred Wees, letter to Mary Grannan, 18 September 1937. PANB1.

24. Amy J. Roe, letter to Mary Grannan, 10 December 1937. PANB1.

25. Amy J. Roe, letter to Mary Grannan, 31 March 1938. PANB1.

26. Mary Grannan, "Magic Cookies," *Country Guide & Nor'-West Farmer*, January 1938, 40.

27. Hayden Leaman, interview by the author, 29 October 1993.

28. Scott Webster, interview by the author, 4 October 2001.

29. Moira Day and Marilyn Potts, "Elizabeth Sterling Haynes: Initiator of Alberta Theatre," *Theatre History in Canada*, 8, 1 (Spring 1987): 32.

30. Mary Grannan, letter to Fletcher Peacock, 21 December 1937. PANB2.

31. Ibid.

32. Fletcher Peacock, letter to Mary Grannan, 8 January 1938. PANB2.

33. Ibid.

34. Sterling Haynes, interview by the author, 18 July 2001.

35. J. Frank Willis, letter to Carl Watson, 10 August 1936. PANB1.

36. J. Frank Willis, letter to Carl Watson, 8 December 1936. PANB1.

37. J. Stewart Neill, letter to William Gladstone Murray, 11 December 1936. PANB1.

38. Mary Grannan, letter to Robert Bowman, 15 May 1937. LAC2 & PANB1.

39. *Daily Gleaner*, 4 March 1937.

40. R.T. Bowman, letter to Mary Grannan, 1 June 1937. LAC2 & PANB1.

41. Mary Grannan, letter to R.T. Bowman, 5 June 1937. LAC2 & PANB1.

42. R.T. Bowman, letter to Mary Grannan, 12 June 1937. LAC2 & PANB1.

43. R.T. Bowman, letter to J. Frank Willis, 12 June 1937. LAC2.

44. Frank Willis, letter to Mary Grannan, 30 June 1937. PANB1.

45. W.H. Brodie, letter to E.L. Bushnell, 2 December 1937. LAC2.

46. Elizabeth Sterling Haynes, letter to Radio Commission, 16 December 1937, LAC2.

47. Elizabeth Sterling Haynes, letter to Hugh Morrison, 5 July 1938. LAC2.

48. H.W. Morrison, letter to Mary Grannan, 4 July 1938. PANB1.

49. Malcolm Neill, interview by the author, 11 August 1999.

50. Mary Grannan, *Just Mary Anniversary Programme*, CBC Radio, 30 July 1948: 20. CON.

51. J. Stewart Neill, telegram to Mary Grannan, 17 August 1938. DR.
52. W. Gladstone Murray, letter to E.L. Bushnell, 6 December 1938. CBCMG.
53. E.L. Bushnell, letter to W. Gladstone Murray, 7 December 1938. CBCMG.
54. Ibid.
55. W. Gladstone Murray, letter to Mary Grannan, 5 January 1939. DR.
56. Mary Grannan, letter to W. Gladstone Murray, 10 January 1939. CBCMG.
57. W. Gladstone Murray, letter to Mary Grannan, 21 January 1939. CBCMG.
58. Mary Grannan, letter to W. Gladstone Murray, 1 February 1939. CBCMG.
59. W. Gladstone Murray, letter to Mary Grannan, 8 June 1939. CBCMG.
60. Devon teachers, card to Mary Grannan, June 1939. DR.
61. Mary Galen Cassidy, interview by the author, 27 June 2001.

Chapter Five: Toronto Beginning, 1939–1940

1. H.W. Morrison, letter to Mary Grannan, 15 May 1939. CBCMG.
2. Helen Grannan, letter to Fergus Cronin, 11 October 1982, [2].
3. Mary Grannan, letter to W. Gladstone Murray, [4 July 1939]. CBCMG.
4. Mary Grannan, interview script, *Just Mary Anniversary Programme*, CBC Radio, 30 July 1948, 3. CON.
5. W. Gladstone Murray, testimony, Special Committee on Radio Broadcasting, Minutes of Proceedings and Evidence, no. 8, 17 March 1939, 173.
6. Mary Grannan, letter to Fletcher Peacock, 10 July 1939. PANB2.
7. Fletcher Peacock, letter to Mary Grannan, 13 July 1939. PANB2.
8. Mary Grannan, letter to Fletcher Peacock, [September 1939]. PANB2.
9. Ibid.
10. CBC Annual Report, 1939-1940, 1. CBCRF.
11. Mary Grannan, letter to W. Gladstone Murray, 23 October 1939. LAC1.

12. Mary Grannan, "The Cowboy and the Pony," in *Just Mary* (Toronto: Gage, [1941]), 85.
13. "Children's Entertainment Specially Designed by CBC," *CBC Programme Schedule, Ontario Regional*, Week of October 15, 1939, 15.
14. Austin Willis, interview by the author, tape recording and transcript, 28 September 1999, 1, 3, 5.
15. Sydney Brown, interview by Ronald Hambleton, tape recording, 16 March 1977. LAC, Canadian Broadcasting Corporation, Radio: Oral History, 1981-0076, ISN 304814.
16. Austin Willis, interview by the author, tape recording and transcript, 28 September 1999, 2-3, 9.
17. Frank Perry, interview by the author, 21 March 2000.
18. Austin Willis, interview by the author, tape recording and transcript, 28 September 1999, 13.
19. *Daily Star*, clipping, 22 April 1940.
20. Mary Grannan, *Children's Scrapbook*, 9 February 1946, 1-2, 1 AC3.
21. Mary Grannan, letter to Georgina Murray Keddell, 21 May 1971, [1] 2. DR.
22. Ibid., 2-3.
23. J. Frank Willis, "Nocturne." CBCRF.
24. Mary Grannan, letter to Catherine Grannan, n.d. DR.
25. Helen Grannan, interview by the author, tape recording & transcript, 30 October 1993, 1.
26. Austin Willis, interview by the author, tape recording and transcript, 28 September 1999, 8.
27. Ibid., 10.
28. Mary Grannan, letter to Fletcher Peacock, 18 December 1939. PANB2.
29. Austin Willis, interview by the author, tape recording and transcript, 28 September 1999, 21.
30. H.W. Morrison, letter to E.L. Bushnell, 26 October 1939.
31. Mary Grannan, letter to Fletcher Peacock, 18 December 1939. PANB2.
32. Fletcher Peacock, letter to Mary Grannan, 18 December 1939. PANB2.

33. Notation appeared inside Seymour Hicks, *Me and My Missus: Fifty Years on the Stage* (London: Cassell, 1939).

34. Notation appeared inside John Gassner, ed., *Twenty Best Plays of the Modern American Theatre* (New York: Crown Publishers, 1941).

Chapter Six: Making the Grade, 1940

1. Mary Grannan, *Just Mary* (Toronto: Gage, [1941]), 1, 35; *Just Mary Again* (Toronto: Gage, 1941), 22, 27, 50.

2. Mary Grannan, *Just Mary* (Toronto: Gage, [1941]), 1.

3. Mary Grannan, *New Just Mary Stories* (Toronto: Allen, 1946), 40.

4. Ibid., 72.

5. Ibid., 189.

6. Ibid., 106-107.

7. Mary Grannan, "Little Andy Little," in *Just Mary Again* (Toronto: Gage, 1941), 24.

8. Mary Grannan, "The Magic Hood," in *Just Mary Again* (Toronto: Gage, 1941), 38.

9. Mary Grannan, "Sylvia and the Golden Cat," in *Just Mary Again* (Toronto: Gage, 1941), 77.

10. Mary Grannan, "Chocolate Fudge," in *Just Mary Again* (Toronto: Gage, 1941), 80-81.

11. Mary Grannan, "The Blue Fox," in *Just Mary Again* (Toronto: Gage, 1941), 89.

12. Mary Grannan, "The Princely Pig," in *New Just Mary Stories* (Toronto: Allen, 1946), 69.

13. Mary Grannan, "Barnyard Capers," in *Just Mary* (Toronto: Gage, [1941]), 74.

14. Mary Grannan, "The Little Green Lamb," in *Just Mary Again* (Toronto: Gage, 1941), 60.

15. W.H. Brodie, letter to E.L. Bushnell, 2 December 1937. LAC2.

16. Norah Creaghan, "Sincerity Essential with the Children, Reasons 'Just Mary,'" *Daily Gleaner*, 11 August 1951.

17. Mary Grannan, "Radio Artist Must Have Something Good to Satisfy Juniors," *C.W.P.C. Newspacket*, VI, no. 3, 1 May 1940.

18. *CBC Programme Schedule, Ontario Regional*, 1 December 1941, 5.

19. Austin Willis, interview by the author, tape recording and transcript, 28 September 1999, 1.

20. Mary Grannan, "Katy Kinsella's Kitty Cat," *Just Mary* script, 23 January 1955.

21. Ibid.

22. Austin Willis, interview by the author, 16 July 2002.

23. Ibid.

24. Austin Willis, interview by the author, tape recording and transcript, 28 September 1999, 1-2.

25. Mary Grannan, *For the Children,* 11 May 1940: 1-2, 7. LAC2.

26. Austin Willis, interview by the author, tape recording and transcript, 28 September 1999, 25.

27. Mary Grannan, "Straw Hats and Pin Cushions," in *New Just Mary Stories* (Toronto: Allen, 1946), 165.

28. Ibid.

29. Austin Willis, interview by the author, tape recording and transcript, 29 September 1999, 25.

30. Richard S. Lambert, *School Broadcasting in Canada* (Toronto: University of Toronto Press, 1963), [19]-20, [35].

31. "A Vitamin Diet," *Radio,* September 1950, 9.

32. *Annual Report of the Canadian Broadcasting Corporation,* 31 March 1943, 11. CBCRF.

33. Donald Roberts, interview by the author, 6 June 2000.

34. H.W. Morrison, letter to Walter Anderson, 21 February 1940. LAC1.

35. H.W. Morrison, letter to C.R. Delafield, 19 March 1940. LAC1.

36. Beatrice Barker, letter to W. Gladstone Murray, 27 April 1940. LAC1.

37. Fred LeR. Mawer, letter to Mary Grannan, 18 June 1940. DR.

38. J. Frank Willis as told to Jock Carroll, "J. Frank Willis: My Life on the Air," *Weekend Magazine,* 28 October 1961, 22

39. Austin Willis, interview by the author, tape recording and transcript, 29 September 1999, 14.

40. Ibid., 13-14.

Chapter Seven: First Books, 1941–1943

1. *CBC Programme Schedule*, v.2, week of September 1, 1940, 2.
2. Mary Grannan, letter to Fletcher Peacock, 4 October 1940. PANB2.
3. Ibid.
4. Ibid.
5. Mary Grannan, letter to Fletcher Peacock, 19 November 1940. PANB2.
6. Austin Willis, interview by the author, tape recording and transcript, 28 September 1999, 16.
7. Mary Grannan, "The Chinese Bracelet," *New Just Mary Stories* (Toronto: Allen, 1946), 59.
8. Mary Grannan, "Blue Breeches," *Just Mary* (Toronto: Gage, [1941]), 37.
9. E. Austin Weir, letter to W. Gladstone Murray, 26 October 1940. LAC1.
10. Mary Grannan, *Just Mary* (Toronto: Gage, [1941]), [v].
11. E. Austin Weir, letter to W. Gladstone Murray, 23 January 1941. LAC1.
12. W. Gladstone Murray, letter to Mary Grannan, 31 March 1941. CBCMG.
13. Gwenyth Grube, *The Canadian Forum*, May 1941, 61.
14. Mary Grannan, letter to W. Gladstone Murray, [April?] 1941. CBCMG.
15. E. Austin Weir, letter to Augustin Frigon and W. Gladstone Murray, 2 July 1941. LAC1.
16. E. Austin Weir, letter to W. Gladstone Murray, 18 July 1941. LAC1.
17. W.O. Findlay, letter to E.A. Weir, 26 July 1941. LAC1.
18. W. Gladstone Murray, letter to E.A. Weir, 30 October 1941. LAC1.
19. Jacqueline Webster, interview by the author, 1 October 2001.
20. J. Stewart Neill, telegram to Mary Grannan, 5 December 1941. DR.
21. Mary Grannan, "Orville Bug," in *Just Mary Again* (Toronto: Gage, [1941]), 99.

22. "How the 'Just Mary' Tales Went to War," *Radio-Vision*, 1946, 30.

23. Mary Grannan, interview by Bill McNeil, tape recording, n.d., LAC, ISN 141687.

24. Mary Grannan, "Georgie the Little Rat Who Didn't Listen," in *Just Mary Again* (Toronto: Gage, [1941]), 1.

25. S.W. Griffiths, letter to W.O. Findlay, 18 March 1942. LAC1.

26. E.A. Weir, letter to W. Gladstone Murray, 23 March 1942. LAC1.

27. W. Gladstone Murray, letter to E.A. Weir, 26 March 1942. LAC1.

28. E. L. Bushnell, "Report on Efficiency of Personnel – M. Grannan", 16 January 1942. CBCMG.

29. Sydney Brown, interview by Ronald Hambleton, tape recording, 16 March 1977, LAC, Canadian Broadcasting Corporation, Radio: Oral History, 1981-0076, ISN 304814.

30. CBC *Programme Schedule, Eastern Regional*, 17 May 1942. CBCRF.

31. Mary Grannan, letter to Beatrice Belcourt, 10 June 1942. LAC1.

32. Bob Morton, telegram to Mary Grannan, 11 May 1942. DR.

33. Mary Grannan, letter to W. Gladstone Murray, ca. July 1942. CBCMG.

34. W Gladstone Murray, letter to Mary Grannan, 4 July 1942. DR.

35. Nash, *The Microphone Wars*, 175.

36. W. Gladstone Murray, letter to Mary Grannan, 31 December 1942. DR.

37. Mary Grannan, "A Silly Tale," in *Just Mary* (Toronto: Gage, [1941]), 73.

38. E.A. Weir, letter to Augustin Frigon, 2 October 1943. LAC3.

39. F.D. Tolchard, letter to James S. Thomson, 11 January 1943. LAC3.

40. James S. Thomson, letter to J.F. MacNeill, 29 January 1943. LAC1.

41. E.A. Weir, letter to James S. Thomson, 3 February 1943. LAC1.

42. J.F. MacNeill, letter to James S. Thomson, 16 February 1943. LAC1.

43. H.H. Love, letter to E.A. Weir, 9 February 1943. LAC1.

44. E.A. Weir, letter to James S. Thomson, 15 March 1943. LAC1.

45. "Radio in the War and After," Fourteenth Institute for Education by Radio, Official Program, 30 April–3 May 1943, 6, 14. DR.

46. Mary Grannan, ed., "Children on the War," n.d., ca. 1943. PANB1.

47. Mary Grannan, letter to Fletcher Peacock, 21 January 1942. PANB2.

48. Mary Grannan, "Blue Boots," in *Three Music Plays for Schools* (Toronto: Ontario Public Relations Committee, Second Victory Loan, [1942]), 5. DR.

49. Mary Grannan, "Builders of Canada," in *Three Music Plays for Schools* (Toronto: Ontario Public Relations Committee, Second Victory Loan, [1942]), 9. DR.

50. Mary Grannan, letter to Ann and Helen Grannan, [1943]. DR.

51. "Mary Grannan of 'Just Mary' Fame Visitor in City," clipping Moncton newspaper, August 1943. DR.

52. Mary Grannan, letter to George Young, 25 May 1943. CON.

53. Mary Grannan, letter to George Young, [June 1943]. CON.

54. George Young, letter to Mary Grannan, 13 July 1943. CON.

55. Ibid.

56. Mary Grannan, letter to George Young, 2 August 1943. CON.

57. Mary Grannan, letter to George Young, 7 July 1943. CON.

58. Mary Grannan, letter to Ann and Helen Grannan, [August 1943]. DR.

Chapter Eight: The Birth of *Maggie Muggins*, 1944–1945

1. E.A. Weir, letter to J.S. Thomson, 15 March 1943. LAC1.

2. E.A. Weir, letter to A. Frigon, 6 January 1944. LAC1.

3. Mary Grannan, letter to Beth Morris, circa 1955. Courtesy Beth Morris.

4. Ibid.

5. Mary E. Grannan, *Maggie Muggins* (Toronto: Thomas Allen, 1944), [24]

6. Kay McMullen, letter to Mary Grannan, 15 October 1944. DR.

7. Mary Grannan, letter to Fletcher Peacock, 29 November 1940. PANB2.

8. *Contemporary Authors New Revision Series*, vol. 83 (Detroit: Gale, 2000), 273-274.

9. Mary Grannan, letter to Ann and Helen Grannan, [spring 1944]. DR.

10. James S. Thomson, letter to Deputy Minister of Justice, 17 September 1943. LAC1.

11. F.P. Varcoe, letter to the General Manager, Canadian Broadcasting Corporation, 14 October 1943. LAC1.
12. F.W. Savignac, letter to CBC General Manager, 6 August 1943. LAC1.
13. F.W. Savignac, letter to CBC General Manager, 19 May 1943. LAC1.
14. G.M. Kelley, letter to D. Allen, 14 April 1944. DR.
15. Gerard Ruel, letter to E.L. Bushnell, 8 May 1944. DR.
16. Ibid.
17. E.A. Weir, letter to General Supervisor of Programs (E.L. Bushnell), 26 June 1944. LAC1.
18. F.W. Savignac, letter to E.L. Bushnell and E.A. Weir, 26 July1944. LAC1.
19. E.A. Weir, letter to F. Willard Savignac, 27 July 1944. LAC1.
20. Mary E. Grannan, letter to Dr. Augustin Frigon, 19 October 1944. LAC1.
21. Augustin Frigon, letter to Mary E. Grannan, 4 December 1944. LAC1.
22. E.A. Weir, letter to General Supervisor of Programs (E.L. Bushnell), 26 June 1944. LAC1.
23. E. Bushnell, Report on Efficiency of Personnel: M. Grannan, 1944-1945. CBCMG.
24. F.W. Savignac, letter to Mary Grannan, 24 January 1958. DR.
25. Mary Grannan, inscription to E.A. Weir in *New Just Mary Stories* (Toronto: Thomas Allen, 1946). Book courtesy of Mary Louise Weir Penrose.
26. Mary Grannan, letter to Georgina Murray, 23 March 1945. Courtesy Margaret Graham.
27. Georgina Murray, letter to Mr. and Mrs. George Murray, n.d. Courtesy Margaret Graham.
28. Elmore Philpott, "Big Shark Story," *The Vancouver Sun*, 15 October 1948: 4.
29. Mary Grannan, "Bonnie, Kate and Ellen," *Happy Playtime* (Toronto: Thomas Allen, 1948), 32-33.
30. Ibid, 38.
31. Charles Jennings, letter to E. Bushnell, 5 December 1945. CBCMG.

32. E. L. Bushnell, notation to Charles Jennings, December 1945. CBCMG.

33. Austin Willis, interview by the author, tape recording and transcript, 28 September 1999, 4, verso of 2.

34. E.L. Bushnell, letter to General Supervisor of Programmes (Charles Jennings), 15 December 1945. CBCMG.

35. Charles Jennings, letter to Supervisor of Presentation (John Kannawin), 20 December 1945. CBCMG.

36. Charles Jennings, letter to Mary Grannan, 20 December 1945. CBCMG.

37. J.R. Finlay, letter to General Supervisor of Programmes (Charles Jennings), 28 May 1947. CBCMG.

38. Noel Langley, inscription to Mary Grannan inside Irving Stone, *Lust for Life: A Novel of Vincent Van Gogh* (New York: Heritage Press, [1936]). DR

39. Noel Langley, letter to Mary Grannan, 6 November 1945. DR.

40. Mary Grannan, "Memorandum From 1945." DR.

Chapter Nine: Advent of *Maggie Muggins* on the Radio, 1946–1948

1. John Allen, interview by the author, 14 May 1999.

2. Wells Ritchie, letter to Assistant General Manager et al., 25 September 1946. LAC1.

3. *Toronto Star*, 16 November 1946.

4. *Globe and Mail*, 16 November 1946.

5. Mary Grannan, "Willie Wee Rabbit," in *New Just Mary Stories* (Toronto: Thomas Allen, 1946), 202-203.

6. Noel Langley, letter to Mary Grannan, 16 March 1946. DR.

7. Charles Jennings, letter to Programme Director et al., 26 September 1947. CBCMG.

8. Bonnie Buckingham, "Here Comes Maggie Muggins!" *New/Nouveau Brunswick* 11, no. 3 (1987): 28.

9. Canadian Broadcasting Corporation, *Annual Report*, 31 March 1947: 21. CBCRF; Sandy Stewart, *From Coast to Coast* (Toronto: CBC Enterprises, 1985),136-138; *CBC Programme Schedule*, BC Region, 28 December 1947, 4.

10. Canadian Broadcasting Corporation, *Annual Report*, 31 March 1947, 21. CBCRF.

11. Charles Jennings, letter to Mary Grannan, 21 May 1945. DR.

12. Mary Grannan, "The Gypsy's Prediction," in *Land of Supposing*, 7 May 1950, 1, CON.

13. Mary Grannan, letter to Beth Morris, circa 1955. Courtesy Beth Morris.

14. Beryl Hart, interview by the author, tape recording and transcript, 8 October 2000.

15. Ibid.

16. Mary Grannan, "Maggie and the Porcupine," in *New Maggie Muggins Stories* (Toronto: Thomas Allen, 1947).

17. Mary Grannan, letter to Beth Morris, circa 1955. Courtesy Beth Morris.

18. Beryl Hart, interview by the author, tape recording and transcript, 8 October 2000.

19. Ibid.

20. Ibid.

21. *Canadian Broadcaster* 6, no. 6 (22 March 1947): 1.

22. Canadian Broadcasting Corporation, *Annual Report*, 31 March 1947, 21. CBCRF.

23. Jack Mather, interview by the author, 7 May 2002.

24. Max Braithwaite, "Just Mary," *Maclean's*, 1 June 1947, 8, 56+.

25. Ibid.

26. Ibid.

27. Mary Grannan, letter to Helen Grannan, December 1947. DR.

28. Mary Grannan, "Why O'Casey Barked at the Moon," in *New Just Mary Stories* (Toronto: Thomas Allen, 1946), 21.

29. Canadian Broadcasting Corporation, Press Release, 23 July 1948. CBCMG.

30. "Just Mary" Anniversary Programme script, "Just Mary, Vol. 1" File. CON.

31. Ibid.

32. Donald Manson, letter to Supervisor of Press & Information Service, 4 August 1948. CBCMG.

33. Noel Langley, letter to Mary Grannan, 15 April [1949?]. DR.

Chapter Ten: Visit to the Old Countries, 1949

1. Paul Smith (presumed author of letter as last page missing), letter to Mary Grannan, 30 August [1949?]. DR.
2. Mary Grannan, diary "My Trip," July-August 1949, [1]. DR.
3. Ibid., [10].
4. Ibid., [8].
5. Ibid., [13].
6. Ibid., [16].
7. Ibid., [17-18].
8. Ibid., [18, 20].
9. Ibid., [23-26].
10. Liam Gannon, interview by the author, 5 April 2004.
11. Mary Grannan, diary "My Trip," July-August 1949, [30]. DR.
12. Ibid., [31].
13. Donald Roberts, interview by the author, 6 February 2002; Regina Clarke, interview by the author, 4 March 2002.
14. Donald Roberts, interview by the author, 6 February 2002.
15. Mary Grannan, diary "My Trip," July-August 1949, [33-34]. DR.
16. Ibid., [35].
17. Ibid., [36].
18. Ibid., [37-38].
19. Ibid., [39].
20. Alan Cole and Paul Smith remained together at least until the early 1960s, moving to Sweden, the United States, and Australia after Cole completed his doctorate at Trinity in 1952. Cole was a senior lecturer in the English Department at the University of Melbourne from 1961 until his death in 1976. Smith became a writer, eventually returning to Dublin, where he died in 1997.
21. Mary Grannan, diary "My Trip," July–August 1949, [46]. DR.
22. Ibid., [55].
23. Ibid., [54].
24. Chanticleer, "Notebook," *Daily Herald*, 28 July 1949, 2.
25. Mary Grannan, diary "My Trip," July-August 1949, [66-67]. DR.
26. Looker On, "Whispers from the Wings," *Theatre World*, April 1949, 29-30.

27. Jacqueline Langley, interview by the author, 30 December 2001.

28. Noel Langley, letter to Mary Grannan, 23 November 1949. DR.

29. Noel Langley, letter to Mary Grannan, 5 December [1949?]. DR.

30. Noel Langley, letter to Mary Grannan, 14 August 1949. DR.

31. "'Just Mary' Back from U.K.Visit," *Daily Gleaner*, 25 August 1949.

32. Mary Grannan, diary "My Trip," July-August 1949, [82]. DR.

33. Noel Langley, letter to Mary Grannan, 3 December 1949. DR.

34. Mary Grannan, "A 'Mary' Merry Christmas," *Radio* 5, no. 11 (December 1949): 4. LAC

Chapter Eleven: Prelude to Television, 1949–1954

1. *Globe and Mail*, 2 December 1949, 9.

2. Dominion Bureau of Statistics, "Radio and Television Receiving Sets," 9, no. 1 (January 1954), 1. VPL.

3. CBC *Programme Schedule, BC Region*, 15-21 May 1949, 4.

4. Mary Grannan, letter to Director General of Programmes et al., 19 September 1950, 1. DR.

5. Ibid., 5-6.

6. Mary Grannan, letter to H.J. Boyle et al., 28 May 1954, 5. PANB1.

7. Mary Grannan, "Big Bite's Mistake," in *Maggie Muggins and Mr. McGarrity* (Toronto: Thomas Allen, 1952), 15.

8. Ibid., 9.

9. Ibid., 8.

10. Ibid., 5.

11. Mary Grannan, "The Ironing Board," in *Maggie Muggins and Her Friends* (Toronto: Thomas Allen, 1954), 3-4.

12. June Callwood, "Meet Maggie Muggins," *Maclean's*, 1 July 1949, 19, 35-36.

13. Institute for Education by Radio, the Ohio State University, certificate presented to *Maggie Muggins*, 1950. DR.

14. John Allen, interview by the author, 9 May 2002.

15. Mary Grannan, *Just Mary Blue Stories* (Toronto: Thomas Allen, 1950), 25-37.

16. Mary Grannan, *Just Mary Green Stories* (Toronto: Thomas Allen, 1951), 37-47.

17. Ibid., 135-147.

18. Mary Grannan, *Just Mary Red Stories* (Toronto: Thomas Allen, 1953), 95-104.

19. Ibid., 84-85.

20. Mary Grannan, *Just Mary Blue Stories* (Toronto: Thomas Allen, 1950), 13-24.

21. Mary Grannan, "Penny Webb and the Spider," 15 May 1949. PANB1.

22. "A Grandmother Spider and her Magic Web," *CBC Times,* 27 January – 2 February 1952.

23. "Grandmother and Her Spider Web," *The Prairie Messenger,* 21 February 1952. CBCRF

24. Bill McNeil and Morris Wolfe, *Signing On: The Birth of Radio in Canada* (Toronto: Doubleday, 1982), 279.

25. Ivy Webb, letter to Mary Grannan, December 1954. DR.

26. Maxine Miller, interview by the author, tape recording & transcript, 7 June 2005.

27. Bille Mae Richards, interview by the author, tape recording & transcript, 29 June 2005.

28. Maxine Miller, interview by the author, tape recording & transcript, 7 June 2005.

29. Ibid.

30. Ibid.

31. Bille Mae Richards, interview by the author, tape recording & transcript, 29 June 2005.

32. Maxine Miller, interview by the author, tape recording & transcript, 7 June 2005.

33. Mary Grannan, *Jubilee Road,* 14 October 1953. CON

34. Ann M. Grannan, letter to Commander Ted Briggs, 19 October 1952. CON

35. Donald Roberts, interview by the author, tape recording & transcript, 28 October 1993: 2.

36. Austin Willis, interview by the author, tape recording & transcript, 28 September 1999, 14-15.

Chapter Twelve: *Maggie* Comes to Television, 1954–1958

1. Mary Grannan, letter to sisters, [November 1954]. DR.
2. Mary Grannan, letter to sisters, 26 November [1954]. DR.
3. Mary Grannan, letter to sisters, [30 November 1954]. DR.
4. Margaret Rainsberry, interview by the author, 8 May 2002.
5. Peggy Liptrott, interview by the author, 10 May 2002.
6. F.B. Rainsberry, *A History of Children's Television in English Canada, 1952-1986* (Metuchen, N.J., Scarecrow Press, 1988), 4-10.
7. Joanne Soloviov, interview by the author, 12 January 2002.
8. Ibid.
9. Beth Morris, interview by the author, 15 September 2002.
10. Beth Morris, interview by the author, 11 October 2002.
11. Beth Morris, interview by the author, 15 September 2002.
12. Mary Grannan, letter to sisters, [January 1955]. DR.
13. [Report on Mary Grannan's television scripts], 16 March 1955. PANB1.
14. Peggy Liptrott, interview by the author, 20 January 2002.
15. Peggy Liptrott, interview by the author, 10 May 2002.
16. Ibid.
17. Joanne Soloviov, interview by the author, 10 May 2002.
18. Peggy Liptrott, interview by the author, 10 May 2002.
19. Joanne Soloviov, interview by the author, 10 May 2002.
20. Peggy Liptrott, interview by the author, 20 January 2002.
21. Ibid.
22. Ibid.
23. Mary Grannan, letter to sisters, [winter 1955]. DR.
24. Mary Grannan, letter to sisters, [April 1956]. DR.
25. Mary Grannan, letter to sisters, [December 1954]. DR.
26. Mary Grannan, letter to sisters, [November 1954]. DR.
27. Mary Grannan, letter to sisters, [April 1956]. DR.
28. Mary Grannan, letter to sisters, [April 1956]. DR.
29. Mary Grannan, letter to sisters, [22-27 September 1955]. DR.
30. Noel Langley, letter to Mary Grannan, 15 August 1951. DR.
31. Noel Langley, letter to Mary Grannan, 9 April 1958. DR.
32. Newspaper clipping, Violet Armstrong's scrapbook.

33. Beryl Hart, interview by the author, tape recording and transcript, 8 October 2000.
34. *CBC Times*, 3-9 February 1952.
35. Mary Grannan, letter to sisters, [early December 1954]. DR.
36. Mary Grannan, letter to sisters, [24 May 1957]. DR.
37. Mary Grannan, letter to sisters, [28 September 1956]. DR.
38. Deanne Taylor, interview by the author, tape recording & edited transcript, 17 May 1999.
39. Violet Armstrong, interview by the author, 29 April 1999; letter to author, 17 August 2005.
40. Mary Grannan, letter to sisters, [28 October 1956]. DR.
41. Mary Grannan, *Maggie Muggins* script, 22 May 1958. Courtesy V. Armstrong.

Chapter Thirteen: Many Books but No Cartoons, 1956–1960

1. Mary Grannan, letter to sisters, [April 1956]. DR.
2. F.B. Rainsberry, "Reclassification of Position and Salary Adjustment," 13 April 1959. CBCMG.
3. John Twomey, interview by the author, tape recording & transcript, 22 June 2000.
4. Joyce Bradshaw, letter to the author, 18 June 2002.
5. Ibid.
6. Ibid.
7. John Twomey, interview by the author, tape recording & transcript, 22 June 2000.
8. Joyce Bradshaw, letter to the author, 18 June 2002.
9. Joyce Bradshaw, letter to the author, 26 April 1999.
10. Ibid.
11. Mary Grannan, letter to Georgina Murray Keddell, 21 May 1971: 9-12. DR.
12. CBC, *The Rustler and the Reindeer*, LAC video, 110796.
13. Mary Grannan, letter to sisters, 24 May 1957. DR.
14. Michael Spivak, interview by the author, 22 June 2000.
15. Ibid.
16. Ibid.
17. Ibid.

18. F.D. Allen, card to Deanne Taylor, [28 March 1959]. Violet Armstrong's scrapbook.

19. Violet Armstrong, interview by the author, 29 April 1999.

20. Mary Grannan, letter to Deanne Taylor, [2 April 1961]. Violet Armstrong.

21. Thor Arngrim, interview by the author, 31 May 2002.

22. Ibid.

23. Ibid.

24. Ibid.

25. Ibid.

26. Mary Grannan, *Maggie Muggins and the Fieldmouse* (Toronto: Thomas Allen, 1959).

27. Mary Long, interview by the author, tape recording & transcript, 21 June 2000.

28. Ibid.

29. Ibid.

30. Ibid.

31. Ibid.

Chapter Fourteen: Last Years at CBC, 1960–1962

1. Andrew Cowan, telegram to Frank Willis, 26 February 1960. DR.

2. A.K. Morrow, letter to Mary Grannan, 29 March 1960. DR.

3. W. Gladstone Murray, letter to Mary Grannan, 5 March 1960. DR.

4. Mary Grannan, letter to Bud Knapp, [February 1960]. DR.

5. Noel Langley, letter to Mary Grannan, 14 September 1960. DR.

6. Mary Grannan, letter to sisters, [December 1960 or 1961]. DR.

7. Mary Grannan, letter to sisters, [Fall 1960]. DR.

8. Mary Grannan, letter to sisters, [circa 1960]. DR.

9. Mavor Moore, interview by the author, 20 August 1999.

10. Mary Grannan, letter to Deanne Taylor, [2 April 1961]. Violet Armstrong.

11. Sid Adilman, "What's Happened to … Just Mary," *Daily Star*, 12 January 1963.

12. Mary Grannan, letter to sisters, [April 1962]. DR.

13. Fergus Cronin, "Remembering Mary Grannan," *The Atlantic Advocate*, November 1981, 50.

14. [Fergus Cronin], "End of the Tale," *Time*, Canada ed., 80, no. 1 (6 July 1962): 8.

15. Mary Grannan, interview by J. Frank Willis, *In Reply*, transcription recording, 17 June 1962. DR.

16. J. Frank Willis, *In Reply*, transcription recording, 17 June 1962. DR.

Chapter Fifteen: Journey Homeward, 1962–1975

1. Trent Frayne, "One for the Show," *Canadian Weekly*, 8-14 September 1962, 9.

2. J. Frank Willis, letter to Mary Grannan, 29 September 1962. DR.

3. J. Frank Willis, letter to Mary Grannan, 4 January 1963. DR.

4. Helen Grannan, letter to Fergus Cronin, 20 January 1982, 5. Fergus Cronin.

5. Ibid., 6-7.

6. Helen Grannan, letter to Fergus Cronin, 10-11 March 1983, 4. Fergus Cronin.

7. Helen Grannan, letter to Fergus Cronin, 20 January 1982, 4. Fergus Cronin.

8. F.D. Allen, letter to Mary Grannan, 20 November 1968. DR.

9. Helen Grannan, interview by the author, tape recording & transcript, 30 October 1993, 8-9.

10. Jack Fenety, interview by the author, 8 February 2001, 9.

11. Sid Adilman, "What's happened to Just Mary," *Daily Star*, 12 January 1963.

12. "Say, Just What Did Happen to Just Mary?" *Maclean's*, 17 December 1966.

13. John Braddock, "The (Lost?) World of Maggie Muggins," *Atlantic Advocate*, February 1967, 16–23.

14. "Missing Persons: Whatever became of Mary Grannan?" *Canadian Panorama*, 22 February 1969, 15.

15. Austin Willis, interview by the author, tape recording and transcript, 28 September 1999, 23.

16. Ibid: 5.

17. Muriel-Ann McKenna, interview by the author, tape recording & transcript, 18 May 1999, 9.

18. Donald Roberts, interview by the author, tape recording and transcript, 28 October 1993, 1.
19. Mary Grannan, letter to Donald Roberts, 31 March 1965. DR.
20. Donald Roberts, interview by the author, tape recording and transcript, 28 October 1993, 13.
21. Ibid., 27.
22. Mary Grannan, card to Donald Roberts, [circa 1962-1974]. DR.
23. J. Frank Willis, card to Grannan sisters, December 1968. DR.
24. Muriel-Ann McKenna, interview by the author, tape recording & transcript, 18 May 1999, 7, 16.
25. Ibid., 6-7.
26. Ibid., 8, 17.
27. William Walker, interview by the author, 7 June 2000.
28. Muriel-Ann McKenna, interview by the author, tape recording & transcript, 18 May 1999,16.
29. Mary Grannan, letter to Georgina Keddell, 21 May 1971, 3-5, 7, 12-13.
30. John D. Ross, letter to the author, 17 November [1998]
31 Donald Roberts, interview by the author, tape recording, 7 October 1998.
32. June Graham, "Mary Grannan," *Closed Circuit*, 15 January 1975, 3.

Epilogue: The Last Public Performance, 1967

1. Hayden Leaman, interview by the author, 30 September 2001.
2. Hayden Leaman, interview by the author, 29 October 1993.

Appendix A
Bibliography of Mary Grannan's Books

Just Mary. Illustrated by Georgette Berckmans. Toronto: Published for the Canadian Broadcasting Corporation by W.J. Gage & Co., Limited, [1941].

Just Mary Again. Illustrated by Georgette Berckmans. Toronto: The Canadian Broadcasting Corporation, W.J. Gage & Co., Limited, [1941].

Just Mary Stories: Combining Just Mary and Just Mary Again. Illustrated by Georgette Berckmans. Toronto: The Canadian Broadcasting Corporation, W.J. Gage & Co., Limited, [1942]; distributed in the United States by G.P. Putnam's Sons.

Maggie Muggins. Drawings by Nancy Caudle. Toronto: Thos. Allen Limited, c1944.

Just Mary Stories: Combining Just Mary and Just Mary Again. Illustrated by Georgette Berckmans. Toronto: Thomas Allen, [n.d.].

New Just Mary Stories: A Recent Selection of the Famous Radio Stories. Illustrated by Georgette Berkmans. Toronto: Thomas Allen, 1946.

New Maggie Muggins Stories: A Recent Selection of the Famous Radio Stories. Illustrated by Nancy Caudle. Toronto: Thomas Allen Limited, c1947.

Happy Playtime, More Just Mary Stories: A Recent Selection of the Famous Radio Series. Illustrated by J. Frank Willis. Toronto: Thomas Allen, 1948.

Happy Playtime, More Just Mary Stories: A Recent Selection of the Famous Canadian Radio Stories. Illustrated by J. Frank Willis. Philadelphia: John C. Winston Co., 1948.

Maggie Muggins Again. Toronto: Thomas Allen Limited, c1949.

Just Mary Blue Stories. Illustrations by Pat. Patience. Toronto: Thomas Allen, 1950.

Maggie Muggins Stories: A Recent Selection of the Famous Canadian Radio Stories. Drawings by Edwin Schmidt. Philadelphia: John C. Winston Company, 1950.

Just Mary Green Stories. Illustrations by Pat. Patience. Toronto: Thomas Allen, 1951.

Maggie Muggins and Mr. McGarrity. Illustrations by Pat. Patience. Toronto: Thomas Allen Limited, c1952.

Just Mary Red Stories. Illustrations by Nancy Caudle. Toronto: Thomas Allen, 1953.

Maggie Muggins and Her Friends. (Cover title: *Maggie Muggins and her Animal Friends.*) Illustrations by Pat. Patience. Toronto: Thomas Allen Limited, c1954.

Just Mary Yellow Stories. Illustrations by Pat. Patience. Toronto: Thomas Allen, 1955.

Kim and Katy: Their Summer Holiday. (Cover title: *Kim and Katy on their Holidays.*) Jacket design by Pat. Patience. Toronto: Thomas Allen, 1956.

Kim and Katy: Circus Days. Jacket design by Pat. Patience. Toronto: Thomas Allen, 1956.

Maggie Muggins in the Meadow. Illustrations by Pat. Patience. Toronto: Thomas Allen Limited, c1956.

Just Mary's Brown Book. Illustrations by Pat. Patience. Toronto: Thomas Allen, 1957.

Kim and Katy: Schooldays. Jacket design by Pat Patience. Toronto: Thomas Allen, 1958.

Maggie Muggins Tee Vee Tales. Illustrations by Pat. Patience. Toronto: Thomas Allen Limited, c1958.

Appendix A

New Just Mary Stories: A Recent Selection of the Famous Radio Stories. Illustrated by Georgette Berkmans. 5th abridged ed. Toronto: Thomas Allen Limited, 1958.

Just Mary Stories. Pictures by Jennetta Vise. Rev. ed. London: Frederick Warne & Co., [1958].

More Just Mary Stories. Pictures by Jennetta Vise. Rev. ed. London: Frederick Warne, 1959.

Maggie Muggins and the Fieldmouse. Illustrations by Pat. Patience. Toronto: Thomas Allen Limited, c1959.

This is Maggie Muggins. Illustrations by Bernard Zalusky. Cleveland, Ohio: Pennington Press, c1959.

More Maggie Muggins. Illustrations by Bernard Zalusky. Cleveland, Ohio: Pennington Press, c1959.

Maggie Muggins and her Animal Friends. Illustrations by Bernard Zalusky. Cleveland, Ohio: Pennington Press, c1959.

Maggie Muggins by the Sea. Illustrations by Lonnie Stern. Cleveland, Ohio: Pennington Press, c1959.

Maggie Muggins Bedtime Stories. Illustrations by Lonnie Stern. Cleveland, Ohio: Pennington Press, c1959.

The Wonderful World of Maggie Muggins. Illustrations by Lonnie Stern. Cleveland, Ohio: Pennington Press, c1959.

Maggie Muggins and the Cottontail. Illustrations by Pat. Patience. Toronto: Thomas Allen Limited, c1960.

Maggie Muggins Gives a Party. Illustrations by Pat. Patience. Toronto: Thomas Allen Limited, c1961.

Maggie Muggins and Benny Bear. Illustrations by Pat. Patience. Toronto: Thomas Allen Limited, c1962.

More Just Mary Stories. Pictures by Jennetta Vise. Toronto: Thomas Allen, 1981.

Maggie Muggins and Mr. McGarrity. Illustrations by Pat. Patience. 1st paperback ed. Toronto: Thomas Allen & Son Limited, 1985.

Appendix B
Mary Grannan's
Broadcast Programs

Radio Programs

CFNB

Musical Scrapbook, April 21, 1936 to 1939
Aggravating Agatha, April 21, 1936 to 1937
Just Mary, November 1937 to June 1939

CBC

Just Mary, July–September 1938; December 1938–January 1939; September 1939–June 1962
The Children's Scrapbook, 1939–1946
The Magic Chord, Christmas, 1942–1945, 1950–1951
Magic in Spring, Easter, 1943–1946
Sonnie and Susie (Commercial for Simpson's on CJBC & later CFRB), 1944–1945
Evening Scrapbook, 1945
The Land of Supposing, spring 1946 to 1948, 1950
The Enchanted Pine, Christmas and Easter, 1946–1949, 1956
Maggie Muggins, 1947–1953
Sarah and Peter (Commercial for Grolier Society), 1948–1950

Karen Discovers America, summer 1952
The Christmas Roundup, Christmas 1952
The Cotton Sprouts, summer 1953
Jubilee Road, 1953–1956
Mr. McGarrity's Garden, summer 1954–1955
Miss Goldie's Gift Shop, December 4, 1954
Digger Jones, summer, 1956
Kim and Katy Circus Days, summer 1958

Television Programs on CBC

Maggie Muggins, February 4, 1955 to June 1962
Just Mary, April–December 1960

Television Specials

Gift for the Princess, 1955
Jewels of Fermanagh, 1956
The Rustler and the Reindeer, 1957

Acknowledgements

Throughout the many years of work on Mary Grannan's biography, I have been overwhelmed by the generosity and kindness of so many people who were just as eager as I was to see her life story in print. To all who have helped in so many ways, large and small, I extend hearty thanks.

Donald and Joan Roberts deserve a special tribute, for without them the story could not have been told. Don, with his vivid, detailed memory, gave countless hours of interviews and generously offered access to his carefully preserved collection of Mary Grannan's personal papers, photographs, and artifacts. Joan patiently allowed me to take over her dining room and kitchen for many days, fed me, and offered her own memories.

In 1993, I was fortunate to interview Helen Grannan (who died on her ninety-eighth birthday, July 13, 2001), but I also gained much valuable insight and witness to her sister's life from Helen's other taped interviews and through the letters she wrote to Fergus Cronin. To Fergus Cronin, who so kindly shared his extensive correspondence and photographs, I owe deep gratitude.

The four women who played Maggie Muggins — Beryl Braithwaite Hart, Beth Morris, Deanne Taylor, and Mary Long — received me so warmly, sharing in abundant, flowing detail their rich experiences of playing the beloved heroine. I extend special thanks to them and to Deanne's mother, Violet (Taylor) Armstrong, for her enthusiastic sharing of information and memorabilia.

Many of Mary Grannan's friends, neighbours, former students, relatives, and colleagues were exceptionally helpful in providing information about her time in Fredericton: Pat Barry, Nancy Beltrandi, Mary Cassidy, Regina Clarke, Gertrude Davis, Marguarita Dorcas, Mavis Dunn, Jack Fenety, Mary Grandy, Sterling Haynes, Mary Hayes, Gwen Herbin, Jessie Hodgson, Roberta Holdsworth, Charles Hughes, Doug Jackson Sr., Doug Jackson Jr., Ted Jones, Marie Kiever, Eugene Lawrence, Hayden Leaman, Walter Long, David McCormack, Muriel-Ann McKenna, Lila McPherson, Henry Murphy, Jane Murphy, Malcolm Neill, Mae Nicholson, Helen O'Connor, Jim O'Neill, Donna Rickard, John Ross, Marie Rushbrook, Carol Slocum, Eleanor Stillwell, Helen Tippett, Bill Walker, Eileen Wallace, Jackie Webster, and Scott Webster.

Those who knew Mary at the CBC eagerly told me reams of stories, in particular Austin Willis and former television producers Peggy Liptrott, Joanne Soloviov, Michael Spivak, and John Twomey. Many others kindly contributed valuable information about Mary's CBC years: Thor Arngrim, Thom Benson, Joyce Bradshaw, June Callwood, Dinah Christie, Liam Gannon, Margaret Graham, Vladimir Handera, Gary Katz, Nina Keogh, Christopher Langley, Jacqueline Langley, Jack Mather, Mary Rose McMaster, Maxine Miller, Mavor Moore, Mary Catherine O'Brien, Mary Lou Penrose, Frank Perry, Margaret Rainsberry, Billie Mae Richards, Anna Russell, Herb Samuels, and Robert Weaver. Sheila Egoff provided comments on libraries' reaction to Grannan's books.

John and Jim Allen of Thomas Allen & Son Limited generously shared information, books, and photographs. Jim Allen thoughtfully offered some excellent advice early in my work.

I am indebted to Ernest Dick for his incredible assistance in helping me locate information in Library and Archives Canada and the CBC. Several people provided substantial research information on particular topics: Roger Boulter on Alan Cole and Paul Smith; Moira Day

Acknowledgements

on Elizabeth Sterling Haynes; Jim O'Neill on circuses; Ronald S. Ritchie on trains. David Nelson also provided train information.

The CBC has been most helpful and a rich resource for information: CBC Research Library, Michele Melady and Leone Earls; CBC Design Library & Still Photo Collection, Lynda Barnett; CBC Television Archives, Roy Harris; CBC Radio Archives; CBC Records & Information Management, Georges Lee; Radio Licensing, Barbara Brown.

Libraries and archives, whose rich collections make research into our history possible, played pivotal roles, while their knowledgeable staffs were most kind. Valuable collections and helpful staff members include: Provincial Archives of New Brunswick, Marion Beyea, Director; Library and Archives Canada, Anne Goddard, Rosemary Bergeron, and Jean Matheson; Centre for Broadcasting Studies at Concordia University, Howard Fink, Roger Des Ormeaux, and Shirley Sibalis; Vancouver Public Library; Toronto Reference Library, Heather Wilson; Harriet Irving Library and Eileen Wallace Children's Literature Collection, University of New Brunswick; University of British Columbia Libraries; Minto Public Library, Mary Lambropoulos and Rosalyn Gray; Archives of Ontario, Erin Coulter; University of Natal, Durban, South Africa, Revd. Stacie Gibson.

Many skilled people assisted me in the process of writing: David Macfarlane and Gary Ross at Booming Ground; Terry Glavin at the Victoria School of Writing; Robert Ray, Jack Remick, and Elizabeth Lyon at the Surrey International Writers' Conference; Bernice Lever of the Canadian Authors Association; Marilyn Bittman, Melody Hessing, Rosemary Patterson, Sylvia Shirran, and Jessica Swail of the Bykota Writers' Group. Michael Holroyd kindly offered some advice in a letter. Naomi Pauls prepared the index.

I extend warm thanks to the Dundurn Group and its wonderful staff — Kirk Howard, Beth Bruder, Tony Hawke, Barry Jowett, Jennifer Gallant, Jennifer Scott, and all the rest — for their enthusiasm and hard-working efforts for this book.

In particular, I would like to thank Dr. Gwendolyn Davies for her foreword and wonderful suggestions. Thank you also to Sheree Fitch for her enthusiasm and help.

In that most precious area of emotional support and encouragement, as well as plenty of practical help, I have some special people to thank: my dear husband Forrest, Katherine, Rosa, Stan, my father Albert, Joanne, Jim, Mary, the rest of our great family, and Ed Hicks. Some special friends have long encouraged me, especially at the beginning when it was most important: Marc Richard, Julia Taminiau, and the late Anne Galler.

Many thanks to one and all.

Permissions

Excerpts from the works of Mary E. Grannan, including her letters, diary, published and unpublished works, and her books originally published by Thomas Allen Limited from 1944 to 1962, and excerpts from letters and published work by Helen J. Grannan are reproduced here with the kind permission of the late Helen J. Grannan.

Excerpts from *Just Mary, Just Mary Again,* and *Just Mary Stories: Combining Just Mary and Just Mary Again,* originally published for the Canadian Broadcasting Corporation by Gage & Company Limited in 1941 and 1942, and material from the CBC Archives are reproduced here with the kind permission of CBC.

Permission to quote from J. Frank Willis's letters and poem *Nocturne* and to reproduce his illustration "Mary Grannan Autograph Party 1957" from Gwen Willis.

Permission to quote Joanne Hughes's report on Mary Grannan's scripts from Joanne Soloviov (neé Hughes).

Permission to quote from Max Braithwaite's article "Just Mary," which appeared in *Maclean's* magazine June 1, 1947, from Sharon Siamon.

Permission to quote from the letters of:

Elizabeth Sterling Haynes from Dr. Sterling Haynes;
Georgina Keddell (neé Murray) from Margaret Graham;
Noel Langley from Dr. Jacqueline Langley;
J. Stewart Neill from Graham Neill;
Fred B. Rainsberry from Elizabeth Rainsberry; and
E. Austin Weir from Mary Louise Penrose.

Index

Index

Index

Index